Discourses of
the Environment

To Bernadette (1926–1996)

Discourses of
the Environment

EDITED BY ÉRIC DARIER

Copyright © Blackwell Publishers Ltd 1999

Editorial matter and organization copyright © Éric Darier 1999

First published 1999

2 4 6 8 10 9 7 5 3 1

Blackwell Publishers Ltd
108 Cowley Road
Oxford OX4 1JF
UK

Blackwell Publishers Inc.
350 Main Street
Malden, Massachusetts 02148
USA

British Library Cataloguing in Publication Data

A CIP catalogue record for this book is available from the British Library.

Library of Congress Cataloging-in-Publication Data

Discourses of the environment / edited by Éric Darier.
    p.   cm.
    Includes bibliographical references and index.
    ISBN 0–631–21122–5 (alk. paper). — ISBN 0–631–21123–3 (pbk. : alk. paper)
    1. Environmental sciences.   2. Environmentalism.   3. Foucault, Michel.   I. Darier, Éric.
GE105.D58   1998
363.7—dc21   98–26079
                                                                                CIP

Commissioning Editor: Jill Landeryou
Picture Researcher: Michael Craven

Typeset in 10.5 on 12.5 pt Sabon
by Graphicraft Limited, Hong Kong
Printed in Great Britain by TJ International, Padstow, Cornwall.

This book is printed on acid-free paper

Contents

Contributors

Sylvia Bowerbank teaches in the Arts and Science Programme and English Department of McMaster University in Hamilton, Ontario. Her present research interests include women and ecology and the theorizing of eco-criticism. She is completing a book on early modern women's contributions to ecological thought, entitled *Speaking for Nature: Women and Ecology in Early Modern England*. Her recent publications include an essay on the greening of literary studies in the *Canadian Review of Comparative Literature/ Revue Canadienne de Littérature Comparée* (Sept. 1995); (with Dolores Wawia) 'Literature and Criticism by Natives and Métis Women in Canada', *Feminist Studies* (Fall 1994); and 'Does Women Speak for Nature?: Toward a Genealogy of Ecological Feminism', in Nina Lykke and Rosi Braidotti (eds), *Between Monsters, Mother Goddesses and Cyborgs* (Zed Books 1996).

Éric Darier is a Research Associate at the Centre for the Study of Environmental Change at Lancaster University, England. In 1995–6, he was a Post-Doctoral Fellow at the Environmental Policy Unit, Queen's University, Canada. He taught in several graduate and undergraduate environmental studies programmes. He obtained his Ph.D. in Political Studies in 1993 from McGill University, Montreal. His doctoral thesis was entitled 'L'Environnement au Canada: une approche foucaltienne'. His publications include 'Time to be Lazy: Work, the Environment and Modern Subjectivities', *Time and Society* (1998); 'Environmental Governmentality: The Case of *Canada's Green Plan'*, *Environmental Politics*, 5(4) (1996a); 'The Politics and Power Effects of Garbage Recycling in Halifax, Canada', *Local Environment*, 1(1) (1996);

and 'Environmental Studies in Context: Knowledge, Language, History and the Self', in Michael D. Metha and Eric Ouellet (eds), *Environmental Sociology: Theory and Practice*, Toronto: Captus Press, 1995. He is co-author (with Simon Shackley) of an article entitled 'The Seduction of the Sirens: Global Climate Change and Modelling' (*Science and Public Policy*, forthcoming).

Thomas Heyd teaches philosophy in the Department of Philosophy of the University of Victoria. He has written on indigenous knowledge ('Indigenous Knowledge, Emancipation and Alienation', *Knowledge and Policy*, 8(1) (Spring 1995), performance art ('Understanding Performance Art: Beyond Art', *British Journal of Aesthetics*, 31(1) (1991) and installation art ('Blair Brennan: Art and the Sacred', *Artichoke*, 7(3). His other areas of research and publication include history of philosophy (Modern period) and philosophy of the environment. He is the former (1990–5) Chair of the Canadian Society for the Study of European Ideas, and organized a session on Ideas of Nature and Land at the Society's Annual Conference (28–9 May 1996) held in conjunction with the Learned Societies at Brock University, Canada.

Isabelle Lanthier obtained a B.A. in political science from the University of Quebec at Montreal. She was a parliamentary intern for Canadian Member of Parliament Francine Lalonde. She is completing an M.A. in political science on 'The Genealogy of Happiness: Birth of a Political Stake'. She has published in the Canadian daily, *The Globe & Mail*, and has presented several papers to political science conferences.

Neil Levy was educated at Monash University, in Melbourne, Australia, where he received his Ph.D. in comparative literature and critical theory. He is currently a tutor at the Centre for Critical Theory at Monash, and is working on a comparative study of Continental and Anglo-American approaches to ethics.

Timothy W. Luke is Professor of Political Science at Virginia Polytechnic Institute and State University in Blacksburg. He conducts research in the areas of comparative politics and international political economy as well as in political philosophy and social theory. Author of *Shows of Force* (Duke University Press 1992), *Social Theory and Modernity* (Sage 1990) and *Screens of*

Power (University of Illinois Press 1989), he is now completing a book on contemporary ecological criticism and social theory.

Lawrence Olivier has a B.A. in political science and a M.A. in political philosophy from université Laval, Canada. He obtained his Ph.D. in history and civilization at the université Aix-Marseille, France. Professor in the Department of Political Science at the University of Quebec in Montreal, Canada, he specializes in epistemology, political philosophy and the issue of Francophones and Acadians in Canada. He taught at the université de Moncton and université Laval. Author of a recent book entitled *Michel Foucault – Penser au temps du nihilisme* (Liber 1995), he has also edited books to which he has been a contributor, and has published several scientific articles.

Peter Quigley obtained his Ph.D. from Indiana University of Pennsylvania in 1990, focusing on cultural studies, Marxist aesthetics, poststructural theory and environmental literature. He then won a Fulbright Scholarship and went to lecture and do research on American literature and culture at the University of Bergen, Norway. Invited to stay for a second year, he took a permanent position as Associate Professor of American Studies at the University of Tromso, Norway. He currently holds tenured positions at both Embry–Riddle Aeronautical University in Arizona and the University of Tromso. He continues to do research in environmental, technological and literary issues, and is developing a B.A. programme in science, technology, and society for ERAU, where he intends to stay. In addition, he is working with University of Utah Press to bring out a collection of articles on the much maligned and ignored environmental author Ed Abbey.

Paul Rutherford teaches environmental politics in the Department of Government and Public Administration at the University of Sydney, Australia, and is currently completing a Ph.D. in the Research School of Social Sciences at the Australian National University, Canberra. His current area of research deals with the problematization of natural environment in contemporary political and social theory, and in particular seeks to use the notion of 'governmentality' to understand the growth of environmental politics and regulatory practices. He has had extensive experience as a policy advisor and political advisor in the areas of environmental protection and natural resource management, with both non-governmental organizations and state agencies in Australia.

Catriona Sandilands is an Assistant Professor in the Faculty of Environmental Studies at York University, Canada. Her work inhabits a liminal zone between feminism, political theory and environmental thought; she has published on these and other topics in *Environmental Ethics, Canadian Women's Studies, The Z Papers*, among other places. She has also been involved in other political arenas, including the Women and Environments Education and Development (WEED) Foundation in Toronto.

Acknowledgements

Like most writing, I suspect, this book is the result of academic frustration and intellectual loneliness. While working on my doctoral thesis on Foucault and the environment at McGill University, I became frustrated, as it seemed that I was the only person on this planet doing this kind of research, despite the fact that I knew there must have been others. Thanks to these creative academic frustrations and the diligent and stimulating support of James Tully, my thesis supervisor, I managed to complete the thesis in 1993.

It was only in 1995–6, during my year as a Post-Doctoral Fellow at the Environmental Policy Unit, at Queen's University, Canada, that I finally decided to make a systematic attempt to discover other Foucauldian scholars working on the issue of the 'environment'. Through the process of editing this collection of articles, I discovered an active group of Foucauldian scholars working on this topic. Finally I was not alone any more! I shall be eternally thankful to William Leiss, the Eco-Research Chair in Environmental Policy, who generously offered me a Post-Doctoral Fellowship, thus creating the material conditions for the realization of this book. In these dark days of education and research 'cut-backs', 'down-sizing', 'fiscal austerity', and other poor excuses, I felt privileged, not unlike winning the lottery. I am also grateful to Bill Leiss for creating an extremely friendly and creative Environmental Policy Unit with remarkable colleagues: Christina Chociolko, Georgia Hanias, Michael Mehta, Holly Mitchell and Debora VanNijnatten.

Despite the fact that Queen's University tends to be too 'white' and too 'middle class' for my personal taste, and is located in the provincial town of Kingston, Ontario, I am thankful for the dozens of intellectually stimulating individuals I met, most notably through the Institute of Women's Studies, the departments of sociology, history, and English, and the Queer Study Group. I am particularly grateful to Paul Jackson for stimulating conversations, friendship, coffees and bicycle rides.

Back in Montreal, I am specially thankful to Kevin Crombie for his patience and his editing and formatting skills, and to Eric Laferrière for his comments on the manuscript.

I want to thank my current colleagues at the Centre for the Study of Environmental Change (CSEC) and in other departments at Lancaster University, including among others Robin Grove-White, Phil Macnaghten, Leslie Moran, Simon Shackley, John Urry and Brian Wynne.

Finally, I want to thank the following individuals who directly or indirectly have created the conditions for the emergence of this volume: Eugenio Bolongaro, David T. Brown, Jacqui Burgess, Ravi Chimni, Raymond Côté, Michael Craven, Ann Dwire, Alain-G. Gagnon, Nick Garside, Susan Guppy, Sue Hendler, Steve Jordan, Innocent Kabenga, Martha-Marie Kleinhans, Andréa Lévy, Bill Marshall, Rhonda Mawhood, Steven Maynard, Maureen McNeil, John Middleton, Viviana Patroni, Thierry Schickes, Gale Stewart, Carl Stychin, Charles Taylor, Michael Temelini and people at Blackwell, including Jill Landeryou, Cameron Laux, and Jean van Altena.

1

Foucault and the Environment: An Introduction

Éric Darier

Grazing sheep can be beautiful, very different from 'sulphureous vapours' though actually . . . no more natural.
– Raymond Williams

The desire for knowledge has been transformed among us into a passion which fears no sacrifice, which fears nothing but its own extinction. It may be that mankind will eventually perish from this passion for knowledge. If not through passion, then through weakness, we must be prepared to state our desire or choice: do we wish humanity to end in fire and light or to end on the sand?
– Nietzsche

The law doth punish man or woman
That steels the goose from off the common,
But lets the greater felon loose,
That steals the common from the goose.
– author unknown; eighteenth-century protest against the Enclosure Act in England, quoted by Parsons

[I]f it is extremely dangerous to say that Reason is the enemy that should be illiminated, it is just as dangerous to say that any critical questioning of this rationality risks sending us into irrationality.
– Foucault

Contexts

Despite – and because of – 30 years of environmental legislation, regulation, institution building at national and international level, and the emergence of a diverse and relatively powerful environmental movement, there is a general concern and anxiety about the 'environment' in the North. As a result, there has been a proliferation of discourses about the environment from most quarters of society which has also coincided with a general increase in scepticism about scientific knowledge and the meaning and efficacy of political and social change. For example, at least since Thomas Kuhn (1962), there has generally been less confidence that scientific knowledge and technological innovations are the necessary conditions for human betterment. This scepticism manifests itself through discourses of scientific 'uncertainty' and 'complexity'. Jerome Ravetz accurately noted that 'while our knowledge continues to increase exponentially, our relevant ignorance does so even more rapidly. And this is ignorance generated by science' (1987: 100). In this context of 'generated ignorance', there is increased anxiety among the population of the North about the possible consequences of rapid scientific and technologically induced changes on humans and the environment. Apart from business, which has vested interests in always justifying changes in positive terms like 'benefits' and 'improvements', very few experts would volunteer a resolutely optimistic outlook for the environment in the future (Simon and Kahn 1984; Easterbrook 1995). The absence of obvious credible solutions and the knowledge to implement them sustain concerns and anxiety for the environment. This is reflected in the extreme diversity of assumptions and solutions offered by many in the 'environmental movement' (Eckersley 1992: 33–47; Marshall 1992; Merchant 1992: 85–210; Murphy 1994: x–xi). As Andrew Ross has noted, 'Except for the name of "ecology" itself, virtually nothing unites the bioregionalists, Gaians, eco-feminists, eco-Marxists, biocentricists, eco-anarchists, deep ecologists and social ecologists who pursue their ideas and actions in its name' (1994: 5).

According to some of the environmentalists from the spectrum identified above, one of the obstacles to addressing the environmental crisis has been the perceived extreme relativism and the 'anything goes' attitude of what they call 'postmodernism' (Bookchin 1990; Gare 1995; Sessions 1995a; Soulé and Lease 1995) or 'moral pluralism' (Callicott 1990). Their position seems to be based on nostalgia for a presumed lost coherence. For example, Callicott feels

that we must maintain a coherent sense of self and world, a unified moral world view. Such unity enables us rationally to select among or balance out the contradictory or inconsistent demands made upon us when the multiple social circles in which we operate overlap and come into conflict. More importantly, a unified world view gives our lives purpose, direction, coherency, and sanity. (Callicott 1990: 121)

Bookchin echoes Callicott in condemning postmodernism as 'a veritable campaign . . . to discard the past, to dilute our knowledge of history, to mystify the origins of our problems, to foster dememorisation and the loss of our most enlightened ideals' (Bookchin 1990: 73–4). Because of the vagueness and general confusion regarding what is understood by 'postmodernism',[1] it would probably be sterile and simplistic to embark on a prolonged debate pitting 'postmodernism' against 'environmentalism'. Recent works have recontextualized this debate (Andermatt Conley 1997; Bennett and Chaloupka 1993; Bird 1987; Darier 1995; Haraway 1991; Jagtenberg and McKie 1997; Macnaghten and Urry 1998; Oelschlaeger 1995: 1–20; Redclift and Woodgate 1997; Ross 1994; Soper 1995, 1996; Zimmerman 1994, 1996). One of the central issues in this debate is the tension between, on the one hand, the argument that for humans, 'nature' can only make sense through the various filters of 'social construction'[2] and, on the other hand, the argument that nature has an irreducible positivist reality outside human interpretations. Kate Soper calls these two views 'nature-skeptical' and 'nature-endorsing' respectively (Soper 1995; 1996: 23). In part, this debate reflects the two broad general perspectives and worldviews offered by the social sciences and the natural sciences. It also reflects the 'primacy of epistemology' in the natural sciences over the more interpretative practices in the social sciences (Connolly 1992; Taylor 1987). Even within the 'primacy of epistemology', this disciplinary divide reflects irreconcilable differences regarding the possibility of knowledge, ranging from 'value-free' positivism to absolute relativism (Feyerabend 1981a, 1981b, 1991; Taylor 1971, 1980). Nevertheless, there are examples of cross-over between the two broad categories of disciplines and epistemological premises, of natural scientists adopting a constructivist approach (Latour and Woolgar 1986; Latour 1987; Woolgar 1988) and of social scientists opting for a more positivist approach. Beyond this excessively Manichaean framing of the controversy, it is important to note that others have attempted to find an intermediate position which doesn't epistemologically deny – or affirm – the material existence of what is referred to as 'nature' or 'environment', but stresses the diversity and changes in human interpretations of 'nature' through history, which might in turn explain the 'domination', the 'destruction', the 'protection' and/or the 'transformation' of 'nature' by human activities (Benton 1994; Ellen 1996; Hannigan 1995; Murphy 1994;[3] Simmons 1993).

It may be time to reframe the controversy in different ways. In a rare, probably unique insight into this topic, Michel Foucault perceived the heated debate in environmentalism in terms not of epistemological options from which one has to choose, but, on the contrary, of essential and necessary conditions for the emergence of an ecological/environmental movement itself.

> [T]here has been an ecological movement – which is furthermore very ancient and is not only a twentieth-century phenomenon – which has often been, in one sense, in hostile relationship with science or at least with a technology guaranteed in terms of truth ['*nature-endorsing*']. But in fact, ecology also spoke a language of truth. It was in the name of knowledge concerning nature, the equilibrium of the processes of living things, and so forth, that one could level the criticism ['*nature-sceptical*']. (Foucault 1988b: 15)

Ulrich Beck has restated Foucault's observation in a similar manner:

> The observable consequence is that critics [i.e. environmentalism] frequently argue more scientifically than the natural scientists they dispute against . . . [but] fall prey to a naïve realism about definitions of the dangers one consumes. On the one hand, this naïve realism of hazards is (apparently) necessary as an expression of outrage and a motor of protest; on the other it is its Achilles' heel. (Beck 1995: 60)

One of the main objectives of this book is to explore this essential, necessary tension between currents in environmentalism as noted by Foucault and Beck, and, more precisely, the controversy between the 'nature-endorsing' claim of a truth-discourse about nature and the 'nature-sceptical' radical critique about the inescapable power effects of all knowledge, of all truth-claims. Despite the fact that the work of Foucault seems to promise a challenging contribution to our understanding, there has been a tendency to omit Foucault from most critical studies in environmental theory (Andermatt Conley 1997; Eckersley 1992; Goldblatt 1996; Hayward 1994; Merchant 1994). Hopefully, this book will fill the obvious gap and explore the possible creative synergy between two large corpora of critical literature which surprisingly haven't yet met in a systematic fashion: (a) the works by, and about, French theorist Michel Foucault and (b) environmental criticism.

Foucault and the Environment:
'My Back is Turned to It'

Before embarking further on an exploration of the possible relevance of Foucault for environmentalism, it is important to state a few points.

Michel Foucault (1926–84) is probably one of the most influential thinkers of our time, at least in France, the English-speaking world and parts of Latin America. The evidence is the large number of books and articles about Foucault published since his death. However, this is only the tip of the Foucauldian iceberg. The real extent of his influence is far more extensive than books with the name 'Foucault' on their cover, in their chapter titles, in their index or in their bibliography. To get an idea of the extent of the influence of Foucault, one must also take into account the gigantic body of works which use some of the concepts developed by Foucault without making any explicit reference to him. Those concepts include 'discourse analysis', 'power/knowledge', 'disciplinary techniques', 'field of power', 'governmentality', 'normalization', 'resistance', 'non-strategical ethics' and 'aesthetic of existence'. What is also surprising is the breadth of the influence of Foucault across virtually every academic domain, ranging from legal studies, gender and queer studies, cultural studies, anthropology, sociology, political studies, to philosophy, history, literary criticism, media and communication studies, geography and so on. Foucault's influence can also be encountered in non-academic, openly activist contexts such as the gay, lesbian, bisexual movement, the women's movement, the anti-racist movement, the prisoners' rights movement and community activism generally. In North America, Foucault – alongside non-essentialist strands of feminism and queer theory (Bersani 1995; Halperin 1995; McNeil 1993; Terry 1991) and a 're-discovery' of aboriginal peoples in the context of an 'age of diversity' (Tully 1995) – is also having a profound impact on the reworking of pluralism, or rather in the 'ethos of pluralization' (Connolly 1995).

To my knowledge, there are no systematic studies aimed at exploring the possible connections and relevance of Foucault to environmental thinking, although the idea has been suggested (Gare 1995: 94). This is a puzzling lacuna when one examines Foucault's intellectual legacy in more detail: for example, his concept of 'biopolitics' is a strong, direct reflection of a 'politics of life' which is close to the concerns of environmentalism. It is true that Foucault never addressed the environmental issue directly, or the ecological crisis as such, except in the brief insightful quote already given. It is also true that Foucault 'detested nature', or rather, that he preferred 'visiting churches and museums'. Éribon's biography recounts a car trip through the Italian Alps that Foucault took with a colleague, Jacqueline Verdeaux, which revealed his attitude to nature. '[Verdeaux] remembers . . . well that Foucault detested nature. Whenever she showed him some magnificent landscape – a lake sparkling in the sunlight – he made a great show of walking off toward the road, saying, "My back is turned to it" ' (Éribon 1991: 46).[4]

If one shouldn't look in Foucault for an obvious aesthetic appreciation and/or some empathy with nature, it doesn't mean that Foucault's work is irrelevant or unimportant for environmental thinking. In fact, as this collection of essays illustrates, Foucault's concepts can be made highly relevant to environmental thinking, whatever attitude to 'nature' Foucault himself might have held. Therefore, bracketing Foucault's attitude toward 'nature' is not an attempt to side-step an embarrassing 'character' trait in Foucault! It is also a way to put into practice Foucault's own position regarding the highly historical contingency of the function of 'author' and 'text' in our societies. Foucault noted that the disappearance – or death – of the author was due to the fact that the 'author function is . . . characteristic of the mode of existence circulating, and functioning of certain discourses within society' (Foucault 1984g: 103, 108). This means that increasingly, in our current society, texts 'could be read for themselves' without the anchoring presence of an 'author' (ibid. 110). Consequently, Foucault was advocating the 'total effacement of the individual characteristics of the writer' (ibid.). He also systematically resisted the boxing of his work in the existing intellectual categories such as 'structuralism', 'poststructuralism', 'modernism' or 'postmodernism'. In order to achieve this, he employed several 'de-locations' in the focus of his research (the literal translation of the French word *déplacements* is more accurate than the too mild word 'shifts'). The rupture between 'author' and 'text' explains how concepts can have unintended, unpredictable effects in 'back of the author'. I would argue that despite his having 'turned his back to nature', Foucault's writings are having profound, albeit indirect, effects on environmental thinking. The virulent critique of Foucault by many environmental thinkers, via the postmodernist category, may also indicate that Foucault is having an effect 'in the back' of environmental thinkers themselves.

Mapping Foucault in Contexts

Mapping Foucault's work may help us to understand and appreciate the various possible Foucauldian contributions to critical environmental theory. But before embarking on this task, I wish to make the following general remarks.

First, it is generally recognized that there are not one or two but at least three Foucaults (archeological, genealogical and ethical). Foucault 're-located' his research agenda several times. However, this doesn't mean that each period in Foucault's intellectual life was totally divorced from the others or was part of an overall singular project. Because of the existence of multiple Foucaults, it is important to be as clear as possible about the periods in which concepts emerged before engaging in a critique of Foucault's work. For example, the early archeological period may indeed have been structuralist in tone. However, it is more difficult to make the structuralist label stick for the intermediate genealogical period, and it is quite irrelevant to use it for the final ethical period.

Second, Foucault's books and articles were written in typical scholarly style, which may make them difficult to read at times. This is why so many commentators use the numerous interviews he gave all through his life. The problem with the interviews is that Foucault, as a member of the French intellectual star system[5] (centred of course in Paris), was very aware of the audience he was addressing when interviewed. For example, if he was giving an interview to a Marxist journal, he would employ Marxist vocabulary. Therefore, one has to go beyond Foucault's textual answers to the context of the particular interview to gain an accurate appreciation of what he was trying to say. Unlike some, such as Habermas, who considered the activities of intellectuals as serious matters – such as shaping the communicative expression of the transparent and increasing manifestation of 'Reason' – Foucault saw his intellectual production as 'tactics', 'strategies', 'toolbox', 'laughter' (de Certeau 1994), 'irony' (Connolly 1992; Rorty 1989: 61), 'games' (Kroker 1987) or 'fiction'. 'I have never written anything but fictions. . . . It seems to me that the possibility exists for fiction in truth, for a fictional discourse to induce effects of truth, and for bringing about that true discourse engenders or "manufactures" something that does not as yet exist' (Foucault 1980c: 193).

Third, there are major differences in the interpretations of Foucault's work. For example, the English-speaking world (especially Americans) tends to see Foucault, in the best case, as some kind of closeted ironic liberal (Rorty 1989) or as 'normatively confused' but with 'empirical insights' (Fraser 1989); whereas in France (and in southern Europe more generally), he tends to be seen as closer to Nietzsche than to the liberal tradition. Foucault was able to get lots of attention because of the generally privileged position of intellectuals in France as cultural icons extensively involved in political and social life. Although Foucault has now become an intellectual icon, his academic career in France was not easy or straightforward. This was due to what I have called elsewhere his 'marginal belonging' (*appartenance marginale*) in the French university milieu (Darier 1993: 5–51). Despite being marginal in the sense that he didn't fit into any of the dominant intellectual schools or in any precise academic discipline, Foucault did manage to obtain a Chair at the prestigious Collège de France, a symbol of the intellectual establishment in France, but experienced the 'solitude of the acrobat' (Éribon 1991: 212–13). Elsewhere, especially in the Anglo-Saxon world, Foucault's influence – and the influence of intellectuals generally – is more limited, to pockets inside the walls of university campuses. At best, intellectuals are tolerated as long as they don't disrupt the dominant preoccupations of society, such as 'economic efficiency and competition', 'fiscal responsibility' and widespread 'commercialism'. The differences in intellectual contexts lead to different readings of Foucault (Dumm 1996: 9–15; Gordon 1996: 253–70). However, one should not underestimate the influence of Foucault, especially in the current reworking of liberalism (Connolly 1993b; Dumm 1996; Flathman 1992; Kateb 1992) into what William Connolly prefers to call 'an ethos of pluralization' (Connolly 1995).

The Three Foucaults

With others (Davidson 1986; Smart 1994), I believe that there are three broad periods in Foucault's intellectual *oeuvre* which involve different 'methodological'[6] approaches: (1) an archeological approach to scientific discourse and knowledge generally; (2) a genealogical approach analysing social practices; and (3) an ethical concern for the possible conditions for the creation of the self by itself. Furthermore, there are at least two ways of entering the Foucauldian constellation. First, one can survey the three periods one at a time; or one can choose a key concept from one of the three periods and show how (and if) it relates to the other two periods. For example, the concept of 'governmentality' developed in the genealogical period not only offers a way into a historical survey of the conditions for the emergence of the modern form of power called 'government'; it also incorporates an archeological understanding of knowledge (hence 'power/knowledge') and a tool with which to examine conditions for the emergence of the pro-blematization of subjectivities, as the 'ethical', 'final' Foucauldian period suggests.[7] For the purpose of this book, I hope to show that not only are both ways of entering the Foucauldian constella-tion valid, but that both should be used simultaneously. By negoti-ating this dual entry into Foucault, one may be able to avoid transforming Foucauldian thought into either a discontinuous collage of three periods or a single coherent 'meta-theory'. To try to live up to this dual entry approach, I suggest the following: for mainly pedagogical reasons, I shall briefly review separately each of the three Foucauldian periods. However, in my subsequent general introduction to the contributions to this book, it should become obvious that most of them, although using concepts from one of the periods as a starting-point, end up making linkages to the other periods. Consequently the titles of the three parts of this volume don't 'follow' the periodization of Foucault's work.

The archeological approach

This first period is that of the early Foucault, and includes books published in the 1960s (Foucault 1961, 1963, 1966, 1969).[8] The most comprehensive and systematic critical examination of Foucault's archeological approach to date is that of Gary Gutting (1989). At least one theorist has explicitly adopted Foucault's archeological approach to his study of the environment (Berman 1981: 74).

The method, or more precisely the approach, is called 'arche-ological' because it attempts to undertake excavations of historical texts. The purpose of these intellectual archeological digs is to reveal the various historical layers of what constitutes, or con-stituted, knowledge. Foucault was interested in what he called *épistème*, which is a historically specific, coherent configuration of how knowledge is organized (around disciplines, concerns, themes, etc.) and what kind of justifications are deemed acceptable to support that knowledge. It is important to stress two points. First, 'archeology is not an isolated method reflecting Foucault's idio-syncratic approach to the history of thought. Rather, it is rooted in the French tradition of history and philosophy of science' (Gutting 1989: x–xi) represented by, among others, Jean Cavaillès, Gaston Bachelard and Georges Canguilhem (Canguilhem 1988, 1989). However, this 'tradition' doesn't represent the established intellectual mainstream even in France. It may be a 'tradition', but it is a marginal one in the ocean of Marxisms, ranging from Garaudy through Althusser to Bourdieu, and of the different schools of the 'philosophy of experience' (J. Miller 1993: 59) represented by Sartre, Merleau-Ponty and post-Freudian/Lacanian psychoanalysis. This illustrates further what I described earlier as Foucault's 'marginal belonging'. Secondly, archeology is not a coherent theory or 'method' from which flow Foucault's studies of madness (Foucault 1961, 1963) and the human sciences (Foucault 1966). Rather, archeology is a *post facto* reconstruction/ justification of his earlier case studies. In fact, archeology is an 'ill-defined methodology' (Gutting 1989: 109) emerging from specific historical studies. Foucault only attempted to systematically work through his archeological method in the last book of this period – *The Archaeology of Knowledge* – which already pointed to the subsequent *déplacement* toward 'genealogy' (Foucault 1969).

The main point that Foucault tried to make throughout this period was that knowledge is relative to the historical context from which it emerges. 'We are doomed historically to history, to the patient construction of discourses about discourses, and to the task of hearing what has already been said' (Foucault 1963: xvi). For Foucault, there can be no adjudicating positivist external 'reality' by which to evaluate the 'truth', the validity of a discourse about knowledge. However, this position doesn't make Foucault a relativist in the sense that 'anything goes', that it is impossible to know anything and so forth. On the contrary, Foucault's archeology adopts 'truth-claims' in themselves as the factual background on which he builds his detailed studies. The only level of factual 'reality' that interests Foucault is statements about a presumed objective reality. This makes Foucault a contextualist of the statements of observers of 'objective reality', an observer of 'situated knowledge' (Haraway 1989), an observer of the 'manufacturing of knowledge' (Knorr-Cetina 1981, 1983).

Foucault's main focus during his archeological period was on scientific discourses and how objects of legitimate scientific investigations emerge. His principle interest was the emergence of discourses about human nature through the 'human sciences', and how humans become the objects of their own scientific enquiries.

For example, one of the specific scientific discourses that Foucault studied was 'madness' and the creation of social medical institutions in the European context around the eighteenth century (Foucault 1961, 1963). In *Order of Things* (1966) Foucault offers a more global, or at least structural, view of the historical landscape of knowledge. According to him, there was a clear rupture, a clear break (sometime around the sixteenth century), between what he calls the 'Classical Age' and 'Modernity'. In *Order of Things*, he takes three areas of knowledge, which we now might call linguistics, economics and biology. Foucault found that around the end of the eighteenth century there was a rupture in the epistemological field, which led to the emergence of these disciplines. For example, in the Classical Age, there was a direct link between words and things. This was the point that the French title of *The Order of Things* – *Les Mots et les choses* ('words and things') – was trying to convey. Words directly represented the objects they named. The Classical Age was the age of 'representation'. After the Classical Age, a gap between 'reality' and language opened up, which meant that representation ('representationalism' to use Charles Taylor's term) was no longer credible (Taylor 1985). 'Representation no longer exists; there's only action – theoretical action and practical action which serve as relays and form networks' (Deleuze in Bouchard 1977: 206). The new focus became the meaning and significance of linguistic signs. The second example is the transition from an analysis of 'wealth' as static, which was prevalent during the Classical Age (Adam Smith), to an economic analysis based on the dynamic circulation of production and consumption (Ricardo and Marx).

The third example is more directly pertinent to the contemporary environmental debate. It is about the emergence of the biological sciences. During the Classical Age, knowledge about the natural world was based on the construction of categories built around 'resemblance'. Thus, Carolus Linnaeus the well-known Swedish naturalist (1707–78) established a comprehensive nomenclature of plants and animals based on their similarities. For flowers, this nomenclature was based on the number of flower parts. After the Classical Age, classification was based no longer on Linnaeus's visual similarities of flower parts, but on a radically new concept centred on hidden dynamic mechanisms of life called now 'biology' (Foucault 1970). It is the knowledge of this new discipline called 'biology' which created the conditions for an articulation of the contemporary environmental critique. For

Foucault the emergence of 'biology' as a new scientific discipline signals the 'entry of life into history', what Foucault later calls 'biopower'. This historical contextualization of biology makes some environmental theorists worried about the tactical use of non-epistemological grounded environmental knowledge in the current struggle against polluters who could argue that there is no 'objective' yardstick by which to measure 'pollution', that the 'environmental crisis' is relative, and therefore that there is no need to change existing practices (Soulé and Lease 1995). Because Foucault was not a relativist but a contextualist, this charge cannot be sustained. Furthermore, because validated environmental scientific knowledge often retains a certain degree of uncertainty, and is subject to challenge and change over time, there is little point in trying to anchor it in a static epistemological justification system. In my view, it is more productive to follow Foucault's path and highlight some of the historical contingencies in the construction of knowledge about the 'environment', including the justifications for what some might call 'environmental pollution' and others a minor price to be paid for 'progress'. A Foucauldian discursive approach might help us to understand 'science as an environmental claim-making activity' (Hannigan 1995: 76–91) or the process of 'constructing environmental risks' (ibid. 92–108). It might be more productive than investing effort in establishing a homogenized, fundamentalist environmentalist epistemology as desired by Callicott, for example (1990).

However, there are at least four problems with Foucault's archeological approach (Gutting 1989: 222–6). First, in Foucault's archeological method, 'there is nothing that goes beyond the methodology of Canguilhem's history of concepts' (ibid. 218) and, I might add, very little beyond the British school of science historians (Porter 1977; Rousseau and Porter 1980). Furthermore, Foucault's historical case studies present 'major gaps at crucial points in the argument' (Gutting 1989: 226). Second, Foucault's archeology remains, in the final analysis, a structuralist approach, in the sense that it tries to reveal the deep historico-epistemological structure of the conditions of knowledge that Gutting calls the 'structuralist temptation' (ibid. 266). There is indeed a tension between Foucault's truth-claim about revealing the structure of knowledge and the contextuality of all knowledge, including presumably Foucault's own archeology. Foucault's subsequent response to this critique was to say that he was never a structuralist, but instead offered a critique of structuralism. The irony is that this critique of structuralism happened to be structural in approach.[9] Foucault may have tried to 'turn his back' to structuralism, but structuralism remains stuck to his back! Third, the 'structuralist temptation' of Foucault's archeology creates what Charles Taylor would call a 'kind of distance from its own value commitments, which consists in the fact that it alone is lucid about their status as fruits of a constructed order, which lucidity sets it apart from other views and confers the advantage on itself on being free from delusions' (Taylor 1989: 100). Ultimately Taylor finds 'this view as deeply implausible as its empiricist cousins' (ibid. 99).[10] Fourth, the archeological approach was criticized mainly – but not exclusively – by Marxists for being too focused on ideal categories of knowledge and for ignoring social relations and power relations in the everyday life (Gutting 1989: 224–6). Reading the early Foucault, one might indeed get the impression that what makes history tick are the ruptures/discontinuities which occurred in the historico-epistemological structures of knowledge. In the next section, we'll see how Foucault responded to this criticism through his genealogical approach.

In conclusion, Foucault's archeological 'history is sufficiently responsible and challenging to be worth serious attention, but it is also often greatly oversimplified and lacking in evidential support' (Gutting 1989: 262).[11] His archeological approach has definitively challenged some environmentalists in either reassessing or coming to the defence of their epistemological justification – and the need for such epistemological justification – to articulate their own environmental critique. In this context, it is important to restate what Foucault said later about environmental knowledge (i.e. 'ecology'): '[I]n fact, ecology also spoke a language of truth. It was in the name of knowledge concerning nature, the equilibrium of the processes of living things, and so forth, that one could level the criticism' (Foucault 1988b: 15).

However, this 'language of truth' about nature can also lead to a form of environmental / green fundamentalism. As Andrew Dobson reminds us,

[T]he foundation-stone of Green politics is the belief that our finite Earth places limits on our industrial growth. This finitude, and the scarcity it implies, is an *article of faith for Green ideologues*, and provides the fundamental framework within which any putative picture of a green society must be drawn. (Dobson 1990: 73, my emphasis)

Even if Foucault's archeological methodology is shaky, one of its political effects might be to help environmentalists resist the 'fundamentalist temptation' of unreflexively reducing the justification for environmental activism and actions to a presumed epistemologically solid ground of what is understood by 'nature' as defined by the natural sciences. It is becoming more urgent to resist this fundamentalist temptation, because, while the 'geopolitical reach of environmental science has become more and more expansive, its intellectual temper has become more reductionist' (Wynne 1994: 171).

The genealogical approach

This second period – the 'middle' or 'genealogical' Foucault – includes Foucault's writings published in the 1970s. It includes not only his main books (Foucault 1969, 1975, 1976) but also numerous articles, book reviews, interviews and course descriptions (Defert and Ewald 1994).

The genealogical approach is in part an attempt to respond to critiques levied against archeology. By adopting genealogy, Foucault tried to distance himself further from structuralism and detached empiricism. This genealogical *déplacement* operates at two levels. First, as a method, genealogy 'rejects the metahistorical deployment of ideal significations and indefinite teleologies' (Foucault 1984c: 77). On the contrary, genealogy

> record[s] the singularity of events outside of any monotonous finality, it must seek them in the most unpromising places, in what we tend to feel is without history, in sentiments, love, consciousness, instincts, it must be sensitive to their recurrence, not in order to trace the gradual curve of their evolution, but to isolate the different scenes where they engaged in different roles. (Foucault 1984c: 76)

Foucault borrowed strongly from Nietzsche's analysis of 'descent', which is 'not the erecting of foundations: on the contrary, it disturbs what was previously considered immobile; it fragments what was thought unified; it shows the heterogeneity of what was imagined consistent with itself' (Foucault 1984c: 82).

Secondly, genealogy adds to the archeological and contextualizing understanding of knowledge within a scientific discursive rationality, the broader context of social practices. This broader genealogical context refers to the vast heterogeneous webs of social practices criss-crossed by relations of power, which include the human 'body – and everything that touches it: diet, climate, and soil' (1984a: 83). Instead of searching for a grand structural narrative explaining the various layers of knowledge, his project became more specific in the scope of his studies, and more modest in his objectives. He wanted to offer a description of the conditions of emergence of the present ('a genealogy of the present') at the micro-level of 'forgotten' social practices.[12] For Foucault the genealogist, the structure and structuration of knowledge became less important than what he identified as a 'will to knowledge', which seems to be the main driving motivation behind modern sciences. Furthermore, Foucault is not only highly sceptical about the one universal truth sought by this 'will to knowledge'; he also pointed out some of the unintended effects, including environmental effects, of the 'will to truth' (Sheridan 1980).

> Even in the greatly expanded form it assumes today, the will to knowledge does not achieve a universal truth; man is not given an exact and serene mastery of nature. On the contrary, it ceaselessly multiplies the risks, creates dangers in every areas, it breaks down illusory defenses . . . ; it releases those elements of itself that are devoted to its subversion and destruction. (Foucault 1984c: 95–6)

Beyond the general ranting against 'postmodernism' by some environmental theorists (Sessions 1995a; Bookchin 1990: 73–4), it is interesting to note the similarities between the critique of environmental 'management' (i.e. instrumental knowledge) by the same environmental theorists and Foucault's concept of the 'will to knowledge'.

> [I]ncreasingly intensive management produces a host of unintended consequences which are perceived by the managers and the public, and specially by the environmental/ecology movement, as real and severe problems. The usual approach, however, is to seek more intensive management, which spawns even more problems. And each of these problems is seen as separate, with separate experts and interest groups speaking to each other across a chasm of different technical vocabularies. (Devall and Sessions 1985: 146)

These similarities between the environmental theorists' critique and Foucault's suggest that there may be common ground in their analyses of contemporary social practices despite differences in their epistemological premisses. However, nature sceptics like Foucault would remain deeply suspicious of the 'belief that society ought to conform to nature' because of the normalizing effects of this belief and the danger identified by Andrew Ross 'that the authority of nature, and hence of the status quo, will become a despotic vehicle for curtailing rights and liberties' (Ross 1994: 12).

Through genealogy, Foucault also responds to the Marxist critique of archeology by looking not only at discourses about knowledge ('discursive practices'), but also at the social practices through which people live ('non-discursive practices').[13] This genealogical *déplacement* led him to consider power relations which occur in social practices, specially at the micro-level, and at the 'practice of everyday life' (de Certeau 1984). Foucault refrains from explicitly defining his concept of 'power'. In fact, he spends a lot of effort stating what power *is not*, rather than what power *is*. This radical 'negation' has to be situated in the context of Foucault's tactical writing.[14] By constantly defining power as what it *isn't* and refusing to say what it *is*, Foucault resists the temptation to adopt 'power' as an essentialist, empiricist category. Or at least, this enables Foucault to keep the concept of 'power' within the various contexts which led to its emergence, and removes the need to anchor it in any precise fixed location. Genealogy is the approach which enables Foucault to show that any anchoring point for the concept of 'power', for example, is historically contingent. Far from adopting a privileged objectivist/empiricist position, as Taylor seems to believe, Foucault's 'own value commitment' (Taylor 1989: 100) is explicitly Nietzschean in theory *and* in practice through his tactical writings.[15] Foucault's refusal to define concepts like 'power' is not a 'failure', as Taylor would argue, but, on the contrary, highlights the constraints imposed on us by the contingency of language and vocabulary in which we are embedded and by which we are constituted. Therefore, Foucault's 'own value commitment' is the systematic, constant transgression of the limits of the given language, as with the term 'power' (Lemert and Gillan, 1982) Foucault has no interest in defining/anchoring a theory of power 'outside' the limits of what power is currently understood to be. On the contrary, his only purpose is to constantly challenge the limits as defined by the various discourses and practices. Within these constraints, it is possible, nevertheless, to make the following points about the various concepts emerging from Foucault's genealogy.

First, 'power' is not something which the State or a dominant class *has* or *possesses* and which others don't have. Power is not a zero-sum game. Power is mostly relational; it rarely entails absolute domination. Even in the most unequal situations of relations of power, those subjected to power do exercise some choices, however limited. In Michel de Certeau's view, Foucault attempts

> to bring to light the springs of this opaque power that has no possessor, no privileged place, no superiors or inferiors, no repressive activity or dogmatism, that is almost autonomously effective through its technological ability to distribute, classify, analyse and spatially individualize the objects dealt with. (de Certeau 1984: 46)

The Foucauldian idea of power can be conceptualized as a 'field of power' similar to the field of forces and vectors described by physics or the workings at the level of the 'microcellular' described by biology (Baudrillard 1987: 12). However, it is important to stress that Foucault wasn't making a strong epistemological claim about a presumed superiority of physics and biology to explain social phenomena; he was using the imaginary of physics and biology as a tactical allegory to undermine prevalent discourses about 'power'.[16]

Second, 'power' for Foucault is more than simply preventing or forcing others to do something they would not do on their own. It is more than just 'naked' violence. In fact, under the specificity of European 'Modernity', the practice of power

> has been characterized on the one hand, by a legislation, a discourse, an organisation based on public right, whose principle of articulation is the social body and the delegative status of each citizen; on the other hand, by a closely linked grid of disciplinary coercions whose purpose is in fact to assure the cohesion of this same social body. (Foucault 1980h: 106)

These two simultaneous, 'heterogeneous' aspects of modern power – 'a right of sovereignty' and a 'mechanism of discipline' – mean that, for Foucault, the exercise of power has *normalizing* effects on the population. Disciplinary mechanisms can indeed restrict the possibilities regarding what individual and collective identities can do, be or become. However, the existence of disciplinary mechanisms with a 'right of sovereignty' also enables individuals or groups to take on an identity which might be the condition for subsequent, unintended actions. It is because of this process of constructing identities – through the 'heterogeneity between a public right of sovereignty and a polymorphous disciplinary mechanism' (ibid.) – that Foucault qualified power as being 'positive', in contrast to the more conventional view of power ('royal' form of power) as solely repressive. For example, current 'gay', 'lesbian' or 'queer' identities are the unintended effects of, on the one hand, legal and medical discourse creating and disciplining 'homosexuality' in late nineteenth-century Europe and, on the other hand, the 'delegative' urge of the discourse on public right.[17] For Foucault, the 'strategies of normalization' (like constructing 'heterosexuality' as the norm, by contrasting it with the 'abnormality' of 'homosexuality') constitute one effect of power which in many cases is resisted by those who are supposed to be normalized as 'abnormal'. One of the central objectives of Foucault's genealogy was to reveal these 'tactics of resistance' which may have been forgotten and use them as 'counter-memories'. The distinction between strategies of normalization and tactics of resistance[18] can be appreciated only at the micro-analytical level, in the sense that only detailed, localized studies of events can capture that distinction within the specificity of its own context. Because instances of normalization and resistance constantly interact in a dynamic manner, reversals occur. Yesterday's resistance can become today's normalization, which in turn can become the conditions for tomorrow's resistance and/or normalization. The concept of normalization / resistance cannot be understood as a fixed meta-narrative describing 'power' in the abstract, but, on the contrary, should be approached as a constant recontextualization of power relations as lived and experienced by humans. For example, it is important to understand how populations living in industrialized countries had their daily conduct normalized to become throw-away 'consumers' (de Certeau 1984: 30–4; Luke 1993b), and how parts of the radical environmental movement can be seen as tactics of resistance against it (e.g. Darier 1996b). Environmental tactics of resistance can include the systematic use of irony against an extremely 'serious' normalizing discourse like the one coming from the pro-nuclear lobby (Chaloupka 1992; Seery 1990).

Third, the field of power is not a structuralist framework in which humans are passive objects and mere products. Humans have some degree of 'liberty' or 'freedom'. However, 'liberty' as understood by Foucault is not an ontological quality of humans or an ideal state of suspended power relations – as it is for Liberals,

Marxists and humanists generally – but an expression of individuals' very own existence in the specificity of power relations.[19] For Foucault, there cannot be liberty in a space without power relations. Total liberation from 'oppression', from power relations, is a delusion, because power is not exclusively repressive, and because power is 'capillary', diffused and everywhere. Those who still want to believe in a grand teleological narrative of liberation see Foucault as being pessimistic because of the impossibility of escaping power relations. However, Foucault's view is simultaneously more accurate in terms of the conceptualization of power ('repressive' *and* 'positive'; constitutive *and* enabling) and ultimately more optimistic for several reasons. First of all, Foucault's concept of power is less deterministic than that of those who believe that humans are limited by their inherent nature or by the economic structure or by the iron law of historical materialism. Foucault's focus on the 'conditions of emergence' and 'resistance' suggests that power relations in the 'field of power' are not deterministic, but, on the contrary, a form of what I would call an 'open-ended determinism'. The field of power imposes constraints about the possible options open to individuals and groups, but it is those individuals and groups which ultimately make choices to accept these constraints or to challenge them. Foucault reminds us that

> [i]f one or the other were completely at the disposition of the other and became his thing, an object on which he can exercise an infinite and unlimited violence, there would not be relations of power. . . . In order to exercise a relation of power, there must be on both sides at least a certain form of liberty. (Foucault 1988b: 12)

Even in situations of extreme domination, there are possibilities of freedom. Thomas Dumm's interpretation of the biography of Nazi camp survivor Primo Levi is an illustration of Foucault's point (Dumm 1996: 144–52). Secondly, this 'open-ended determinism' is very unnerving for believers in a grand narrative of liberation or for some of those who are 'nature-endorsing'. Their critique can be summarized in relation to the following question: what is the clear direction / the teleological purpose which can guide humans in their resistance and in the choices open to them? Before even trying to answer this question, it is important to point out that Foucault was highly suspicious of any grand narratives of liberation such as humanism, liberalism or Marxism, because they also turned into new disciplinary regimes. Humanism's anthropocentrism led to justification for the 'domination' of nature; Liberalism justified disciplining humans as workers and consumers; Marxism – or at least its Stalinist experimentation – resulted in fast industrialization; and all three created the conditions for ecological 'crises'. For Foucault, ignoring the possibilities of a 'dark side' of any liberation project is the sure recipe for the demobilization of social activists once the liberation project turns sour or becomes obviously unfulfillable. It is in this context that one can see how Foucault would be suspicious of the brand of environmentalism which desires a world free of pollution, in which life is simpler, and social and natural harmony are established upon presumed 'natural limits'.[20] Foucault's counter-suggestion is that humans should be constantly vigilant and critical of all actions, especially those undertaken in the name of liberation or in the name of 'saving the environment' or obeying 'natural limits'.[21] In brief, social change, revolution or environmental activism is a never-ending activity in which tactics and 'goals' are constantly re-evaluated and adapted to changing circumstances within the field of power. Foucault's position on this point is not far from Marx's refusal to give precise details about what Communism would be: Marx thought that it was presumptuous to define precisely the form of a future society which could only be imagined by individuals and groups located in radically different sets of power relations in a different historical context.

Foucault was attacked not only by 'modernists', but also by postmodernists like Jean Baudrillard. His critique of Foucault centres on Foucault's alleged (over-) preoccupation with 'power'. For Baudrillard, 'Foucault's discourse is a mirror of the powers it describes' (Baudrillard 1987: 10) in the sense that 'with Foucault, we always brush against political determination in its last instance' (ibid. 40). For Baudrillard, Foucault's 'theory of control by means of a gaze that objectifies, even when it is pulverized into micro-devices is passé. With the simulation device we are no doubt as far from the strategy of transparence as the latter is from the immediate, symbolic operation of punishment which Foucault himself describes' (ibid. 16).

Baudrillard complains that Foucault 'does not tell us anything *concerning the simulacrum of power itself*' (ibid. 40, emphasis original). For Baudrillard,

> [i]t is useless . . . to run after power or to discourse about it *ad infinitum* since from now on it also partakes of the sacred horizon of appearances and is also there only to hide the fact that it no

longer exists, or rather to indicate that since the apogee of the
political has been crossed, the other side of the cycle is now starting in which power reverts into its own simulacrum. (ibid. 51)

There are at least two ways of responding to Baudrillard's critique. First, Foucault's preoccupation was *not* about power *per se*.
It is not by design that Foucault defined power by saying what
it is not. For Foucault, 'power is not an institution, and not a
structure; neither is it a certain strength we are endowed with'
(Foucault quoted in ibid. 42). The systematic use by Foucault of
'negatives' to define – or rather to '*n*/efine' – a concept is evidently
a tactical move to avoid having to redefine concepts that one might
not want to employ in the first place. Foucault lifts the concept of
power (its simulacrum?) from its context (by the use of the negative), and leaves it suspended in order to lose the conventional
meaning of 'power'. Baudrillard would probably answer that 'it is
a good thing that terms lose their meaning at the limits of the
text', but would still complain that Foucault doesn't 'do it enough'
(ibid. 38). Secondly, when Foucault doesn't use a negative to
describe 'power', he gives an open definition which might not be
too far from what Baudrillard might consider to be a definition of
the 'simulacrum of power itself': 'it is the name that one attributes
to a complex strategical situation in a particular society' (Foucault,
cited in ibid. 93). Although Baudrillard would argue against the
'strategical' aspect of Foucault's definition, might it be possible to
say that this 'complex strategical situation' is the *mise-en-scène* of
the 'simulacrum of power itself'? After all, isn't a *mise-en-scène* a
strategy even if it is without any strategist or strategical intentions?

Toward a genealogical critique of environmental practices: environmental governmentality, eco-politics and space

There are at least three concepts emerging from the genealogical
period which can be particularly helpful for an environmental
critique: 'governmentality', 'biopower' and 'space'.

'Governmentality' is the broadest term, and occurs in the context of Foucaults historical interpretation of the literature on 'reason of state' in Europe from around the sixteenth century. Foucault
identifies and qualifies the emergence of modern deployment of
power in the context of three axes: institutional centralization
around governmental agencies, the emergence of new instrumental
knowledge, and the capillary diffusion of power effects across the
entire social body. For Foucault, 'governmentality' is:

1   The ensemble formed by institutions, procedures, analyses and
    reflections, the calculations and tactics that allow the exercise
    of this very specific albeit complex form of power, which has as
    its target population, as its principle form of knowledge polit-
    ical economy, and as its essential technical means apparatuses
    of security.
2   The tendency which over a long period and throughout the
    West, has steadily lead towards the pre-eminence over all other
    forms (sovereignty, discipline, etc.) of this type of power which
    may be termed government, resulting, on the one hand, in the
    formation of a whole series of specific governmental appara-
    tuses, and, on the other, in the development of a whole com-
    plex of *savoirs*.
3   The process, or rather the result of the process, through which
    the state of justice of the Middle Ages, transformed into the
    administrative state during the fifteenth and sixteenth centur-
    ies, gradually becomes 'governmentalized'. (Foucault 1991a:
    102–3)

The concept of governmentality has potential for an environmental
critique, because it explicitly deals with issues of (state) 'security',
techniques of control of the population, and new forms of knowledge (*savoirs*). Contrary to more traditional analyses of 'public
policy', which focus narrowly on 'objectives', 'results' within an
instrumental framework of linear causalities and quantifiable data,
governmentality focuses on the deeper historical context and on
the broader power 'effects' of governmental policy (Dean 1994b;
Pal 1990). A certain number of studies explicitly using the concept of 'environmental governmentality' already exist (Rutherford
1994a, 1994b; Darier 1996a).

The more specific concepts of 'biopower' / 'biopolitics' emerged
initially from Foucault's archeological studies of the natural sciences and, more precisely, biology, but were recontextualized in
the framework of governmentality and power/knowledge. Biopolitics is the series of governmental strategies centred on this
new concept called 'life'. More precisely, for Foucault, biopolitics
is 'the manner by which it has been attempted, since the sixteenth
century, to rationalize the problems posed to government practices by phenomena concerning the totality of human beings constituted as a population: health, hygiene, natality, longevity, race'
(Foucault 1989d: 109, my trans.).

This concern for life ('biopolitics') identified by Foucault is largely
anthropocentric, in that the prime target is the control of all aspects

of human life, especially the conditions for human biological reproduction. Current environmental concerns could be seen as an
extension of 'biopolitics', broadened to all life-forms and called
'ecopolitics' (Rutherford 1993). On this scenario, the normalizing
strategy of ecopolitics is the most recent attempt to extend control
('management') to the entire planet (Sachs 1993). In this context,
the promotion of ecocentrism by deep ecology, for example, can
be seen as not only a critique of prevalent, increasing instrumental
control of the natural world, but as inserting itself very well into
the new normalizing strategy of an ecopolitics. My point here
should not be interpreted as a negative evaluation of deep ecology
per se. Instead, I want to illustrate the complexity of power relations and the constant dangers – but also opportunities – lurking
in the field of power. In this context, the adoption of a Manichaean
approach to environmental 'issues' by many environmental theorists fails to acknowledge that their tactic of environmental resistance is always what de Certeau calls 'maneuver "within the enemy's
field of vision",' and cannot be positioned as a referential 'external-
ity' (de Certeau 1984: 37). This is why Foucault's genealogical
approach is so important for an environmental critique.

Foucault's approach to 'space' is the third concept which might
also be extremely relevant to an environmental critique. Foucault
explored the problematization of 'space' within a historical context
(Foucault 1984e; 1989d: 99–106). According to the framework of
governmentality, the 'security' of the state is guaranteed not so
much directly by the control of a territory (space), but rather
through the increasing control of the population living in that
territory. In fact, Foucault suggested that at the beginning of the
seventeenth century the government of France started to 'think of
its territory on the model of the city'. According to Foucault,

> The city was no longer perceived as a place of privilege, as an
> exception in a territory of fields, forests and roads. . . . Instead, the
> cities, with the problems that they raised, and the particular forms
> that they took, served as the models for the governmental rationality
> that was to apply to the whole of the territory. A state will be well
> organised when a system of policing as tight and efficient as that of
> the cities extends over the entire territory. (Foucault 1984b: 241)

Consequently, one historical rupture which became a condition for
the environmental 'crisis' was the attempt to extend the system
of social control in place in the cities to the countryside. This historical analysis of the increasing control of the non-urban space (the

more 'natural' environment) is similar to the critique of social ecologists who might agree with Foucault that the domestication of
nature was part of a system of (urban) power relations among
humans which had for its objective the maintenance of the given
social order (Bookchin 1982). As the environmental 'crisis' was
one of the results of specific power relations – such as social
inequalities and political hierarchy – it would presumably have to
be addressed before – or at least at the same time as – the environmental 'crisis'. Obviously, deep ecologists, like George Sessions,
would interpret this focus on human issues as the continuation of
anthropocentrism which created the environmental 'crisis' in the
first place (Sessions 1995b). Locating Foucault with social ecologists
against deep ecologists is not accurate either. Foucault's studies of
the emergence and rise of 'human sciences' in the context of
governmentality – as a specific 'reason of state' based on security
– could also be the basis for a critique of anthropocentrism. However, unlike deep ecologists, Foucault would not suggest replacing
anthropocentrism by ecocentricism, which also presents its own set
of traps. For example, Foucault would probably agree with Timothy
Luke's critique of ecocentrism (i.e. anti / non-anthropocentrism)
as being also, ultimately, a humanly constructed category which is
policed by all-too-human ecocentrists. Justifying human actions in
the name of 'nature' leaves the unresolved problem of whose
(human) voice can legitimately speak for 'nature' and the inherent
dangers of such an approach.

As Luke remarks admirably,

> deep ecology could function as a new strategy of power for nor-
> malising new ecological subjects – human and non-human – in
> disciplines of self-effacing moral consciousness. In endorsing self-
> expression as the inherent value of all ecospheric entities, deep
> ecology also could advance the modern logic of domination by
> retraining humans to surveil and steer themselves as well as other
> beings in accord with 'Nature's dictates'. As a new philosophy of
> nature, then, deep ecology provides the essential discursive grid for
> a few enthusiastic ecosophical mandarins to interpret nature and
> impose its deep ecology dictates on the unwilling many. (Luke
> 1988: 85)

This longing for 'nature', either through the self-effacement of
humans before 'wilderness' (deep ecology)[22] or through nostalgia
for a simpler social order in harmony with nature (social ecology)[23]
is possible only in the context of an 'intimate distance' brought

about by the 'dislocation of nature in modernity' (Phelan 1993). Consequently, the 'space' that Foucault is talking about is not the unproblematized physical and material environment of the environmentalists, but the various problematizations of 'space' raised, for example, by feminists (Lykke and Bryld 1994). In this sense, Foucault and the environmentalists are not located in quite the same space! However, the reconceptualization of space – for example, as 'heterotopias' (Foucault 1986) – enabled Foucault to create a break in our current 'physical' understanding(s) of space. We shall come back to the important concept of 'heterotopias' as two of the contributors to this volume, Thomas Heyd and Peter Quigley, apply it.

The final Foucault

After the publication of the first volume of his *History of Sexuality* (1976), Foucault remained silent until just before his death in 1984. Foucault's silence was relative in the sense that he carried on giving numerous interviews. In retrospect, however, one can see a shift occurring sometime in the 1977–84 interval. Just before dying of AIDS, Foucault published the second and third volumes of *The History of Sexuality* (Foucault 1984a, 1984f). The introduction to *The Use of Pleasure* constitutes another *déplacement* from the second Foucault and from the first volume (Foucault 1976). Until *The Use of Pleasure* was published, the assumption was that, for Foucault, the forms taken by our subjectivities were the contingent effects of power relations and nothing more. For this reason alone, Foucault was highly suspicious of any teleological project such as, for example, 'ethics', which he saw as a technique for the normalization of the population, a technique whose objective was to control daily human conduct.[24] In this sense one could argue that Foucault was strongly against ethics. What surprised many readers after the publication of the second and third volumes was the focus on Greek ethics or, more precisely, on conditions for the emergence of the self-construction, by some Greeks, of how humans related to themselves. Now the question for Foucault was: how can individuals or groups of individuals shape / construct their own self / their own subjectivity / their identity and consequently their conduct in the world / in relative distance / autonomy from the process of normalization? This exercise illustrates what Foucault called a 'practice of freedom'. Some readers

saw in Foucault's final volumes the affirmation of an ontological
subject which he spent all his life seeking to escape. I believe that
this is a gross misreading of Foucault. In the first place, Foucault
was not an 'anti-humanist' in the sense of rejecting humanity; he
simply offered a critique of 'one style of being human' (Dumm
1996: 15). The only thing he was doing in the second and third
volumes was debunking over-determinist readings of normalization, as outlined by the genealogical Foucault and more precisely in
the first volume of *History of Sexuality*. Up to the end, for Foucault,
there was no ontological subject, as humanists would have everyone believe. However, for him the subjectivities of individuals
were not the sole effects of the normalization process. The various
forms that the subject takes also emerge from the specificity of the
field of power: this is to say, the occasional cracks in the *dispositif*
between normalization and resistance.

According to the second and third volumes, the subject can also
be self-constituted in 'a more autonomous way, through practices
of liberation, of liberty'. This 'autonomous way' is not based
on an ontological autonomy of the subject. 'I do indeed believe
that there is no sovereign, founding subject, a universal form of
subject to be found everywhere. I believe, on the contrary, that
the subject is constituted through practices of subjection, or, in a
more autonomous way, through practices of liberation, of liberty'
(Foucault 1988a: 50).

What Foucault was *not* doing in the last two volumes of *The
History of Sexuality* was giving a prescriptive ethical norm. He
was not suggesting that the ethics of the Greeks should be our
norms. On the contrary, the final volumes should be interpreted
as containing examples of non-strategic ethics – that is, ethics
which are not part of a strategy to normalize / control the population, but an ethics which emerges in relative autonomy from the
normalization process. The central objective of Foucault was to
tell his contemporaries that, in some cases, it is possible to remake
ourselves, to remake our self-identity independently of the normalization process, and for us to 'understand the ways in which
we are free' (Dumm 1996: 63). Thus the 'ethics' described in the
second and third volumes are merely examples of radical alterity,
of practices of freedom, from other spaces and from other times,
not a universal, ahistorical ethical prescription to be followed
to the letter. Foucault's ultimate position / ethical stand is well
summarized by Lawrence Kritzman, for whom 'the quintessential
challenge in the post-Sartrean age is to invent new forms of life

based on an ethical stance endlessly disengaging itself from all forms of discourse based on the familiar and accepted' (Kritzman 1988: xxiv–xxv).

Foucault's non-ethics has important consequences for environmental ethics in that the focus shifts away from the presumed discovery or 'rediscovery' of a true permanent 'ecological self'[25] to the active constitution of subjectivities which constantly rework humans' relations with themselves, with other life-forms, and with the world generally. The ethical constitution of what might be called 'green' subjectivities might be the endless process of 'ethicization' of being human in the world.

Where Do We Go from Here?

In summary, we have seen a degree of overlap between Foucault and environmentalism. In general, there is an irreconcilable conflict between the contextualizing premisses of Foucault's archeology and the frequent recourse by many environmental theorists to a naturalistic position in the last instance. However, Foucault and the environmental activists have potentially more in common when it comes to practical political tactics of resistance and to understanding the construction / deconstruction of subjectivities. Foucault wasn't interested in defining what is 'good' or 'bad' in the abstract, because these terms make sense only within the specificity of their contexts. Rather, Foucault's ethico-political project is to 'determine which is the main danger'. For him, 'not everything is bad, but everything is dangerous'. And if this is the case, then 'we always have something to do', which 'leads not to apathy but to a hyper- and pessimistic activism' (Foucault 1984d: 343). Surely this is the way that most environmentalists approach their political practices, asking 'What are the main dangers we are facing – including the normalizing dangers of environmental discourses themselves?' Even if there is deep pessimism in the environmental movement about the chances for the ecological survival of humans and many other life-forms on this planet, it hasn't lead to quietism. On the contrary, it has stimulated both a 'hyper-activism' of environmental resistance and a constant refashioning of one's own subjectivities. Despite 'turning his back to nature', Foucault's provocative and creative thinking may help us to face up to the environmental challenge.

Because of the stimulating diversity and richness of Foucault's approaches, themes and concepts, it is only possible to touch on some of them. This collection of essays intends to illustrate only the diversity of unintended Foucauldian effects on environmental critique. The first part of this volume approaches discourses of the 'environment' from a Foucauldian historical angle – that is, a genealogy of the present with several 'histories'.

In his chapter ' "The Entry of Life into History" ', Paul Rutherford focuses on 'biopolitics', which is probably the closest Foucault ever came to addressing the environmental issue from the perspective of how the mechanisms of biological life themselves became an object of 'reason of state' calculations and strategy. In this sense, 'life' as an object of scientific knowledge, as a state preoccupation, and as an ethical / normalizing guiding principle for individual conduct enters 'history', because it becomes an articulated, explicit strategy. Building on the Foucauldian concept of 'biopolitics', but pushing it beyond its central concern for human life, Rutherford shows that the current interest in ecology can be characterized as an 'ecological governmentality' in which all life-forms become objects of scientific enquiry, a series of state calculations based on 'security' and on the disciplining / normalization of the population. He illustrates this 'ecological governmentality' by reviewing in detail the procedures for *environmental impact assessment* as an emergence of discourse about eco-risks.

Using a Foucauldian-inspired 'archeo-genealogical' approach, Isabelle Lanthier and Lawrence Olivier also address the theme of 'biopolitics', and identify a recent rupture in the discourse of medicine and human health which introduces the concept of 'life-style', linking issues of human life to the quality of air, water, urban space and working environment. It is the technique of normalization of individual conduct through 'life-style' practices which created the conditions for the emergence of an environmental 'awareness'. Lanthier and Olivier show that the current environmental 'awareness' is not simply an extension or a deepening of biopolitics, but also an unexpected effect.

For her part, Catriona Sandilands's 'Sex at the Limits' critically explores the theme of ecological 'limits' and, more precisely, 'population control' in the recent history of environmental discourses. For Sandilands, 'calls for limits' have disciplinary and normative consequences which environmentalism rarely acknowledges. For example, the problematization of population control translates 'natural limits' into 'sexual limits', which have racialized, gendered and heterosexualized power relations. Sandilands concludes by advocating 'the reassertion of an overt sense of "polymorphous" pleasure into environmental discourses' as a tactic of resistance to the normative constraints of the discourses about 'population control'.

In 'Ecological Modernization and Environmental Risk', Paul Rutherford reviews part of the debate between German social theory and Foucault and its possible consequences for an understanding of the current problematization around the issue of 'environment'. It seems that the concerns for 'security' which emerge out of the 'reason of state' result in taking more environmental risks in order to guarantee more 'security'!

The second part of this collection is devoted more specifically to the effects of various techniques of enviro-normalization on the construction of subjectivities and conceptions of space. To reflect the plurality and heterogeneity of these techniques, this second part is entitled 'Environmentalities'.

The article by Timothy W. Luke on 'Environmentality as Green Governmentality' is a practical case study of 'ecological / green governmentality' in the current American environmental political context, which includes among others the Wise Use / Property Rights movement, the pro-business agenda of the Republican Congress, and President Clinton and Vice-President Gore's 'environmental musings'. Luke illustrates very well how 'environmentality' is one central characteristic of the new political economy of 'globalization' which includes 'eco-knowledge' and 'enviro-discipline'.

In his article, 'Art and Foucauldian Heterotopias', Thomas Heyd explores the concept of space in Foucault, especially heterotopias as an example of resistance against the homogenization and normalization of space. Heyd suggests that 'medicine wheels' located on the plains of North America and their occasional use as a source of inspiration in contemporary arts are an illustration of the importance of 'other places' in imagining other possibilities for the present and the future.

Sylvia Bowerbank's article 'Nature Writing as Self-Technology', warns us about the dangers in techniques of nurturing a 'green self' by a growing number of environmentalists. Bowerbank reminds us that 'self-technologies' such as nature retreats and 'eco-pastoral' exercises used by contemporary environmentalists are not new, but are part of a broader history of disciplinary strategies.

The third and final part of the volume deals with the intense debate between the 'nature-endorsing' and 'nature-sceptical' sides of environmental theory and the deployment of many strategies of resistance.

In 'Nature as Dangerous Space', Peter Quigley offers a fierce critique of the 'grounded responsibility' suggested in recent publications, most notably by Aaron Gare, Charlene Spretnak, Neil Evernden and George Sessions. To get away from problematic 'grounded responsibility' and/or 'nature-endorsing', Quigley proposes using Foucault's concept of resistance. As an example of resistance, Quigley mentions Foucault's 'heterotopias' as 'places where sites of opposition are created'.

For his part, Neil Levy resists the discourses associated with poststructuralism and Foucault because they tend to be 'profoundly anti-naturalistic', 'dangerously relativistic' and 'abstract'. If Levy identifies overlaps between the anti-humanist critique of poststructuralism and the anti-anthropocentrism of some of the environmental discourses, he also identifies profound differences. For Levy, 'if there is nature in Foucault's work, we can have no knowledge about it'. Nevertheless, he acknowledges the importance of the Foucauldian concept of resistance as one which works 'without committing us to a belief in an ontological referent'.

In the final chapter I build on Quigley's critique and also try to resist environmental ethics, which I see as moralistic and justified ultimately on the 'naturalistic fallacy'. I suggest instead a contextualized concept of resistance *à la* Foucault and use the example of non-essentialist gay/queer political tactics to outline what a Green aesthetic of existence might look like.

Notes

1   Madan Sarup identifies four features of poststructuralism, which he equates with postmodernism: (1) dissolution of the subject and subversion of the notion of structure; (2) critique of historicism; (3) critique of meaning; (4) critique of philosophy (1989: 2–3, 118). For a general introduction, see also Smart 1993. For a critique of postmodernism, see Norris 1990.
2   The 'filters' can also be considered as the only reality. The metaphor of the filter as filtering an objective reality for humans might be part of the illusion. Paraphrasing Derrida, one could say, 'il n'y a pas d'hors filtres'! For a stimulating discussion of textuality in Foucault and Derrida, see Said 1978b.
3   For an illustration of an acrobatic statement on the topic, see Murphy 1994: ix: 'The sociological construction of the relationship between the social and the natural must be done in a way that maintains the importance of social constructions without reducing reality to a social construction.'

4   There are three important biographies of Foucault (Éribon 1991; Macey 1993; J. Miller 1993) and a more recent rebuttal of critiques by Éribon (1994).

5   This is probably why Thomas Dumm see Foucault as a performer, as 'a sort of intellectual Elvis'. '[Foucault's] referentiality is not a sign of his lack of originality but is instead, an artifact of the unusually meticulous preparation of the archival retrieval' (Dumm 1996: 72).

6   I agree with Olivier (1995: 20) that Foucault's intentions were more philosophical than methodological.

7   For a similar 'bothends' way of approaching Foucault, see Mahon 1992, which, starting from a Nietzschean genealogical perspective, explores the foci of research of the three Foucaults: viz. 'truth', 'power' and the 'subject'.

8   For the purpose of chronological coherence and clarity, I give the date of the first publication in French, but in the Bibliography, I also give (in square brackets) the date of the first publication of the English translation, followed by the title in English.

9   Gutting shows that Foucault removed the word 'structural' from the later reprinting of *The Birth of the Clinic*. With archeology, it may be 'possible to make a *structural* analysis of discourses that would evade the fate of commentary by supposing no remainder, nothing in excess of what has been said, but only the fact of its historical appearance' (Foucault 1963: xvii; quoted in Gutting 1989: 134, my emphasis).

10 It is important to note that the target of Taylor's critique in this passage (1989: 99–100) is 'neo-Nietzscheans', which explicitly includes Foucault. Taylor's critique was directed not against the archeological approach, but against the Nietzschean position taken by Foucault in response to the limitations of the archeological approach. I took Taylor's critique out of its context on purpose, because, although I may disagree with Taylor's view of the Nietzschean Foucault, I believe that Taylor's critique is perfectly pertinent to the archeological period.

11 For an example of a subsequent archeological study of scientific knowledge which incorporates a genealogical 'power' dimension (i.e. 'power/knowledge'), see Rouse 1987.

12 For an example of genealogical re-memorization of forgotten practices, see Kubrin 1981, which shows that the founding father of 'modern' physics, Isaac Newton, was also an adept of magic.

13 It is interesting to note that the most supportive 'Marxian' (not Marxist?) evaluation of Foucault focuses exclusively on the genealogy, not the archeology (Smart 1983). For another stimulating Marxian reworking of Marxism through Foucault, see Poster 1985. Foucault also offered his own genealogical critique of Marxism: 'What strikes me in the Marxist analyses is that they always contain the question of "class struggle" but they pay little attention to one word in the phrase, namely "struggle" . . . But when they speak of the "class

struggle" as the mainspring of history, they focus mainly on defining class, its boundaries, its membership, but never concretely on the nature of the struggle. One exception comes to mind: Marx's own non-theoretical, historical texts, which are better and different in this regard' (Foucault 1988d: 123).

14 Another technique of tactical writing employed by Foucault is the use of quotation marks to create a rupture between the accepted meaning of a word and the object it is suppose to signify. For a discussion of the use of quotation mark by Foucault, see Visker 1995: 74–135.

15 For an account of Foucault as a 'self-professed' Nietzschean, see Olivier 1995.

16 For a similar likening of 'chaos theory of contemporary physics and postmodern critique of modernity's search for a univocal, stable structure that organizes all phenomena', see Zimmerman 1994: 13, 318–77.

17 Among many 'gay' historical studies, see Halperin 1990; Weeks 1985. From a historico-legal perspective, see Moran 1996; Stychin 1995.

18 I borrow this useful distinction from de Certeau. 'I call a *strategy* the calculation (or manipulation) of power relationships that becomes possible as soon as a subject with will and power (a business, an army, a city, a scientific institution) can be isolated. It postulates a *place* that can be delimited as its *own* and serve as the base from which relations with an *exteriority* composed of targets or threats (consumers or competitors, enemies, the country surrounding the city, objectives and objects of research, etc.) can be managed' (de Certeau 1984: 35–6). '[A] *tactic* is a calculated action determined by the absence of a proper locus. No delimitation of an exteriority, then, provides it with the condition necessary for autonomy . . . it is maneuver "within the enemy's field of vision". . . . It does not, there-fore, have the options of planning general strategy and viewing the adversary as a whole within a district, visible, and objectifiable space' (ibid. 36–7).

19 I am not using the word 'individual' to affirm an individualist onto-logy and/or epistemology. On the contrary, one should see the 'individualization' of self-identity as one of the effects of modern power relations. Again, we are trapped in the boundaries of lan-guage, for we don't have vocabulary for describing what is not!

20 '[E]nvironmental consciousness has . . . helped to reinforce the cur-rent recessionary messages about self-sacrifice and deprivation in our daily lives' (Ross 1994: 266). 'While it may be necessary to rebut the calls for limits – sounding across a whole spectrum from the economics of corporate environmentalism to the cultural pol-itics of traditional values – it would be historically naive to suggest that cultural freedoms can be uncoupled from the social conditions

in which they were won and are maintained today. On the one hand, popular consciousness tenaciously insists that people are less free when they have less to consume even though many consumers recognise that higher levels of consumption involve them in socially constraining networks of dependency and debt that are not always visible or economically quantifiable. But it is rank First World arrogance to suggest that people in non-consumer societies are somehow more free in their less commodified ways, or more healthy in their freedom from diseases associated with life in high-consumption societies' (ibid. 267). For a study of the social construction of human 'needs', see Leiss 1976.

21 Baudrillard makes a direct link between 'consumption' and the 'desire for totality' which implies that, for example, the longing for a coherent ecological totality in fact sustains 'consumption'. For Baudrillard, '[t]he desire to "moderate" consumption or establish a normalising network of needs is naive and absurd moralism. At the heart of the project from which emerges the systematic and indefinite process of consumption is a frustrated desire for totality' (Baudrillard 1982: 25). It is because we cannot achieve a totalizing objective world-view that we are consuming the world.

22 The discourse of 'wilderness' by deep ecologists is indeed the 'litmus test of whether someone has firmly adopted a non-anthropocentric ecological ethic that transcends mere environmental pragmatism and enlightened human self-interest' (Chase 1991: 18).

23 'The fourteenth and fifteenth centuries may well have marked a unique watershed for Western humanity. History seemed to be poised at a juncture: society could still choose to follow a course that yielded a modest satisfaction of needs based on complementarity and the equality of unequals. Or it could catapult into capitalism with its rules of equivalence and the inequality of equals, both reinforced by commodity exchange and a canon of "unlimited needs" that confront "scarce resources"' (Bookchin 1982: 214–15).

24 For a superb application of the conceptual framework of the normalization of 'conduct' to the seventeenth century, see (Tully 1993a). See also Rose 1990.

25 For an example of this position, see Mathews 1991. For Mathews the issue is to 'find a metaphysical and ethical expression for the intuition of "oneness" and interconnectedness' (p. 3). Despite the obviously fundamentalist character and non-Foucauldian approach of Mathews's search for the 'ecological self', it is possible to read Mathews as a strategic counter-example to current non-ecological modern selves. However, it is quite clear that Mathews does literally 'believe' in her metaphysical ethics. Again, this illustrates the tension that Foucault identified in the environmental movement between a critique of existing truth-claims and a political practice justified by similar truth-claims (Foucault 1988b: 15).

Part I

Histories

2

'The Entry of Life into History'

Paul Rutherford

Introduction

In the decade since Foucault's death there has been a proliferation
of academic literature applying what could broadly be described
as poststructuralist insights to the study of gender, social policy,
health policy and medicine, education, international politics, etc.
However, in the area of environmental issues, works adopting
this approach have been most notable for their rarity, despite
occasional exceptions.[1]

Modern thinking about the natural environment is characterized by the belief that nature can be managed or governed through
the application of the scientific principles of ecology. This chapter
considers how governing the environment in this sense involves
more than the familiar political activities of the modern administrative state. Environmental governance in advanced liberal societies is far more dependent on the role played by scientific expertise
in defining and managing environmental problems than the more
traditional state-centric notions of politics and power would suggest. Scientific ecology has become a political resource that in
important respects constitutes the objects of government and, at
the same time, provides the intellectual machinery essential for
the practice of such government.

Foucault's ideas of biopolitics and governmentality can help
provide a critical perspective on contemporary environmental problems. In this chapter I attempt to demonstrate this by developing
three basic propositions: first, that the concern with ecological
problems and environmental crises can be seen as a development of
what Foucault called 'the regulatory biopolitics of the population';

second, that this contemporary biopolitics has given expression to a mode of governmental rationality that is related to the institutionalization of new areas of scientific expertise, which in turn is based on a bio-economic understanding of global systems ecology; and third, that this relatively recent articulation of biopolitics gives rise to new techniques for managing the environment and the population that can be termed 'ecological governmentality'.

Discipline and Biopolitics: Foucault

In *Discipline and Punish,* Foucault examined in detail the emergence of a form of disciplinary power that acted directly on the body of individuals. Disciplinary power did not completely displace other forms of power; rather, it invested these with a new capacity to penetrate the most minute, everyday activities of individuals, to produce docile bodies 'that may be subjected, used, transformed and improved' (Foucault 1975: 136).

Discipline and Punish focused on understanding these disciplinary technologies as operating in the 'minute, capillary relations of domination', forming the ongoing substratum for the institutions and structures of the state (Gordon 1980: 255). The microphysics of power suggested that the operation of power relations could be grasped only through analysis of the disciplinary techniques that produced docile bodies within specific institutional contexts, such as prisons, schools or the work-place. A key criticism of Foucault's work in this period was that its emphasis on such local relations of power ignored the 'macro' issue of the relationships between particular institutions ('society') and the state. His later work on governmental rationality provided a direct, important response to this type of criticism (Gordon 1991: 4). In the first volume of *The History of Sexuality* Foucault turned his attention specifically to a consideration of the connection between the operation of power at the micro-level of the individual within particular institutional situations and the problem of the regulation at a global level of entire populations by the state (Dean 1994a: 175–6; Gordon 1991: 4–5).[2]

The context in which Foucault develops this is his description of the emergence in the eighteenth and nineteenth centuries of a new form of power concerned with 'administering life' (Foucault 1976: 139). This *biopower* focuses on the fostering of life and the care of populations, and developed in two distinct yet related forms. The first of these, constituting 'an anatomo-politics of the human body', focuses on disciplining the body of the individual, to increase its utility and manageability through its 'integration into systems of efficient and economic controls'. This element of biopower is generally equivalent to the notion of disciplinary power developed in *Discipline and Punish*. The second, more recent form of biopower focuses on the supervision of what Foucault calls 'the species body', 'the body imbued with the mechanics of life and serving as the basis of the biological processes'. Management of the species body occurs through a range of 'interventions and *regulatory* controls' which he characterizes as '*a biopolitics of the population*' (ibid. 139).

A range of empirical investigations, particularly in demography and geography, were closely connected with the rise of these regulatory interventions, and Foucault argued in general that the social sciences developed to meet the particular demands of the administration of human populations, resources and the economic relations between them (Foucault 1980e: 171–2; 1991a: 93). In these developments, *population* emerges as an economic and political problem in which the central concern is the proper balance between population growth and available resources (Foucault 1976: 25). It is worth noting that *in this process, not only does the idea of a measurable and manageable population come into existence, but so also does the notion of the environment as the sum of the physical resources on which the population depends.* According to Foucault, in the eighteenth century population and environment came to be seen as constituting 'perfect living interrelation', with the task of the state involving the supervision of the 'living interrelations between those two types of living beings' (population and environment)[3] (Foucault 1988c: 160). Elaboration of this 'population–riches problem' occurs within a network of new types of knowledge and techniques of government, having as their primary concern programmes for the statistical description and efficient management and disposition of all elements of the population and its resources.[4]

Foucault regarded biopower as indispensable to the development of modern society. He pointed to the parallel growth of the *institutions* of state power alongside the *techniques* of biopower (both disciplinary anatomo-politics and biopolitics) within the economy and the population. According to Foucault,

it is largely as a force of production that the body is invested with relations of power and domination; but, on the other hand, its

constitution as labour power is possible only if it is caught up in a
system of subjection . . . the body becomes a useful force only if it
is both a productive body and a subjected body. (Foucault 1975:
25–6)

Thus the development of capitalism, the economic modernization
of Europe, was dependent on the emergence of disciplinary power.
Investing social relations with these new 'micro' relations of power
was very much the prerequisite for the success of capitalist modernization (Foucault 1976: 140–1; Rabinow 1984: 18).

It was through the operation of biopower at every level of the
social body, across a diverse range of institutional locations (including schools, clinics, the family, the military and administration),
that the modern capitalist economy became possible and was sustained. The techniques of biopower also played a pivotal role in
processes of social segregation and hierarchization, which not only
guaranteed that the political relations of domination and hegemony
of the modern state were more efficiently perpetuated, but also
ensured a congruence between the 'accumulation of men to that of
capital, the joining of the growth of human groups to the expansion of productive forces' (Foucault 1976: 140–1)

Several other factors were identified by Foucault as arising from
the formation of this new domain of political action focused on
human beings as living entities. One was the eighteenth-century
'rupture' in the way that scientific discourse dealt with the 'two-
fold problematic of life and man': that is, the emergence of the
modern view of human beings based on a new relationship between history and life – the 'dual position' of human life that is
simultaneously 'outside history, in its biological environment, and
inside human historicity, penetrated by the latter's techniques of
knowledge and power' (ibid. 143). This dual problematic itself
can be understood, in large part, as arising from the fundamental
shift that occurred towards the end of the eighteenth century, in
the way in which life in general was conceptualized. The transformation was associated, according to Foucault's account, with
a general discontinuity between the 'Classical' and the 'Modern'
era, and in particular with the development of modern biology.
Unlike classical natural history, modern biology saw life as dependent for its existence on the way in which organisms are functionally linked to their external surroundings: that is, on the way
in which they *exchange resources with their environment*. The
classical view of a timeless continuity of nature was replaced by a

concept of life in which species were understood as discontinuous entities shaped by the evolutionary influence of the environment, and therefore 'tied to the time in which these forces and their effects exist' (Gutting 1989: 192).

Another crucial outcome of the growth of modern biopower was the increasing importance of what Foucault described as the 'action of the norm', at the expense of sovereign power and the law (Foucault 1976: 144). There are several key elements to this argument. There was a decline in the absolute power of the sovereign over his subjects, and a shift to reliance on a series of expert knowledges that endowed the subject with a multiplicity of properties denoting such things as sexual aberration, criminality, states of physical, mental and moral health, etc. In concert with this, there developed a corresponding series of specific disciplinary technologies that operated corporeally to train the body, thereby increasing its economic utility and political docility (Foucault 1975: 128–44). The experts involved in the production of these new discourses also acted as the technicians and 'normative judges' responsible for the application of such disciplinary and corrective programmes. Effecting such detailed, individualized supervision was beyond the blunt, prohibitive capacities of the judicial system. Rather, Foucault argued that what was needed was a subtle, individualizing mode of power that was able to 'take charge of life' and distribute the living, biological subject as efficiently as possible within the social and economic field. Such a task required 'continuous regulatory and corrective mechanisms' with the power to 'quantify, measure, appraise and hierarchise', so as to effect a distribution about the norm (Foucault 1976: 144).

Biopower did not replace juridical power, but rather functioned as its correlative, so that the law increasingly tended to function as a norm rather than as a rigid prohibition. The legal system was more and more 'incorporated into a continuum of apparatuses (medical, administrative, and so on) whose functions are for the most part regulatory' (ibid.), and it was this displacement of sovereign power and the incorporation of the juridical as a correlative to the 'effectivity of the norm' that distinguished biopower (Hewitt 1983: 69). It was the conjunction of the modern biological understanding of *life* and the proliferation of medical and social-scientific knowledge as normalizing disciplines that brought forth a qualitatively different, distinctively modern *biopolitics*. For Foucault, the rise of biopower, from the eighteenth century onwards, represented quite literally the 'entry of life into history'

(Foucault 1976: 141). By this Foucault was not denying that the age-old problems of the biological struggle for existence, as manifested in the threat of famine and epidemic, could exert a political effect on history. Such influences were clearly not new. Rather, he was arguing that with economic development and increased productivity during the eighteenth century it became possible to gain some *control* over the threat of death at this basic biological-demographic level. Foucault's comments on why this occurred are generally in line with standard accounts of modernization. He argued that increases in agricultural productivity and availability of resources in eighteenth-century Europe encouraged rapid demographic growth, and accompanied greater security from starvation and disease. Essential to this was the development of new areas of knowledge, particularly in biology, agriculture, and public health (Foucault 1980e: 168–72; 1976: 142). It is against the background of these transformations that Foucault identified the emergence of the discourses on population and security. He was able to claim that 'life enters history' precisely because these new technical and normative disciplines provided relative control over the actual conditions of life. In doing so, they took upon themselves responsibility for the control and modification of 'the life processes' (Foucault 1976: 142).

In the modern West, knowledge of the biological conditions of life and their relationship to individual and collective welfare thus came to be reflected upon as *political* concerns, and no longer as 'an inaccessible substrate' that emerged only periodically against the randomness of fate and death (ibid.). Political power was no longer primarily sovereign power exercised over legal subjects (over whom the ultimate authority was death), but was concerned with the management of living beings and their relations with all the factors that shape security and welfare. The influence which biopower exercised over living beings was necessarily 'applied at the level of life itself'; and in so operating, biopower simultaneously gained influence over the individual both politically and as a biological entity. The corporeal nature of the body of the subject was brought directly into the explicit calculations of power, and was thereby transformed into a subjected body. The body (individually and collectively) became both the raw material of power and at the same time that which produces and transforms itself as a living being (ibid. 142–3; Hewitt 1983: 69).

Foucault explicitly discounts the suggestion that biopower resulted in the total integration of all aspects of life into the techniques that administer it;[5] indeed, life 'constantly escapes them' (Foucault 1976: 143). Nevertheless, with the increasing penetration of bio-power's normalizing reach into new areas of life activity, and hence the emergence of life as a *political* object, a new conception of rights developed. However, according to Foucault, this was a form of rights radically different from the traditional right of sovereignty, and was incomprehensible from within the frame-work of the classical juridical system. It was in fact a notion of 'rights' that, while couched in the terminology of traditional rights, was 'turned back' against the traditional systems of rights and law. Thus the politicization of life, directed as it was at the satisfaction of essentially *biological* needs (including the psychological), gave rise to a recognizably modern interpretation of rights: 'The "right" to life, to one's body, to health, to happiness, to the satisfaction of needs, and beyond all the oppressions or "alienations", the "right" to discover what one is and all that one can be' (ibid. 145).

Biopolitics and Ecological Risk

Foucault suggests a continuity between this modern right to life and the contemporary concern about risks to the environment. He claims that the 'biological risks' confronting the human spe-cies 'are perhaps greater and certainly more serious, than before the birth of microbiology' (ibid. 143). He further suggests that the economic and social conditions that, since the eighteenth century, allowed the West a measure of relief from the struggle against famine, etc. do not necessarily apply 'outside the Western world', and goes on to link the notion of modernity directly with biopower and the conditions under which it emerged:

> But what might be called a society's 'threshold of modernity' has been reached when the life of the species is wagered on its own political strategies. For millennia, man remained what he was for Aristotle: a living animal with the additional capacity for a polit-ical existence; *modern man is an animal whose politics places his existence as a living being in question.*[6] (ibid., emphasis added)

These comments can be seen as an indication that Foucault's work on biopolitics is capable of addressing the notion of ecolo-gical risk and the problem of the social relation to nature, which are emerging as key problems for contemporary social theory. As will be discussed in another chapter, social theorists Ulrich Beck and Klaus Eder both understand ecological threats as the result of global processes of modernization and rationalization, which have created new *ecological fields of conflict* within contemporary society. Beck in particular points to a link between the success of economic growth and the consolidation of welfare state mechanisms in providing an unprecedented level of security for life in the West. From a different, yet not unrelated perspective, Eder emphasizes the rise of a new, post-industrial 'politics of class' involving competition for the symbolic definition of the social relation to nature. These perspectives inextricably link ecological problems with social systemic processes of modernization.

One useful way of approaching Foucault's notion of biopower is to follow Brian Turner, who has argued that, notwithstanding his apparent hostility to systematic theorizing, Foucault's work nevertheless implicitly embraces a particular causal explanation of the modern world (Turner 1984: 159). Turner identifies the 'unifying theme' of Foucault's work as a dual focus on the '*rationalisation of the body* and the *rationalisation of populations* by new combinations of power and knowledge', and argues that these rationalizations are the effect of increasing population densities, which in the nineteenth century came to threaten 'the political order of society' (ibid. 163, emphasis added). Turner rightly emphasizes the role which population pressures played in Foucault's analysis of the development of biopower, pointing out that

> it is this factor which stands behind the expansion and development of new regimes and regimens of control – a profusion of taxonomies, tables, examinations, drills, dressage, chrestomathies, surveys, samples and censuses. The pressure of men in urban space necessitates a new institutional order of prisons, asylums, clinics, factories and schools in which accumulated bodies can be made serviceable and safe. Just as the space of knowledge experiences accumulations of new discourses, so the social space is littered with bodies and the institutions which are designed to control them. (ibid. 160–1)

The point I would stress is that not only is knowledge pivotal to practices of power; it is also *central to the constitution of the objects upon which biopower operates* – that is, to the 'making-up' of *both* people and *things*. Biopolitics is therefore inherently linked to the development and elaboration of specific forms of expertise. This is an issue I will return to later in the chapter. For the present, suffice it to say that the definition and administration of populations simultaneously requires the constitution and management of the environment in which those populations exist and upon which they depend. Such a conclusion is implicit in Foucault's approach, although not developed, and as a consequence Foucault does not adequately deal with the way in which the political and economic problematization of populations also gave rise, in more recent times, to a similar problematization of nature and the environment.[7] However, it is clear from Foucault's discussions of the biopolitical regulation of populations that this assumes not only the disciplining of individuals and populations, but also, necessarily, a concern with the administration of 'all the conditions of life' as represented by the environment.

For Foucault biopolitics, the task of administering life at the level of the 'species body', represents the multiple points of application to the body (both individually and collectively) of disciplines such as public health, medicine, demography, education, social welfare, etc. (Barret-Kriegal 1992: 194). Ecology and environmental management can also be regarded as expressions of biopolitics, as these originate in, and operate upon, the same basic concerns for managing the 'continuous and multiple relations' between the population, its resources and the environment. Contemporary ecological discourse, in other words, is an articulation of what Foucault calls the 'population–riches problem'. This suggests a specifically ecological or environmental dimension to biopolitics, which renders more complex the way in which we understand the body as the target and site of power. Not only are we forced to deal with the individual 'anatomical' body and the social body, and the relations between these, but we must also take into account an ecological dimension in which the focus is on the relationship between the social body and the biological *species body*.[8] This is not to suggest that there will not be new forms of discipline and normality directed at the body at the individual level (indeed, these would appear to be a necessary component in ecological governmentality[9]), but that, as with areas of social policy such as public health, the ecological is primarily biopolitical in nature – that is, it is manifested in specific regulatory controls aimed at the population, albeit from a somewhat different perspective.

Governmental Rationality

Foucault's work on biopolitics, especially the first volume of *The History of Sexuality*, represents a development that goes beyond his earlier writings on the relation between power and knowledge. As Mitchell Dean argues, the last chapter of *The History of Sexuality*, volume 1, in particular foreshadowed a new concern with the problem of government and the role of the state that Foucault took up during the period 1978–84. This was the only major work in which Foucault considered in some detail the relation between the 'institutionalised micro-forms of work upon the self . . . and the global strategies of the government of the state' (Dean 1994a: 175). Whereas Foucault's earlier work had focused on power in terms of a local 'microphysics of power', this later work recasts the problem of power on a much broader, macro-level of analysis. This is not to suggest that Foucault abandoned recognition of the importance of the micro-level application (and origin) of power, but rather that the problem is reformulated in a more complex, sophisticated manner, in which the analysis of the state (and government) is no longer reliant on a juxtapositioning of micro- and macro-levels of power.

Despite the change in focus that occurs with his writings on biopolitics, and more fully in those on governmental rationality, these later works nevertheless maintain continuity with two key concerns developed in his earlier writings. These are, first, a continuity between the earlier concern to elaborate a microphysics of power (the disciplinary technologies of the body) and relating this to the sorts of biopolitical problems raised by the regulation of entire populations and societies. Second, there is a continuity between both of these concerns and the practice of ethics as a form of 'government of the self' (ibid. 176). Foucault's work on government thus takes as its object of analysis, to use Dean's phrase, the 'triple domain' of government. That is, it is concerned with understanding the multiple means by which human conduct is governed through various practices of individual self-government, the government of others, and the government of the state. Foucault's characterization of government as the conduct of conduct (Foucault 1982: 220–1) delineates the field of government in a very broad sense: it is a 'massive domain' that extends from the minutiae of individual self-reflection to the depersonalized, anonymous rationalities concerned with the political regulation of states, populations and societies (Dean 1994a: 176–7).

Central to modern government was the development of a new political discourse (at the end of the sixteenth and during the first half of the seventeenth centuries) concerning the art of governing. This discourse specifically centred on the state as being its own end and having its own logic and nature, expressed in the theory of *raison d'état.* Reason of state, according to Foucault, grew out of two political technologies that led to the formation of the modern nation-state: the diplomatic-military practices that developed the external capacities of states through the system of military alliances and a political technology internal to the state known as the *police*, which attended to the development of all 'the means necessary to increase the forces of the state from within'. These two political technologies came together in the system of mercantilism or cameralism to give rise to the formation of the modern state (Foucault 1988c: 103–4).

Central to this new perspective was a definition of government that no longer focused primarily on the governing of territory, but rather on the governing of *things* (see note 4). This new police doctrine of government represented a radical shift from the negative emphasis on politics as the 'holding out' of sovereign power within a territory to an emphasis on the positive, detailed management of the entire *social body* – that is, to ensuring the abundance and prosperity of the population. The principal concern of the 'police' state became productive, involving a continuous and remarkably specific series of 'positive interventions in the behaviour of individuals' and groups (Foucault 1988c: 159).

The doctrine of reason of state, in holding that the principles of government were inherent in the state rather than deriving from natural or divine law, posed the problem of determining the needs or interests of the state and acquiring the knowledge and information necessary to manage these. The task of administration rested above all on ever more detailed knowledge of the resources of the state, including all the characteristics of its population and particularly knowledge of geography, demography, natural resources, agriculture, climate, etc. (Foucault 1991a: 93–5). The strength of the state, in police theory, was directly linked to the well-being of the population. The power of the state is increased inasmuch as the physical (and social) condition of the population is *secured* and improved; thus the police state is also the 'state of prosperity' (Gordon 1991: 10). Foucault identified, in the writings of police theorists, the clearest definition of the aim of the modern art of government: 'to develop those elements constitutive of individuals' lives in such a way that their development also fosters that of the strength of the state' (Foucault 1981c: 252). Hence, the police state's concern with acquiring the most exhaustively detailed knowledge, and on the basis of this intervening in the activities of each of its citizens, assumes a pastoral – even totalitarian – dimension (ibid. 248). However, this should not be seen as support for those, such as Habermas (1985) and Honneth (1991), who see in this evidence of Foucault's alleged view of modernity as a totally administered society. What is missed by such an assertion is the genealogical lineage pointed to by Foucault's analysis. Reason of state and police science are elements that contribute to the modern governmental rationality, but do not fully define it. In order to more fully understand Foucault's account of how disciplinary biopower and modern state rationality are brought into play, it is necessary to take into account the influence of liberalism.

Liberalism and Security

Foucault's analysis indicates that modern government derived from two distinct yet related sources: first, the cameralist/police science influence, with its emphasis on an essentially pragmatic knowledge of the state's capacity and resources, and second, liberalism. As has been suggested, police science harboured within it an aspiration to a perfect or total knowledge of all the workings of the state's resources and population. Such knowledge, it was thought, was necessary if the development of the state was to be regulated so as to maximize the realization of its own ends (security, prosperity, etc.) in the most efficient manner. Thus police science, as a governmental technology premised upon the principle of reason of state, always operated on the presumption of there being 'too little government' (Foucault 1981b: 354).

Liberalism, on the other hand, emerged as a *critique of state reason* (Gordon 1991: 15). While liberalism is frequently understood primarily as a political (and economic) theory or ideology concerned with the defence of individual liberty from encroachment by the state, Foucault viewed liberalism as a specific practice of government that embodies a continuous reflection on not only the limits of government but also its *necessity* (Foucault 1981b: 354–6). Where liberalism differs from reason of state is that the state is no longer considered as its own end; nor is government considered to be synonymous with the state. Thus Foucault argued:

> Liberalism, then, is to be analysed as a principle and method of rationalising the exercise of government . . . the liberal rationalisation finds its point of departure in the idea that government would not be considered its own end. Here, government is not to be

understood as an institution but, rather, as an activity which consists in directing human conduct within the setting and with the
instruments of state. . . . Phrased differently, this latter question asked
what makes it necessary for there to be a government and what
objectives ought it to pursue with regard to society in order to
justify its existence. (Ibid. 354–5)

The interests of the population could no longer be understood
as necessarily coextensive with those of the state. Liberalism was
still concerned with governing – that is, with how human conduct
can be *directed* to appropriate ends. Where liberalism differed, as
a governmental rationality, was that it considered what governmental tasks can be efficiently (and legitimately) conducted by the
state and what ambitions must be regarded as outside the competence of state (ibid. 356; Gordon 1991: 15).

The liberal critique pointed to the impossibility, in the economic sphere, of possessing knowledge of the interests and prefer-
ences of individuals such that government could direct and regulate
private economic activities for the public good. Foucault noted
that this also needs to be seen as a problem posed by liberalism for
government in general. The state, according to liberal theorists,
could not in fact possess the sorts of totalizing knowledge upon
which police science sought to base state action. The opacity, the
unknowability, of economic processes precluded the possibility
of the type of economic sovereignty assumed by reason of state.
Thus the familiar liberal assertion that the state's ability to act
(beneficially) is restricted by the inherently fallible and limited scope
of its knowledge.[10] One result of the influence of liberal thought
was to initiate a new relation between knowledge and government
in which political economy assumed a greater autonomy and
distance from pragmatic state needs (Foucault, cited in Gordon
1991: 16). Liberalism did not dismiss the need for government, but
rather – and this is what Foucault saw as distinctive about liberal
governmental rationality – it *dissolved the immediate unity between
knowledge and government*, and consequently the equation of
maximized governmental effectiveness with maximal regulation
(Foucault, cited in Burchell et al. 1991: 138–9). In doing so, liberalism brought into being a new relationship between knowledge
and government, involving what Colin Gordon has succinctly described as 'a new mode of objectification of governed reality', that
resituates 'governmental reason within a newly complicated, open
and unstable politico-epistemic configuration' (Gordon 1991: 16).

This new configuration of knowledge and techniques of government Foucault called 'governmentality'. He described this as the

> ensemble formed by the institutions, procedures, analyses and reflections, the calculations and tactics that allow the exercise of this very specific albeit complex form of power, which has as its target population, as its principal form of knowledge political economy and its essential technical means apparatuses of security. . . . [T]his type of power which may be termed government, (results) on the one hand, in the *formation of a whole series of specific governmental apparatuses*, and on the other, in the *development of a whole complex of savoirs* (knowledges). (Foucault 1991a: 102–3, emphasis added)

This relationship between particular, more or less formalized bodies of knowledge and specific administrative mechanisms has become a crucial feature of government in advanced liberal societies. Increasingly in such complex societies government, the conduct of conduct, necessarily relies on the role of professional expertise. As Donzelot (1979, 1993) has demonstrated, throughout the nineteenth century there was a proliferation of alliances between private and professional agents that led to the formation of a series of welfare programmes directed at perceived problems within the social body. Over time these welfare programmes became linked with the functions and institutions of the state. However, the adoption of these welfare programmes by the state did not lead to the rise of an all-powerful, interventionist state, but instead resulted in the bringing together of a diverse network of arguments, projects and mechanisms through which various political forces sought to pursue a multitude of social and political objectives (Rose and Miller 1992: 192). Thus welfare did not represent a coherent, state plan for social regulation and normalization, but rather was composed of a series of networks assembled from diverse, often antagonistic elements. Modern social welfare did not originate as centrally directed projects of state action, but was 'a composition of fragile and mobile relationships' between non-state professionals, intellectuals and social movements, and state agencies (ibid. 193). Just as the development of social welfare (and subsequently, the welfare state) involved forging and maintaining alliances and networks between diverse experts and political forces, of which the state was only one, so too the development of programmes of environmental security can be understood as drawing on an equally complex, open and unstable 'politico-epistemic configuration'.

Ecological Governmentality

Foucault saw the emergence of biopolitics in the eighteenth century as directly linked to an expanding series of population discourses focusing on health, criminality, education, sexuality, etc. At the same time we can also find, in the historical scholarship, evidence of the beginnings of a new discourse that had as its object *the environment*. David Worster has dated the first systematic documentation of concern about this new problem in 1864, with the publication of George Perkins Marsh's *Man and Nature*, a work which sought to demonstrate the danger to humanity and to nature posed by rapid change in the global environment (Worster 1987b: 91–2).[11] Clarence Glacken has also identified Marsh's work as marking the arrival of a modern perspective on the relationship of humans to nature. The nineteenth century thus saw, in Glacken's words, the advent of 'an entirely different order, influenced by the theory of evolution, specialisation in the attainment of knowledge, (and) acceleration in the transformation of nature' (Glacken 1967: 704–5). Anna Bramwell, in her history of environmentalism, similarly pointed to modern ecological concepts as deriving from 'a set of biological, physical science and geographical ideas that arose separately around the mid-nineteenth century' (Bramwell 1989: 15). The ideas of Malthus and Darwin on population also contributed to themes discernible in the modern ecological analysis of environmental problems (Pepper 1984: 91–100).[12]

This problematization of the relationship between population and the environment can, as previously noted, be linked to three major social developments in the eighteenth and nineteenth centuries: the emergence of modern biology as the science of life, the rapid increase in the population of Europe leading to a series of mass migrations to other continents (Foucault 1991a: 98; Worster 1987b: 92–5), and the development of an international capitalist market (Dreyfus and Rabinow 1982: 135; Rabinow 1984: 17–18; Worster 1987b: 92–5). Environmental historians such as Worster note the importance of the interaction between these three factors in the period pointed to by Foucault's work on the emergence of biopolitics. Foucault identified 'the deep historical link' between the rise of modern biopolitics and the emergence of the population–resources problem. His focus was on the processes which isolated 'the economy as a specific sector of reality and political economy as the science and technique of intervention of government in that field of reality' (Foucault 1991a: 102). Worster has linked the development of the 'two great global forces' of population growth and world markets in the nineteenth century with an 'environmental upheaval' that remade nature 'with geological effectiveness' (Worster 1987b: 95–7). Similarly, Richard Grove has claimed that the techniques of colonial environmental management (1670 to the mid-1950s), involving forestry, irrigation and soil conservation, in shaping environmental perceptions ultimately had a more profound impact on the development of the modern world than other more 'conspicuous and dramatic aspects of colonial rule' (Grove 1990: 17; see also Crosby 1986).

The population–resources problem can thus be seen as one of the central themes of nineteenth-century environmental discourse. It is also taken up in contemporary discourse on ecological crises. Many of the most important popular writings in the environmental debate of the last three decades have as their central focus the notion of the carrying capacity of the Earth, which is seen as a biological law with a profound influence for contemporary environmental and population–resources problems. While the emphasis and political implications stemming from this idea vary, most see population growth as a fundamental factor in ecological crisis. Well-known examples of this approach include Hardin 1968; Ehrlich 1968; Goldsmith et al. 1972; Meadows et al. 1972; and governmental reports (Council on Environmental Quality 1981). Other influential works have placed less emphasis on absolute population levels as the cause of environmental degradation, and instead have focused on the problem of global pollution, and the mode and intensity of resource exploitation, which in turn were seen as related to population levels, and industrialism (and consumerism) as a *system* of production. Here the central concern was the impact of new forms of technology which have proliferated in the post-World War II period,[13] and which are characterized by the extensive manufacture and use of synthetic, toxic chemicals. (Bookchin 1962; Carson 1962; and Commoner 1971 were important examples of this work.)

These and numerous similar works have several important features in common. Each problematizes the environment as the previously taken for granted biological basis for human life, and constitutes it as a domain of social concern and potential political conflict (Cramer et al. 1989: 96). Each seeks to locate its claims to authority within the overall framework of a global ecosystems approach to ecology,[14] whether it be Hardin's and Ehrlich's biological law of carrying capacity, Commoner's four laws of ecology,[15] or the Club of Rome's complex computer modelling of the limits to growth.[16] Central to each is the view that human populations are constrained by the operation of ecological laws that are biological, and therefore both natural and non-anthropocentric. These ecological laws are understood as having significant economic and political consequences, and are frequently expressed in the economic form of externalities impacting on ecologically defined public goods. The concern of this contemporary discourse is how to *manage* populations and resources in relation to their natural environments. This focus remains central to current environmental discourses; it is, for example, a clear theme in the Brundtland report to the United Nations (Brundtland 1987) and the ongoing international debate on sustainable development since the publication of that report, and continues to be manifest in the 1992 United Nations Earth Summit (Brown et al. 1990; MacNeill et al. 1991) and its establishment of the UN Sustainable Development Commission and the 1994 UN Population Conference.

Scientific expertise has been fundamental in defining environmental problems.[17] It is therefore necessary to consider the role of scientific ecology in providing the conceptual framework employed in the contemporary definition of environmental problems. In its modern form, ecology emerged in the 1940s and 1950s, and is based on an 'energy-economic model of the environment' in which the essential feature is the flow of energy through ecosystems (Jamison 1993: 189; Worster 1987a: 311, 339). This bio-economic paradigm, or systems ecology, is a product of twentieth-century science, a distinctly transnational enterprise drawing upon European and US national scientific traditions, but appearing in its contemporary form in the USA in the period since World War II. (Jamison 1993: 193). Despite the popularizing of nature in holistic, and sometimes organicist terms, the bio-economic model at its core expressed an 'agronomic attitude toward nature' which sought to provide the 'analytic tools' needed to 'intensively farm' the Earth's resources. The language of modern systems ecology reflects this, abounding with agronomic and economic terms such as *producers, consumers, total energy income, yield, crop, gross* and *net productivity, nutrient capital, competitive exclusion, energy budget, efficiency*, etc. (Worster 1987a: 311). Modern scientific ecology, says Worster, from the 1940s came to see itself as 'the science of natural economics', in which nature became a 'a modernised economic system, . . . a corporate state, a chain of factories, and assembly line'. 'Conflict', Worster continues, 'can have little place in such a well-regulated economy' (ibid. 311–13). Ecology then, appears as the rationale behind a *new form of political economy*.

The rise of the systems approach to ecology occurred in a very specific historical and cultural context. In a general sense systems ecology appears as one of the consequences of the industrialization of science – that is, with the emergence of 'big science' during and after World War II, which saw the organization of scientific research in the USA along large-scale, capital-intensive, corporate lines, where research output increasingly became an important contributor to economic growth and national power. Applied systems ecology in this period gained significant impetus from work conducted by the US Atomic Energy Commission, originating in the Manhattan Project, into the problems of nuclear waste and radiation ecology (Kwa 1993). Jamison points to three ways in which the post-war development of modern systems ecology was shaped by the US institutional and cultural context in which it emerged. First, as mentioned above, the industrialization of science and the influence of this new industrial setting generated the view of ecology as 'a powerful technique of social engineering . . . (which could potentially) . . . regulate and control the flows of pollutants and other human interventions through large-scale ecosystems' (Jamison 1993: 197–8). Second, the availability and popularity in the USA of powerful computer technology allowed the unparalleled application of mathematical models to natural processes. This was a direct extension of the conceptualization of ecological interactions as cybernetic, 'self-regulating, feedback systems' that had emerged originally from the use of computers in the Manhattan Project for the development of weapons guidance systems. Third, an American tradition combining the influence of a utilitarian Progressive-era conservation philosophy with the legacy of pragmatic regional planning programmes of the 1930s facilitated the development of an approach to ecology that lent itself to large-scale environmental control and management (ibid. 1993: 194–8; Worster 1987a: 312). While the industrialization of science, including ecology, in the USA started towards the end of World War II and grew during the 1950s, environmental concerns throughout the 1950s and early 1960s tended to continue to reflect the professional interests of scientists (Cramer et al. 1989: 96–7). These professional research interests played a significant role in the development of a coherent, science-based environmentalism through the International Geophysical Year (1957–8) and the International Biological Programme (1964–74) (Bocking 1995;

Caldwell 1991: 261; Egerton 1983; Golley 1993: 109–66; Kwa 1987; McIntosh 1985: 213–41). The IBP in particular was a massive transnational enterprise involving research in 97 countries directed towards the understanding of the biological basis of productivity and human welfare, where these were 'calculated to benefit from international collaboration, and were (regarded as) urgent because of the rapid rate of changes taking place in all environments throughout the world'. The focus of the IBP was distinctly ecological, directed towards understanding 'organic production . . . and the potentialities and uses of new and existing natural resources, . . . (as well as) human adaptability to change' (Worthington 1983: 165).

Regulatory Science and Ecological Governmentality

The sorts of extensive, transnational research programmes on ecological issues mentioned above came increasingly to characterize scientific and political discourse on the environment throughout the 1960s and 1970s. From the end of the 1960s, through the establishment of a wide range of environmental legislation and enforcement agencies, the advanced industrialized countries experienced a rapid growth in state intervention directed at environmental regulation and planning. Ecological and environmental research in the 1970s thus laid the foundation for public policies of significant economic and political impact, particularly in terms of the regulatory intervention in the activities of industry. In financial terms alone these are important – for example, the direct cost of complying with US pollution control regulations is estimated to be in excess of US$100 billion per year (Jasanoff 1992: 195). However, of more general importance, the period since the early 1970s has seen the significant institutionalization of new forms of ecological governmentality. Two important aspects of this have been the growth of *regulatory science* and the international spread of procedures for *environmental impact assessment* (EIA).

The notion of regulatory science refers to the widespread reliance by the state on extensive systems of scientific advisory structures which have become an integral feature of environmental (and health) policy making in industrialized societies (Beck 1992a; Jasanoff 1990). These expert advisory groups serve not only a role of political legitimation, but more importantly a role of epistemic policing, both by framing the definition of ecological risks and by certifying what is to count as scientifically acceptable knowledge of the natural world. The complexities thrown up by attempts to define environmental-societal interrelationships in terms of a global systems ecology produces a high level of 'technical' uncertainty and potential social conflict.

The rapid expansion of social regulation associated with the growth of the discourse on ecological problems from the 1970s produced a whole new domain for the biopolitical administration of life. The population became the target for a new form of ecological security and welfare, in which environmental agencies and the professional disciplines required by them set about the task of protecting the public against hazardous and environmentally damaging technologies, demanding 'ever more complex predictive analyses of the risks and benefits of regulation' (Jasanoff 1990: 3). As Brian Wynne has noted, the regulatory 'turn to science', as an attempt to provide greater stability and legitimacy in environmental policy, 'also in important respects . . . defined society, by tacitly defining the scope and nature of social intervention in public policy risk decisions' (Wynne 1992: 746–8). The increasing importance of regulatory ecological science is therefore a particularly significant articulation of the biopolitical character of modern governmental rationality. It is clearly linked to the growth of *big science*. Indeed, a notable feature of regulatory science is the role of the state and industrial interests (especially transnational corporations) in the manufacture, negotiation and certification of knowledge: that is, the central role these institutions play in the normative constitution of ecological knowledge (ibid. 754). Regulatory ecological science does not so much describe the environment as both actively constitute it as an object of knowledge and, through various modes of positive intervention, manage and police it.

As Foucault has suggested, it is often in the mundane and humble procedures of examination and assessment at the micro-level that we can discern the operation of biopower. In this context the environmental impact assessment (EIA) process provides a useful illustration of one aspect of ecological governmentality. As noted above, a major element in the response to environmental problems from the 1960s onwards has involved substantive legislation aimed at regulating particular pollutants. However, the 1969 US National Environment Policy Act (NEPA) marked an important departure from this traditional legal-juridical path. The NEPA adopted a procedural approach to environment protection requiring the preparation of detailed environmental impact statements for major development projects which had the potential to significantly affect the environment. By the 1980s the US EIA process had been adapted and implemented in one form or another in many other industrialized countries. EIA sets out statutory criteria for ecological assessment requiring government agencies to take account of these criteria in their decision making.

However, EIA goes beyond legislating for a science-based, 'rational-comprehensive' assessment and decision-making process. While studies do point to the capacity of EIA to improve the effectiveness, co-ordination and legitimacy of environmental planning decisions, others suggest that these legal-formal mechanisms also utilize a range of 'powerful, informal incentives' within government to 'produce agencies that continuously and progressively think about environmental values' (Wandesforde-Smith, cited in Bartlett 1990: 90). From this perspective EIA can be understood as operating in a highly flexible, *self-regulating* manner, involving continuous mediation between the internal formation of environmental programmes and objectives within organizations (not just state agencies but also non-governmental organizatins and private corporations) and the external political and economic context within which these operate. This suggests that EIA promotes the implementation of environmental management programmes not simply through direct coercion, but through a governmental rationality that establishes norms and procedures which channel problem solving in a particular direction, and which stimulate administrative agencies and other social actors to be both innovative and effective in the implementation of ecological goals (Bartlett 1990).

Bartlett argues that where EIA is successful – that is, where it substantively influences the direction and outcome of environmental planning and economic activity – it does so 'by changing, formally and informally, the premises and rules for arriving at legitimate decisions' (ibid. 91). Thus he argues that EIA creates an 'insidious' mechanism for embedding ecological modes of thought and environmental values into the actions of organizations and individuals.

By establishing, continuously reaffirming and progressively legitimating environmental values and ecological criteria as standards by which individual actions are to be structured, chosen, and evaluated,

EIA institutionalises substantive ecological rationality. . . . It changes patterns of relationships among organisations and among individuals inside and outside organisations. It creates powerful incentives, formal and informal, that thereafter force a great deal of learning and self-regulation upon individual and organisational actors. And it provides opportunities for individuals to develop and affirm environmental values and to press for innovative adaptation of structures and processes to a changing political world. (Ibid. 91–2)

The particular strength of EIA, and that which separates it from the simple legislative imposition of controls (such as permissible discharge levels for pollutants), is that it *structures the institutional and normative fields in which actions and governmental programmes take place without specifying final outcomes.* It establishes a governmental technology which simultaneously guides and problematizes actions in relation to the environment in which juridical techniques are subsumed under the 'effectivity of the norm'. These sorts of techniques also incorporate what Foucault described as a 'pastoral' attitude, where government is understood in terms of the metaphor of 'the shepherd and his flock'. Such a view sees the goal of government as the promotion of 'the well-being of its subjects' by means of an intimate and continuous regulation of behaviour, and is thus more concerned with the *welfare* or *security* of subjects than is the liberal concern with autonomy (Hindess 1996: 118–23).[18] This is a basic normative perspective which is deeply embedded in almost all schools of environmental thought – the notion of wise stewardship as fundamental to the management of all-encompassing ecological relationships.

A criticism sometimes made of EIA and the environmental management techniques it promotes, such as scientific environmental impact studies, is that these are usually conducted by the proponents of development projects, and as a consequence frequently suffer from 'technical flaws' and 'incomplete presentation of information', and therefore cannot be regarded as a substitute for 'overall planning' (Walker 1989: 33). Such an argument misses the point,[19] for it is precisely by incorporating the developer and other non-environmental state agencies into the *process of problem definition* that EIA internalizes and normalizes ecological analysis and behaviour within individual and organizational actors. This of course is not to suggest that such techniques cannot become co-opted to immediate, short-term political manoeuvring by politicians and governments – clearly, they frequently are.

None the less, at the broader strategic level of political rationalities, EIA can be described as an attempt at *institutionalizing ecological rationality* in governmental and social choice mechanisms (Bartlett 1990: 88–9). EIA is of course a regulatory mechanism in the legal-juridical sense, but it is more than this. It attempts to enhance the effectiveness of government (in the Foucauldian sense) in regulating the complex and multiple materiality of the species body, both by institutionalizing a scientized form of administrative apparatus and, more importantly perhaps, by opening up the species body (population) in a new way to that generalized 'modality of intervention' characterized by Foucault as *panopticism*. Hence, a fundamental feature of EIA is that it also functions as a normalizing strategy; that is, it does not mandate specific outcomes from the centre, but sets up a framework for *rationalizing* behaviour in particular ways. In other words, EIA brings into being new relations of power through an interpenetrating cluster of positive norms of internal self-control and external regulation that effect a policing of specific practices of the population, both at a general institutional level and through what Foucault describes as a 'positive intervention in the behaviour of individuals' (Foucault 1988c: 159).

Systems ecology and the highly mathematized natural sciences (such as atmospheric chemistry and physics) involved in global ecosystem modelling exert a powerful influence across a wide range of environmental policy and social planning areas. The ecological sciences are fundamental to key aspects of contemporary biopolitics: ecological discourse both problematizes numerous areas of life and at the same time elaborates programmes of environmental intervention aimed at normalizing the social relation to nature in particular, ecologically benign ways. The contemporary notion of *the environment* is constituted as inherently problematic by the development of specialized scientific (as well as legal and moral) discourse on ecology. This specialized discourse provides what Rose and Miller (1992) have described as 'the intellectual machinery of government', whereby social relations with nature are thematized and brought into the domain of 'conscious political calculation' through the formation of *programmes of government*. Such programmes

> presuppose that the real is programmable, that it is a domain subject to certain determinants, rules, norms and processes that can be acted upon and improved by authorities. They make the objects of government thinkable in such a way that their ills appear

susceptible to diagnosis, prescription and cure by calculating and normalising intervention. (Ibid. 182)

Central to these activities is the production and use of knowledge by experts. The formation of ecological programmes of government occurs to a significant degree within the institutional context of regulatory science, in which environmental experts simultaneously provide scientifically authoritative technical judgements and politically legitimized policies. Programmes of government therefore embody knowledgeable accounts of what are considered legitimate problems, and the goals and objectives to be pursued in addressing them. However, programmes must be capable of being deployed on the population, brought to bear on the 'species body' through a range of interventions and regulatory instruments. The means of making programmes operable can be considered the *technologies of government* (ibid. 175). I have suggested that the technique of environmental impact assessment can be thought of as an example of such a technology of government which expresses most clearly the sorts of *productive* relations of power that Foucault calls 'biopolitics'. In a similar vein Éric Darier's (1996a) study of Canada's Green Plan provides an illuminating example, in the ecological domain, of what Rose and Miller describe as a programme of government.

It is important to emphasize that what is being argued here is not that ecological governmentality is part of some simple, unidirectional, generalized extension of state domination of society, much less an expression of Adorno's totally administered society. Rather, the developments described here reflect what Foucault referred to as 'the "governmentalisation" of the state' (Foucault 1991a). Government, understood as the attempt to implement all those more or less formally articulated plans, projects and practices which seek to systematically shape the conduct of individuals, groups and populations, is not the exclusive domain of the state. Indeed, the complexity of modern society appears to engender an increasing reliance on *liberal* techniques of government which depend on *governing at a distance*, 'seeking to create locales, entities and persons able to operate a regulated autonomy' (Rose and Miller 1992: 173). Thus, as suggested above, non-state actors, particularly professionals, academics and social movements, contribute to the governmentalization of life by entering into complex, potentially unstable relations with state agencies, other institutions and political forces.

Notes

1   See e.g. Cheney 1989; Darier 1996a, 1996b; Luke 1988; Peace 1996; Quigley 1992; Rutherford 1993, 1994a, 1994b, 1996.
2   In this attempt to deal directly with the relationship between the microphysics of power and the broader institutional power structures, we can see a parallel between Foucault's concerns and some of the ecological concerns of contemporary (largely German) social theory. For a discussion of this, see ch. 5 below.
3   Foucault is referring to the work of police theorists, particularly von Justi, who appropriated to political-administrative thought the new demographic knowledge. Here, as elsewhere, Foucault appears to refer to the 'environment' as the totality of natural resources and physical living conditions of human populations.
4   '[W]hat government has to do with is not territory but rather a complex composed of men and things. The things with which this sense of government is concerned are in fact men, but men in their relations, their links, their imbrications with those other things which are wealth, resources, means of subsistence, the territory with its specific qualities, climate, irrigation, fertility, etc.; men in their relations to that other kind of things, customs, habits, ways of acting and thinking, etc.; lastly, men in their relations to that other kind of things, accidents and misfortunes such as famine, epidemics, death, etc.' (Foucault 1991a: 93). See also Foucault 1981a: 238; 1988c: 104.
5   This is an argument mounted by Habermas and Honneth. See Habermas 1985; Honneth 1991.
6   Foucault's use of 'modernity' at other times (e.g. Foucault 1991b) is different.
7   Notwithstanding my suggestion above that Foucault hints at a continuity between biopower and ecological risk, I think there are two reasons for his not developing this link. The first is that he is principally concerned with the development of the *social* sciences and their relation to the formation of modern power. But second, it can also be argued that Foucault's attitude towards the natural sciences was not developed in a manner fully consistent with his own analysis of the relation between power and knowledge. For a critique of Foucault's approach to the natural sciences see Rouse 1993: 137–62; 1987: ch. 7; Rutherford 1994a).
8   The term *social body* can be regarded as a metaphor for 'the collective embodiment of the targets of power, the body as *species*, whether in the form of an entire population or a specific group of prisoners, school children, the insane and so forth, who are subject to specific types of administration and regulation' (Hewitt 1983: 71). Foucault, however, says that the term is *not simply* a metaphor: it refers to a *materiality*. The police 'take charge of the physical element of the

social body'; the object of the police is first and foremost the complete regulation or 'whole management' of the 'complex and multiple materiality' of the social body, the *species body*. The police is both an 'institutional grouping' – i.e. a specific set of social apparatuses and administrative structures – and a 'modality of intervention' [Foucault et al., quoted in Barret-Kriegal 1992: 194] – i.e. a generalized type of political technology, a 'diagram' or 'schema', 'panopticism'. For a discussion of Foucault's 'ambiguous' use of these two aspects of his notion of biopower, see Donnelly 1992: 199–203.

9   For a discussion of how environmental education and environmental drills are combined, in the case of the Canadian Green Plan, to instil new ecological disciplinary practices in the daily lives of individuals see Darier 1996a and ch. 8 below.

10   For discussion of Foucault's analysis of liberalism see Burchell 1991; Gordon 1991: 27.

11   It is also worth noting that 1865 saw the establishment of the first national environmental group in Britain (the Commons, Open Spaces and Footpaths Preservation Society). The US Sierra Club was formed in 1892. See Pepper 1984: 14. It is also worth noting the proliferation of colonial geographic and conservation societies during this period. See Schneider 1990; Grove 1990.

12   See Worster 1987a; Pepper 1984: 100–3. Worster notes that the bio-economic approach of post-World War II systems ecology displays a diminished reliance on earlier Darwinian evolutionary influences (Worster 1987a: 331). See also Grove 1992.

13   It is these sorts of developments and their effects that Beck focuses on as a key distinguishing feature of the 'risk society'.

14   For further discussion of the significance of global ecosystem modelling for a biopolitics of the environment, see Rutherford 1996.

15   Commoner's laws: (1) everything is connected to everything else; (2) everything must go somewhere; (3) nature knows best; and (4) there is no such thing as a free lunch (Commoner 1971: 33–46).

16   These limits are presented as the interaction between 'world population, industrialization, pollution, food production, and resource depletion'. See Meadows et al. 1972: 29.

17   This is particularly evident when one considers the importance of complex mathematical modelling of the global environment (popularized by *The Limits to Growth*, first published in 1968). The current approach to global warming is a far more sophisticated, and more politically influential, response involving more complex computer modelling of global phenomena than that of *Limits to Growth* two decades ago (Buttel and Taylor 1992: 218, 221–2). See Rutherford 1996.

18   Foucault saw the practice of police science as a clear example of this pastoral attitude. See Foucault 1981c.

19   See also Rutherford 1994c.

3

The Construction of Environmental 'Awareness'

Isabelle Lanthier and Lawrence Olivier,
translated by Martine Eloy

A revolution is truly needed – in our values, outlook and economic
organization. For the crisis of our environment stems from a legacy
of economic and technical premises which have been pursued in
the absence of ecological knowledge. That other revolution, the
industrial one that is turning sour, needs to be replaced by a revolution of new attitudes towards growth, goods, space and living things.
                                                                – McCloskey

Introduction

Not a day goes by without the media, governments or the business community referring to the environment. Whether the issue
is an ecological disaster, an environmental impact study requested
by a citizens' group for an industrial or scientific project, the recycling of household waste or public health, the environment has
become an important concern in our society. At the political level,
individuals are organizing into interest groups or political parties
to promote and defend the cause of the environment. In Europe,
the environmental movement is present on the public scene as a
political party. In the United States, although there is no environmental party as such at the federal level, the environmental movement is nevertheless very active through interest groups or political
organizing. In every case, people are fighting to win respect for the
environment, against economic development based on the exploitation of nature. Many other examples could be given to show that
there is today a true concern for the environment, at least for

some of the population in Western societies. Where does such an
interest in the environment, important enough to affect our habits
and in behaviour as citizens, come from? How did an environmental awareness appear, and impose itself?

Certainly, concern for the environment has become a reality.
What is less clear, however, is why an individual or groups of individuals grant such importance to the environment, and struggle
to conserve it. Some will credit the emergence of an environmental
awareness to the destruction of the environment by a system of
production based on exploitation and its consequences for life on
Earth or for the survival of the planet. Such an explanation is
not, in our opinion, convincing: first, because it assumes from the
outset what needs to be explained, the emergence of environmental
awareness. It is not enough to draw attention to certain environmental problems in order for awareness of problems to emerge.
This would suppose that humans have, a priori, a consciousness
that needs only to be awakened.[1] It also supposes a form of altruism
which is not as universal as we would like to believe. We are
more concerned with what happens to us, with our present reality,
than with what could happen, even if the latter is disastrous
or apocalyptic.[2] We must therefore envisage the development of
environmental awareness differently.

Ecology is a science, a branch of biology which studies the
relationship of living beings to their environment, whereas environmentalism refers to a broader field of knowledge that seeks to
rethink our relationship to nature and to take action to transform
the system of values on which this relationship has been based
for a long time. According to Waechter, one of the pioneers of
the militant environmental movement in France, environmentalist
thought entails 'the need to limit one's control over the world,
the need to master own's own power. In short, it is a demand to
exercise our responsibility as a thinking species, capable of ana-
lyzing the past and, consequently, the future' (Waechter 1993: 44).
This means that environmentalism is not only a science, an attempt
to epistemologize a problem so as to transform it into a scientific
subject; it is also a field of knowledge. Before constituting a science,
before determining the types of issues that would belong to such
a science, before defining research strategies, a society has to be
concerned enough about something to make it the object of scientific investigation.

How can we account for the development of this field of knowledge, or rather, how is it that society has turned the environment

into an issue? This question concerns a process that we must now specify. (1) What are the conditions that made possible what we now call 'environmental awareness' or 'environmentalism'? We must identify the elements and events which, when combined, made it possible for the environment to break away from nature and appear little by little as an important reality for a large number of individuals in a society. We will therefore look for the origin (Foucault 1977: 144–52) of this environmental awareness in various movements and social groups – scientific circles, social and political critiques, ideological and philosophical protest – that we find in contemporary Western societies. (2) It is not enough that a combination of favourable conditions exist for a society to make a problem into an important concern. For environmentalism to take hold, it had to develop a legitimizing system of values. Thus, in addition to studying the origin of a field of knowledge, we must study what give rise the conditions for its emergence in a given society (ibid.). No discursive system can impose itself by the mere force of its constitutive elements; at the very moment when they intersect, conflict, interpenetrate – that is, at the time they make a representation of reality possible – a system of values will emerge that will facilitate that representation of reality taking hold in a society. It is here that medical discourse plays an important role, in the creation of a new system of values that obliges the individual to be concerned about his or her environment. Medical discourse relates the health of the individual to an increasingly important condition: a healthy environment. An archeo-genealogical Foucauldian approach will help us to address these issues.

From Cosmology to Spiritual Cosmology

We will begin by identifying the origin of the environmentalist discourse – that is, the set of conditions that promoted the construction of a new way of seeing the relationship of humans to nature. This other relationship to nature, which seems to be the fundamental object of all environmental struggles, is based on a knowledge as old as the Earth: cosmology. The new cosmology calls for the reintroduction of humans within nature as full-fledged members. This representation of the world as a whole is based on a specific criterion: the cosmology depends on the components of the cosmos only to the extent that they are related one to the other and each is related to the whole. Capra speaks of a holistic

vision with reference to the interdependence of all physical, biological, social and cultural elements. He points out that all the
components of the social environment must be considered on an
equal footing, each having the same importance in relation to the
whole. Moreover, these components develop a relationship of
mutualism among themselves. 'None of the new social institutions
will be superior to or more important than any of the others, and
all of them will have to be aware of and communicate and cooper-
ate with one another' (Capra 1982: 265). The concern of cosmology
for the particular is based on the idea that each element of the
cosmos, as well as the environment as a whole, exercises a reciprocal influence on every other element. In fact, this cosmology
addresses the interrelationships between the components themselves
and their relationships with the whole, resituating mankind in a
new relationship to nature – that is, in a relationship of responsibility and accountability *vis-à-vis* the environment. In fact, Capra
adds that this holistic vision, characteristic of cosmology, becomes
more than a mere system of analysis of our relationship to the
world. Cosmology appears as a self-organizing, transcendental and
even spiritual system (ibid. 285), from which our way of thinking,
our conception of the world, our way of behaving, etc. develop.
When it serves as a guide, cosmology takes on a sacred aspect. It
replaces, in a way, the divine model. Henceforth, individuals must
organize their thinking according to a macrocosmic vision of the
world. They must become conscious of the effects of their actions
on the environment as a whole, which now extends to the entire
planet.

According to Berman, economy and quantification are examples
of globalizing methods that enable us to grasp the cosmos in its
entirety.

> The same class that came to power through the new economy, that
> glorified the effort of the individual, and that began to see in
> financial calculation a way of comprehending the entire cosmos,
> came to regard quantification as the key to personal success because
> quantification alone was thought to enable mastery over nature by
> a rational understanding of its laws. (Berman 1981: 55–6)

As opposed to the tenets of the Cartesian system, nature is no
longer seen in a number of modern scientific, social and activist
discourses as an inert resource to be exploited for human benefit.
It is no longer a manageable, manipulable object, to be insensit-
ively subjected to the craziest wishes of human beings. On the

contrary, with the return of cosmology, it appears as an entity that also has the right to be defended and respected in its integrity. It becomes matter that also suffers in the face of the threat of death. It is still central to the project for the well-being of individuals. However, the heedless exploitation of nature is now a source of calamity for mankind. Nature is therefore no longer a good, abundant, renewable commodity.

What has made possible such a turn-about in the conception of mankind's relationship to nature – that is, the passage from inoffensive object in the service of humans to fragile entity entitled to respect? What has given rise to the radical critique of the Cartesian concept of nature? In other words, what are the conditions that led to the emergence of a new human/nature relationship, a relationship that places the exploiter in a new position of responsibility towards the victim?

Rejection of the death culture

In the seventeenth century, in the *Discourse on Method*, Descartes defined humans 'as lords and possessors of nature' (1957: 49). In fact, Descartes discarded any idea that mystifies nature and finds an order in spirituality. For Descartes, nature does not rest on esoteric, arbitrary, undefinable and unjustified laws. On the contrary, nature, which is outside mankind and understood as part of a chaotic whole, obeys physical laws whose mathematical logic we need to discover in order to restore its meaning (Bowler 1993; Popelard 1992). The world is viewed solely as space. It is without movement, deprived of everything: life or soul. The universe is therefore entirely comprehensible to the human mind, a simple mechanics of objects (Ferry 1995). Therefore, knowledge of these constitutive laws of the environment allow us to become aware of the wealth and weaknesses of the environment. Better still, it enables us to organize the exploitation of our natural resources in a logical, productive way, thus best contributing to the development of the health and well-being of individuals (Descartes 1957).

The environmentalist discourse originates in the environmental and human disasters provoked by technology. It is rooted in the critique of positivism: namely, that mastery over matter does not have only beneficial effects, and in the critique of instrumentalism which maintains that, at a certain point, manipulation of nature gives rise to unpredictable counter-productive effects. These critiques reached a culminating point in the first half of the twentieth

century, due, among other things, to the eruption of different technologies. The race to discover the physics of splitting the atom,
as part of the effort to build the atomic bomb, is but one striking example of unbridled ambition to totally control matter. The
nuclear arms race, started by the United States and Germany,
reflects the image of the crazy, unconscious scientist, unconcerned
about the repercussions of his work. Albert Einstein was asked
about the possible practical application of the theory of relativity
which he had discovered. He replied that the baby was born, and
what would it become? A few years later, it became disturbingly
evident that this scientific revolution had given birth to the atomic
bomb. Following the explosions at Hiroshima and Nagasaki,
Oppenheimer, the main physicist involved in the American scientific research, was blamed by the scientific community for having
participated in such a deadly project. He was criticized for his
pretended neutrality, his lack of ethics or scruples with regard to
the atomic project. Oppenheimer gave the following reply: 'When
you see something that is technically sweet, you go ahead and do
it, and you argue about what to do about it only after you have
had your technical success' (Oppenheimer 1954: 81). It is precisely
this conception of a scientist obsessed by a single idea – discovery
– that is called into question by a part of the scientific community
itself and by different social groups.

The importance of the environmentalist discourse lies in the
idea that we have to protect, on the one hand, the sorcerer's
apprentice from himself and, on the other hand, the environment
from human exploits. This critique of Cartesianism is echoed in
the scientific community, the very community which sees the idea
of objectivity and neutrality as essential to its approach. It has
contributed considerably to scientists becoming aware of their
own responsibility. Oppenheimer and Einstein later became fierce
opponents of the military use of nuclear energy.

In the early sixties, other social groups – pacifists, counter-
cultural groups, etc. – challenged the general anthropocentric conception of mankind as exploiter of nature. The environmentalist
discourse is based on the attempt to put nature back at the heart
of our concerns, and to restore an ethic of responsibility to the
frivolous magician. For humans are the architects of their habitat.
It is difficult to deny the fact that human beings have always
reorganized their living environments to suit their needs, even in
spaces as primitive as caves; but environmentalists believe that
this obliges human beings to act responsibly. In other words, the

actions of humans must be guided by this transcendental law that environmentalist cosmology has become (Marty 1992: 31).

Yet, despite the fact that mankind is responsible for controlling the environment, the environmentalist discourse struggles to change the view of mankind as dominator of nature. Engels stated: 'we by no means rule over nature like a conqueror over a foreign people, like someone standing outside nature – but . . . we, with flesh, blood and brain belong to nature and exist in its midst' (1972: 180). The militant environmentalist movement took shape at the end of World War II, with the will to overthrow the 'death culture' (Moscovici 1993: 17) so dear to the modern economicist paradigm. The death culture is characterized by the spirit of domination where by the existence and power of one being becomes effective with this of the other. In fact, this culture is part of the political strategy of death characterized by the attitude which consists of crushing the other to improve one's own life, of threatening the other to preserve one's own gains. Science's obsession with mastering nature, and even dominating it, is in line with the death culture. However, environmentalism is not a radical critique of science. On the contrary, its discourse bases its legitimacy on science.

> Our choices, then, are not easy ones. Giving up bioengineering means sacrificing a measure of control, mastery over the future. Compromising our drive for total mastery over what lies ahead. Making ourselves more vulnerable so that the rest of existence can become more secure. Choosing to serve and nurture even though we have it in our power to dominate and extract. These fly in the face of the human experience to date. When it comes to securing our future, we have never flinched from a total commitment. Over and over again, we have fashioned new, more ingenious ways to organize our future security. Each time nature sacrificed so that we might triumph. And each time we constructed a new image of the universe that glorified and sanctified our new extractive relationship with the world around us. (Rifkin 1984: 253)

Environmentalism is part of a systemic framework. In fact, environmentalists' main criticism of all scientific research is precisely that it does not take into account its global effects on the environment. In other words, environmentalists criticize scientists for having a microcosmic vision rather than a holistic one.

While systemists respect recognized scientific standards, they adopt a holistic framework of analysis, viewing the whole as in a state of constant 'unstable equilibrium' (homeostasis), because it is subject to an aggregate of actions and reactions, adaptation and creation (Capra 1982: 287). 'The systems view looks at the world in terms of relationships and integration. Systems are integrated wholes whose properties cannot be reduced to those of smaller units (ibid. 266).

Law and the new sciences

Environmentalism has also arisen with the end of colonialism. More specifically, it is part of the movement to liberalize the political sphere: that is, to include new elements in the tacit contractual relationship between sovereign and subject. At the beginning of the twentieth century there was a blossoming of legislation. There were struggles for the rights of blacks, women, animals (Ferry 1995), etc., and, much promulgated by environmentalists, for nature as a whole. The idea was to define a new contract between the component parts. The situation no longer involved a social contract where in the interest of the contracting parties was to set up a social order that would protect them from the chaos and danger of nature, where, to paraphrase Hobbes, each person becomes a wolf for the other. The natural contract means that 'nature will no longer be seen as an object of appropriation but as a subject with rights. Man will no longer be responsible for, but responsible to, nature' (Faes 1992: 126). The natural contract thus places nature on an equal footing with humans. It reintroduces humans into nature as members of the same cosmos.

The environmentalist discourse is part of emerging fields of knowledge. For example, the environment is becoming an important element of explanation in new areas of sociology, such as comparative research on urban and rural settings, studies of the impact of industrialization on the surroundings and on the quality of life of citizens. To what extent do urbanization and industrialization contribute to the greater or lesser well-being of individuals? To what extent do urbanization and industrialization render artificial and completely denaturalize human life? What are the consequences of such an artificial construct for the very 'essence' of nature and life? This kind of research certainly arouses, among some individuals, doubts and questions about their relationship to the environment.

Finally, the advent of genetics in the thirties marked another important moment in the emergence of environmental awareness.

Genetic research, today associated with medicine, represented an important field of study in the development of modern armaments such as bacteriological weapons. As a matter of fact, this field expanded considerably during the thirties. It was also the basis for studies of the repercussions of an atomic attack on organic life. From another perspective, genetic research is also responsible for a much more experimental type of medicine, one that goes so far as to perform extraordinary grafts and to manipulate the genetic code of living organisms. Modern medicine even produces living beings in laboratories, as well as clones of living matter, pushing itself almost to the point of reproducing human beings. Finally, with yet another objective, modern medicine makes it possible to conduct other types of comparative research on the effects of the environment on the quality of individual health. It clearly represents an instrument of prime importance in the emergence of a critical discourse with regard to the will to use extraordinary measures to create a better world. In other words, modern medicine is an important element in the growing awareness of the need to develop a new ethics of responsibility. This ethics of responsibility will be interpreted by environmentalists as the introduction of a new life culture – that is, a culture based on the principles of spiritual cosmology (Berman 1981: 58–9).

Thus, we see that the environmentalist discourse was born with the blossoming of legislation in a wide range of fields that have a direct or indirect effect on the life of individuals. This discourse is rooted in the aspiration for a better quality of life, better health, better control over the immediate environment – in short, over any phenomena that influence on our well-being. On the other hand, the aspiration for quasi-total control over matter, pushed to an extreme, leads individuals to create the death culture so justly condemned by environmentalists.

The death culture represents a discourse that was strongly criticized by a number of groups and scientific disciplines. It appears in the imperialist political will, where oppression and exploitation, assimilation and cultural genocide of subjected peoples, constitute the golden rule of the powerful colonizing ruler. 'But more than control over a territory, its subsoil or its wealth, it is a form of cannibalism of values and works of art that devours a culture with all its original creations' (Moscovici 1993: 19). The death culture can therefore be understood in terms of what some environmentalists call genocide and, transposed to the environmental scale, 'ecocide' (ibid. 20), as a mode of governmentality in which exploitation is the organizing principle of social life. Ecocide, decried by environmentalists, is reflected in an absence of respect for the environment, through the pollution of air and water and the destruction of entire forests stemming from a fetishization of concrete. Ecocide is the mutation of the environment by genetic manipulation and cloning, by the nuclear experiment and its production of radioactive waste. Many environmentalists claim that it is the rule of market aesthetics (of ugliness), of waste and of stench.

Work, Health and Citizenship

Knowing that environmentalism arises out of a critique of Cartesianism, productivism, exploitation and the death culture does not explain the importance that it has today, or enable us to grasp how it will impose obligations, restrictions and rights. For such rules to be accepted, environmentalism requires a system of values to establish its legitimacy and allow it to take hold as an important preoccupation for individuals. We believe that this new system of values is being developed by the medical discourse which, by making human beings responsible for their health, forces them to assign a new status to the environment.

The relationship between work and health: the environment as enemy

To demonstrate this, we take the example of occupational medicine to illustrate how the concept of a new relationship of mankind to the environment has been legitimated through health problems. We have known for a long time that the health of individuals is conditioned by the external environment. Hippocrates spoke of how health is shaped by elements like air, water and place (Wolf et al. 1978: 17).[3] In the nineteenth century and at the beginning of the twentieth, the introduction of occupational medicine addressed the conditioning of health by external elements in new terms. Work is considered, by occupational medicine, as pathogenic (Abenhaim 1985: 763), and bad for the individual. The model of analysis is relatively simple: there are several causes of stress that engender health problems: chemical (asbestos – mesothelioma), physical (noise – deafness), mechanical (machinery – amputation), psychosocial (organization of work – anxiety, depression), etc. (ibid.

765). As can easily be seen, occupational medicine is based on a relatively crude causal analysis. For each cause or source of stress, there is one health problem. What can we draw from this model? Three things should be stressed.

First, work or the work environment is viewed in the same way as nature. It has no special status or value, apart from being an object that we must control and master because it is both the source of problems and, in a certain way, an enemy against whom we must struggle and from which we must protect ourselves. This is a relatively negative conception of the work environment. Moreover, though occupational medicine definitely reflects certain major social concerns in that it focuses on external conditions of health, its emphasis on external conditions does not call into question the individual/nature/environment relationship as conceived by the capitalist system of production. The objective is not health as such, but rather the protection of the worker as worker; the objective is to keep the worker capable of performing the task. The aim is not to draw attention to environmental problems as possible or probable causes of a certain deterioration in public health. Finally – and this is the third point to be stressed – occupational medicine cannot be used as a system of values to legitimize environmental awareness in our societies. There is, we believe, a fairly simple explanation for this, besides the fact, of course, that it conveys a negative conception of the environment.

Occupational medicine is part of a medical and legal system that requires that the disease or physical incapacity be caused directly by the work or the worker's occupational environment. The role of the expert-doctor is to 'provide information to the magistrates on the pathological consequences of an accident that occurred "in the course or on the occasion of work"; in particular, the doctor must state if the observed injury is "directly and immediately related" to the accident' (Robineau 1922: 160). One assumes that this requirement is imposed on medicine by the insurance companies responsible for the compensation of workers (Ewald 1991). The consequence is that occupational medicine focuses mainly on the link between working conditions and the environment, on the one hand, and health. It is an internal relation between the individual and the work-place, turned in on itself, that involves no modification of the conception of our relationship to nature. In fact, the health problems of workers are related to unhealthy working conditions or to working habits or behaviours that are damaging to their well-being.

Occupational medicine addresses these two questions in so far as the expert-doctor is asked to determine the exact cause of a health problem, to establish whether it is necessary to compensate the workers affected. Prevention is also part of the expert-doctor's role: prescribing new habits and new behaviours for workers, because disease can come from the workers themselves (poor work habits, refusal to protect themselves, or to follow protective measures, etc.). The doctor has an important role to play in prevention programmes set up to protect the health and ensure the safety of workers, and to improve productivity. This is not a matter of protecting the environment, but rather of protecting workers from themselves. For the relationship between health and the environment to change, the medical model that defined the relationship between work and health had to change. Occupational medicine introduced a new notion or, rather, a new concept: the living environment, or life-style.

The living environment, or life-style

The term used varies, depending on the author. Some speak of life-style, others of living environment or milieu. Whatever the term used, it is increasingly evident that the causal model of occupational medicine has become ineffective. Furthermore, as Abenhaim has demonstrated so well, the causal model was unable to explain the glaring inequality of workers with regard to death (1985: 765–6). In recent years, it has become apparent that the death rate varies enormously, depending on the living environment, and that work does not have the same effect on all individuals (ibid. 766–8). Some workers are more affected by disease, are more vulnerable than others. It is clear, for example, that life expectancy varies according to one's position on the social ladder. The life expectancy of unskilled workers is lower than that of people in the liberal professions (ibid.). The notion of living environment thus wins recognition as a more general explanatory model for health, capable of accounting for the variable of work as well as other sociological variables like economic and social differences and linking them together. Indeed, our conception of health has changed considerably since the beginning of the eighties.[4] Every day, we are urged to take care of our health, to modify our life-style. The Canadian and American government campaigns against smoking and alcohol or to promote physical exercise should suffice to convince us that health has become an important concern. This does not explain how the medical discourse on health has made possible the emergence of an environmental awareness. To see this, we must look deeper into this notion of life-style or living environment that is increasingly present in medical discourse and campaigns to promote health.

In the *Cecil Textbook of Medicine*, among the principles governing therapeutic practice, Stephen B. Hulley insists on the importance of life-style (1992: 33). What is life-style exactly? Hulley demonstrates that medicine must seek to change the behaviour of individuals by explaining, among other things, the relation between certain risk factors and the development of disease (1992). When Hulley speaks of changing behaviour, he uses the expression 'life-style'. The term refers to more than a change of behaviour; it means behaving or acting according to one's values, or, to put it differently, a way of being. More and more, we speak of health rather than disease. The difference is important in so far as it means a new way of seeing the relationship of humans to their environment. Health has become one of the most important concerns in our societies. Many discourses – medical, psychological, social, economic – speak of our health in a new way.

The first thing we must mention is the importance of the environment in the new state of the individual. In fact, health does not depend only on personal habits (smoking, alcohol, eating habits, exercise, etc.); it also depends on a healthy environment. The two cannot be separated, as we can see from the current campaigns about the harmful effect of secondary smoke for non-smokers.[5] There is a lot of emphasis on the fact that the latter suffer undesired ill effects, simply because cigarette smoke pollutes the surrounding air and affects the health of non-smokers who share the same space as smokers. Medical discourse increasingly presents health as the outcome of a multitude of factors – the environment, eating habits, smoking, life-style, etc. – which must be taken into consideration. The medical model is no longer based on direct causality. It is now based on a multi-factor approach which takes into consideration a whole host of factors – professional, personal, social, economic, etc. – and the interaction of these factors to maintain health. However, while the multi-factor approach does not rely on the concept of ecosystem which underlies the environmentalist discourse, it does makes it possible to envisage the problem of health in a broader context, and to make the environment an important concern for individuals.

It is not surprising to see the importance of life-style in medical discourse. While some might argue that this is nothing new, we believe that it represents a very important change, first, in terms of the explanatory model used by medical science, and second, with regard to the individual's conception of his or her relationship to the environment. It shows clearly the role of medical discourse in making the environment an issue in societies such as ours. By linking health to issues such as the quality of air, water and urban space, medicine has helped to make the environment an important concern.

Above all, medicine has helped us rethink our relationship to the environment. Unlike the early hygienists in the nineteenth century (Farr 1975, 1977; Gould 1981), medical practitioners today do not view health and the environment as opponents or enemies, with the environment causing deterioration in health. Medicine is no longer the occupational medicine that detects environmental aggressors which create workers' diseases. Health is now seen as a complex whole, as a balanced relationship between different factors. It is not enough to say that a safe environment promotes good health, because other factors come into play (food, exercise, rest, relaxation, etc.), and health is always a result of a precarious equilibrium among these various factors.

This notion of balance is extremely important in the new medical model. Balance means maintaining a state of health by exercising active control over the various factors that influence or determine it. One can only be healthy by balancing the forces (environment, eating habits, work-related stress, etc.) that influence health. For example, if we cannot eat well at work, we must compensate for the nutritional deficiency by eating more healthily at home. This will be insufficient, however, if we live in a polluted environment – especially if our actions and behaviour help to destroy the environment. For by so behaving, we destroy, the equilibrium on which health is based. This concept of life-style presupposes an individual's agency in relation to him or herself, the recognition of a form of competence, and especially responsibility, with regard to the maintenance of health. This change is particularly important for our argument: individuals have now come to see health as a complex whole of which they are merely a component and in which each element has an influence on the others. In short, while humans are still thinking beings, they are also components of a complex whole which depends for its existence on a fragile equilibrium for which mankind is, in part, responsible. The life and health of individuals depend on harmonious relations with all the other elements of the system. The needs of the individual are no longer opposed to nature; reconciliation with the environment presupposes new awareness, as Thomas Berry states (Berry 1988: 42).

Environmentalism

We now see that the medical discourse entails a new life-style and the adoption of new values (Rosnay 1979: 197–220). This leads to the following two statements: (1) new values are actually emerging through the environmentalist discourse – the environment and the harmony implied in 'life-style' that the medical discourse have helped to make visible and impose in our societies. Several authors speak of this new environmentalist ethic, designating thereby the new emerging values aimed at modifying the behaviour and life of humans (Killingsworth and Palmer 1992: 45–8); (2) these new values define and determine the form of existence that is desired and desirable. They impose a new identity based on environmental awareness and new rules for individuals. An environmentalist is characterized by a life-style that is in harmony with nature and the environment in which he or she lives. But health is not the only issue in the new ethics being introduced. We can speak of a human way of being. Far from turning in on the individual, the life-style being promoted here entails a different approach to living together, based on harmony, co-operation and communication between individuals. Exchange and consensus are substituted for the traditional reference to authority. Environmentalism is not only a struggle against a system of domination of nature: it involves a true political project: a system of values whereby individuals govern themselves and try to govern the universe. Today, the ethics of responsibility, the care that must be given to the environment and nature, dictate the rules by which individuals must abide, because, environmentalists claim, our lives and the survival of our species depend on this.

Conclusion

The new cosmology claims to introduce us to a universe with radically different values (Rosnay 1979: 197–220). Consensus and communication take the place of authority, tolerance replaces intransigence, and aggressiveness gradually gives way to co-operation, enthusiasm and conviviality. In other words, a new set of rules is developing and taking hold, which legitimates, in the 'new society', the way in which an individual can give meaning to his or her existence, and which will become the norm for judging conduct and the way of being in our societies. For a rule or a norm does not seek to counter violence so much as to restrain or legitimate its use. This is an age-old drama: the introduction of 'good' rules of conduct to which individuals must submit, the redefinition of a single, unique way of being that is essential for the happiness and well-being of individuals. In fact, this other, environmentalist way of living, of transcendentalism, is simply part of the endless quest to give a just meaning to life, to give one's life a purpose. The environmentalist discourse is based on hope as a palliative for an absurd, senseless human existence.

Notes

1   This idea of consciousness raising arose out of a form of political practice that existed in the early 1960s. The aim of political struggle was to develop workers' consciousness of their conditions of exploitation, which would then result in major change. Today, the naïvety of such a concept of political struggle is apparent.

2   We do not deny that the apocalyptical argument plays an important part in the development of environmental awareness; however, we do not believe that it is as important as some people claim or believe. It is true that catastrophic hypotheses are often used in political argumentation, but this is not proof of their effectiveness.

3   The authors state that Hippocrates' work *Airs, Waters and Places* (1969) was reproduced until the nineteenth century, and was used as a practical guide by physicians.

4   In Canada, the idea of living environment appeared in political discourse in the middle of the 1970s, as can be seen in the document produced by the Canadian Federal Health Minister Marc Lalonde (1974); but it was only in the mid-1980s that the idea really took hold.

5   This refers to the campaign of the Canadian government against the cigarette.

4

Sex at the Limits

Catriona Sandilands

Introduction: On Limits

As Andrew Ross so pithily put it in *The Chicago Gangster Theory of Life*, 'unlike other social movements, ecology is commonly perceived as the one that says no, the anti-pleasure voice that says you're never gonna get it, so get used to doing without' (Ross 1994: 268). Think of the three R's: reduce, reuse, recycle. Think of the austerity and earnestness of waste-talk, toxics-talk, ozone-talk. It is not only that abundant pleasure is virtually absent in (most) ecological discourse, but that it is often understood as downright *opposed* to ecological principles; frugality and simplicity appear to act as antithetical principles to enjoyment or generosity. The message seems quite clear: we (whoever 'we' might be) have had too much, and that 'having' has depleted the natural world (and, on some accounts, our ecological selves, too); we must now limit our 'having', even our 'being', so that nature can be restored.

Ah, limits: the backbone of environmental discourse. The ecological idea of limits is that they come from nature itself; it then follows that nature, if we know how to assess its warning signs (or listen to it, depending on your shade of green), is telling us that we are (or are nearly) at the limits of growth, of affluence, of consumption. Transgress, and face the consequences. Ross goes on:

In certain environmentalist circles, you do not have to look far to see the principle of scarcity being regarded as a rudimentary circumstance of nature. This applies as much to resource-minded environmentalists (heirs of the conservatism of the Progressive era),

whose apocalyptic prognoses about 'limits to growth' are prag-
matically addressed to the managers of industry, as to biocentric
nature activists (heirs of preservationism), morally moved to conserve and redeem sacrosanct areas of wilderness from human
contamination. . . . [I]ndeed . . . limitation is the cardinal principle
of ecological thought. (Ibid. 261, 264)

As I have argued elsewhere (Sandilands 1995), the 'limits' that
appear in ecology have far more to do with (particular) human,
social ideas of the real, the good and the possible than they do
with some inherent dividing line in nature beyond which we (again,
whoever 'we' might be) cannot go if the planet is to survive.
Understood as such, they lose a great deal of their normative
power; made visible, they can be negotiated. In this mode, as Ross
notes, they may hold a legitimate place in environmental discourse. But the fact remains that 'there are reasons to be careful about the widespread popular deference to [the] criterion of
limitation, especially when it is advanced as a reason for regulation
of social and cultural life' (Ross 1994: 264).

In environmentalism, calls for limitation can be crude or subtle,
physically violent or juridico-political, coercive or normative.
Although it is quite clear that other modes of ensuring deference
to a notion of limits are in operation in contemporary environmental struggles (economic coercion is common unfortunately), it
is normativity that especially concerns me in this chapter. For while
some (unfortunately not all) environmentalists see social justice as
a critical aspect of ecological politics, and thus tend to rail against
obviously coercive strategies of compliance, few speak of the ways
in which environmentalism is itself a normalizing discourse, and
thus produces specific power relations, rather than eliminates them,
in a (supposedly) transparent, common quest for natural harmony.
In particular, the organization of environmentalism around a central notion of limitation, *as if these limits were given in nature*, tends
to produce a form of 'environmentality' that is entirely consistent
with the perpetuation of highly exploitative social relations.

Specifically, much contemporary environmentalism relies on a
discourse of self-limitation and self-denial. This discourse is omni-
present; it is apparent in everything from the 'voluntary simplicity' of deep ecologists to industrialized nations' (hypocritical) calls,
via the normative prescriptions of international eco-regimes, for
'Third World' governments to exercise self-restraint in their
'unruly', ecologically destructive aspirations. The point, it seems, is

to produce both individuals and nations as responsible eco-subjects, not by overt repression or regulation, but by the invocation of a notion of 'the common good' in which 'limit' is the primary discursive term around which people are to organize their ecological practices, self-concepts and pleasures.

To the usual list of particular limits in this general constellation (growth, consumption, affluence, etc.), I would like to add 'limits to sex'. In my view, one of the most disturbing sites of 'self-limiting' ecological wisdom lies in discourses around population. That discipline is inherent in population-talk is neither new nor surprising; as Foucault wrote, 'one of the great innovations in techniques of power in the eighteenth century was the emergence of "population" as an economic and political problem: population as wealth, population as manpower [sic] or labor capacity, population balanced between its own growth and the resources it commanded' (Foucault 1976: 25). While the ecological invocation of population discourse rests on a long tradition of regulatory practice – there are few differences between Thomas Malthus and Paul Ehrlich – its contemporary imbrication in North/South, gendered, racialized and heterosexualized power dynamics suggests a particular series of inflections.

Population-Talk I: Biopower

As Foucault notes, the eighteenth century saw the rise of a mode of government based on the perception of people as a population 'with its specific phenomena and its peculiar variables: birth and death rates, life expectancy, fertility, state of health, frequency of illnesses, patterns of diet and habitation' (1976: 25). While many societies had long since been concerned with population as an indicator of wealth and prosperity, as Foucault writes:

> this was the first time that a society had affirmed, in a constant way, that its future and its fortune were tied not only to the number and the uprightness of its citizens, to their marriage rules and family organizations, but to the manner in which each individual made use of his [sic] sex. . . . There emerged the analysis of modes of sexual conduct, their determinations and their effects, at the boundary line of the biological and the economic domains. There also appeared those systematic campaigns which . . . tried to transform the sexual conduct of couples into a concerted economic and political behaviour. (Ibid. 26)

Population discourse was, and continues to be, a mode of regulation, a series of practices of science in which sex is managed, organized, aggregated and graphically compared across nation-states.[1] Of course, the new 'science' of population did not appear simply as a statistical tool to predict and control the sexual behaviour of individual persons; it appeared as a series of truth-claims about optimal health and well-being to which rational individuals could be expected to orient themselves, and toward which the developing institutions of social welfare (and social purity) were oriented.[2] Population discourse was thus an archetypical expression of modernity; the effective management of people, and especially sex, signalled efficiency, progress, control over nature and enlightenment. It was also, according to Foucault, 'without question an indispensable element in the development of capitalism; the latter would not have been possible without the controlled insertion of bodies into the machinery of production and the adjustment of the phenomenon of population to economic processes' (ibid. 140–1). Think of 'family planning', think of the progressive intrusion of a sort of sexual Taylorism into the previously (supposedly) chaotic and irrational desires of individual prospective parents.

As early as 1798, with the publication of Malthus's *Essay on the Principles of Population*, a crucial component of this discourse has been the possibility that there are, will be, or could be too many people than is good for us. Part of population management thus consists in limitation, and the achievement of modernity seems to rest upon this practice. Indeed, there is a strong relationship between the modern emergence of discourses of population limitation and the centrality of an idea of scarcity to capitalism. As Linda Singer writes, 'The notion of scarcity is crucial to capitalism – both as its justification (there's not enough, especially now, of what we need to survive; therefore, let's control it so that the maximum number of people benefit from it . . . and sometimes, at least, as that for which capitalism is the remedy' (Singer 1993: 35). While there are many facets to this relationship, what is important to note here is that population, rationality and scarcity are inextricably interwoven in the fabric of capitalism.

In this context, the very logic of population management is that its goals cannot be reached merely through the external imposition of codes of appropriate behaviour. While optimal levels and standards may be the terrain of expert negotiation and statistical analysis, efficient management (of reproduction, of eroticism) is really a question of normativity or, more precisely, the mobilization of individual pleasure to the goals of rationality and limitation. As Singer puts it, 'capitalism works not by opposing itself to the pleasure principle, but by finding strategic ways to mobilize it, a form of control by incitement, not by . . . repression but by the perpetual promise of pleasure' (1993: 36). Population discourse thus involves questions of organizing pleasure in particular ways. As a form of biopower, producing and controlling the sexuality of collective and individual human subject-bodies, it operates by enticement, not just by repression; in the case of population limitation, voices whisper a common articulatory thread: 'You will *enjoy* your small(er) family; you will *enjoy* your new-found economic prosperity; you will *enjoy* the process of controlling your fertility.'

This is not to say that population management efforts have never been, or do not continue to be, repressive or coercive. Far from it: one could speak of not-long-past trades of transistor radios for vasectomies among Indian men; one could speak of instances in which poor pregnant women in the USA have been refused hospital obstetric treatment unless they give 'consent' for post-partum sterilization; one could speak of countries in which women are currently lured into trying Depo-Provera, and are refused treatment to have the implants removed when side-effects arise (Trombley 1988, 1996). Early population discourses, including family planning, were overtly tied to eugenic strategies, which resulted in the elimination of reproductive rights for many poor women, women of colour, and women with disabilities (Davis 1981, Mies and Shiva 1993). These and other gross injustices remain, and are soundly condemned by many feminist and social justice activists, and even by some of the more enlightened environmentalists.

But what is perhaps more disturbing is the fact that population management itself remains significantly unchallenged as a goal, a discourse or a disciplinary practice. While some authors are critical of the attribution of singular or even primary causality to population as a source of environmental degradation, even some of the most militant critics of coercive population control measures seem relatively content with family planning education, despite the fact that such normative 'planning' remains a significant instrument of control, and bears the hallmarks of profoundly gendered, racialized and heterosexualized normativity. In many ways, contemporary family planning measures – education, health promotion, access to birth control technologies, etc. – are much more efficient bearers of specifically modern, rational and capitalist relations of reproduction than any bribery or threat could be,

at least in part because the power relations involved are largely
invisible.

Population-Talk II: Environmentality

One of the most significant features of contemporary population
discourse is its intersection with particular ideas of 'nature'. While
for many environmentalists the link between population growth
and environmental degradation seems so obvious as to be a truism,
it must be remembered that the relationship between these two
terms is both historically recent and discursively specific. Indeed,
the population–environment nexus involves a form of what Timothy Luke (1995) calls 'environmentality'. Of this general historical
creation, Luke suggests that '[a]s biological existence was [increas-
ingly] refracted through economic, political, and technological
existence, "the facts of life" passed into fields of control . . . and
spheres of intervention' (1995: 67). 'The environment' emerged as
a significant arena for the play of biopolitics, as constructions of
the natural world became deeply imbricated in the globalizing
spread of capitalist productive (and reproductive) relations and
the regimes of truth/knowledge/power that generate and support
them. Luke writes, following Foucault, that in this context the
environment

> emerges as a historical artifact that is openly constructed, not an
> occluded reality that is difficult to comprehend. In this great net-
> work, the simulation of spaces, the intensification of resources, the
> incitement of discoveries, the formation of special knowledges, the
> strengthening of controls, and the provocation of resistances can
> all be linked to one another. (Ibid.)

Especially with the 1968 publication of Paul Ehrlich's *The Population Bomb*, so-called overpopulation became a question not just
of people but of the planet. Wrote Ehrlich: 'the causal chain of
[environmental] deterioration . . . is easily followed to its source . . .
too many people' (ibid.). The erotic and reproductive bodies of
individuals became inserted not only into the discursive terrain of
human welfare (as had been the case in the commonly posited relationship between population and poverty), but into environmentality. 'Too many people' became a problem for nature. Deforestation,
energy shortages, pollution and other problems were caused by
too many human, consuming bodies. 'Too many people' became

an aberration *of* nature, as we were going beyond our bounds. Nature, via environmental science, must be harnessed to the task of defining a more appropriate number of people for the planet, for the good of both human and non-human life.[3]

As the following excerpt from the 1986 UNFPA report shows dramatically, population discourse posits that contemporary human beings have, presumably with the aid of technology, come perilously close to (or gone beyond) nature's limits. The narrative reads like an epic (it occurs under the subtitle 'the march of the billions', so that is probably not surprising). It is a grand tale about humanity conquering nature but then finding that nature is not to be toyed with lightly.

> There have been many ups and downs in [population] growth rates . . . [that] by themselves have never guaranteed the means to cope with their consequences. The margin of safety has always been thin, and human groups were under constant threat. If they succeeded in escaping famine and disease, their populations might grow faster than their precarious resources and swiftly fall once more. . . . It is only in this century that humans as a group have effectively won control of their demographic fate. But the victory is not final, and one of the factors may be the very weight of numbers which their success has brought into being. (UNFPA 1986: 7–8)

Read: humans must manage themselves more effectively – that is, in respect for nature's limits – if modernity is to be genuinely achieved. It is not that nature should not be managed, but that the management of human nature is now intimately tied to that of resources. And the appropriate guide-lines for the measure of both are to be found in ecological science, demography and, even better, the emerging fields of risk and impact assessment.

Recent commentators are, as a whole, somewhat less essentialist, somewhat less determined to posit overpopulation as the singular cause of environmental degradation than the likes of Paul Ehrlich. In general, there is a tacit recognition of complexity, and some suggestion that poverty, consumption levels, and/or technology may have a role to play in 'excessive' resource usage (few writers in this vein speak about nature in any way other than as 'resources', thus suggesting the strong, continuing influence of capitalist notions of scarcity and management). But what seems to be moderation actually serves to mystify the role that population *does* play in environmental degradation. The above-quoted UNFPA report typically qualifies the contribution of population to environmental degradation. '[P]opulation growth is not', it states, 'the only culprit and no figures can be put on its contribution' (ibid. 19). But the possibility that population has *nothing* to do with environmental degradation (let alone the possibility that there are particular ideas of nature involved in the definition of the problem in the first place) is never considered. The line linking numbers of bodies, numbers of mouths to feed, and numbers of acres of land deforested for marginal agriculture is so firmly drawn through discursive space that its impact is seldom questioned at all. UNFPA's argument? 'To demonstrate the threat in general terms, it is only necessary to invoke the principle of entropy' (ibid. 18–19).

Leaving aside (for the moment only) some of the glaring conclusions that can be drawn about social inequality, there seem to be a number of specific assumptions about human/nature relations going on in recent population–environment discourse. One is that the only possible relationship between humans and non-human nature is antagonistic, as nature exists only as a 'resource' for human use; more people inevitably means more degradation. Following from this, there are only two courses of action to 'save' nature: reduce the number of people or reduce their consumption. Either option signals the necessity of intervention; both imply the invocation of specific notions of natural limits (carrying capacity, etc.) as ways of drawing a line beyond which humans cannot go.

A second, related assumption is that nature's primary appearance in human life is as a limit to human *excess*, including, potentially, an excess of human freedom (especially in the context of a crisis).[4] In the context of the fact that population discourse is also concerned with the achievement of rationality and progress (both of which are discursively opposed to nature in modernity), this seems somewhat paradoxical. But the paradox is easily explained: where the 'ideal' subject of population discourse is rational and has proved capable of subordinating desire to the common good of population control (normative self-limitation), it seems that there are 'other' subjects not so willing or capable. In other words, population discourse at this historical conjuncture relies on the bifurcation of the world into two: 'good' ecological citizens, who have listened to and understood the call for limits and do not require (further) regulatory intervention, and unruly bodies, who have not, might not, and/or do.[5]

Numerous commentators have pointed to the fact that population management strategies differ according to who it is that is being managed. The discrepancy between white, middle-class North

American women, who are encouraged to utilize highly invasive new reproductive technologies to conceive, and poor rural women of countries such as Bangladesh, who are often sterilized without their consent, is too glaring to ignore. The point is not only that racism is a strong feature of population management (unsurprisingly, given the early linkages of family planning to eugenics). The point is also, as authors such as Mies and Shiva allude to (1993: 277–95), that all people (especially women) are in some way or another accountable to the discourse, subject to its prescriptions and prohibitions, *made subjects* through its normative inspirations in the context of economic and political relations that discriminate considerably among different kinds of subjects.

It is my contention that environmentalist discourse often works to amplify both the normativity and the discrimination, by emphasizing the 'natural requirement' of population limitation – the 'natural requirement' of the subordination of human needs to an abstract notion of 'carrying capacity' that passes as an ecological common good. Combined with the fact that so much is *absent* from population discourse, the patina of scientific legitimacy gives the managerial imperative all the more power. And in so far as environmental discourse understands itself to be a continuation of rationalization and modernity,[6] management plus risk science plus nature equals a very powerful normative imperative indeed.

Population-Talk III: Capital, Power and Disappearances

That the mode of sexual subjectivity generated in, and borne by, population-talk is intimately related to the economic and social relations of (globalizing) late capitalism is not a stunning revelation: at the level of physical technologies, of course, family planning and contraceptive development provide a fantastic new global market for the provision of goods and services. But at the level of cultural technologies as well, discourses of the self associated with capitalist liberal individualism, and even particular family forms associated with capitalist productive relations, are part of the normative package sold by the global family planning movement. As Irene Diamond illustrates, these technologies are strongly tied together:

> In order to create a disciplined market that would find Western contraception desirable, family planning professionals utilised

enticing media images that were most always supplemented by monetary and non-monetary incentives. *Women of the South were told 'contraceptives are a woman's right'*. And if in a particular district an insufficient number of women became 'acceptors', zealous recruiters, whose own survival within bureaucratic delivery systems depended on achieving their target goal, did not stop at tricking or compelling a woman to accept. (Diamond 1994: 73–4, emphasis added)

What I would like to suggest is that contemporary population discourses, acting largely (though never entirely) through normative prescriptions of a particular form of managed sexual subjectivity, are part of the increasing global reach of capitalist market economic relations. Just as biopower was intimately involved in the development of industrial capital in the eighteenth and nineteenth centuries, so too it is a foundational element in the globalization of monopoly capital at the end of the twentieth. At one end of the spectrum is international aid tied to the implementation of coercive birth control strategies; at the other is the even more insidious discursive linkage of (economic) well-being with small families through educational programmes sponsored by international development agencies. Whereas the former is relatively easy to condemn (if still, unfortunately, common in some places), the latter is the dominant discourse of organizations such as the United Nations, which are now beginning to speak the language of liberal feminism and women's rights.

Contemporary population management strategies of education and increasing women's 'rights' of access to contraception effectively mask their imbrication in institutionalized discourses of capitalist economic development under a layer of liberal feminist concern for women's social position. This discourse suggests a sort of reproductive structural adjustment; just as the politics of debt and aid force particular economic relations on countries of the South, so too the politics of population management, especially given their transmission via particular reproductive technologies, impose particular family and gender relations. In structural adjustment, countries are to produce *themselves* according to a capitalist productive logic; in reproductive structural adjustment, women and men are to produce *themselves* according to profoundly normative discourses about appropriate gender relations and family structures.

It is certainly the case that many feminist organizations and individuals are critical of the emphasis on population at the level of international policy, citing instead the importance of women's health (reproductive and otherwise), socio-economic conditions and education levels to women's well-being.[7] But it is also the case that almost nobody challenges the assumption that fertility needs to be managed in the first place, or the assumption that 'providing universal access to information, education, and discussion on sexuality, gender roles, reproduction, and birth control' (Mazur 1994: 269) is a necessary aspect of feminist political action (talking about sex, of course, has never meant its liberation). Significantly, it is also the case that the feminism most commonly cited in population circles is inspired by a relatively liberal capitalist enthusiasm for development, with its focus on 'prioritizing women's education, job training, paid employment, access to credit, and the right to own land and other property in social and economics policies, and through equal rights legislation' (ibid. 270). The two prongs of this feminist project – providing family planning information and striving for equal access to economic development – are seen to go together naturally; they coexist in a feminist discourse centred on women's right to choose and the creation of conditions in which women can make the greatest possible variety of 'informed' choices.

Of course, given the fact that all of this is, at some level, about management, the only 'informed' choice that there is to be made seems to be the choice to limit family size. Especially when one takes into account the environmental degradation that is impinging on women's subsistence and other activities in some parts of the world (these are the scenarios that get talked about, never the ones where standards of living actually rise – even if only temporarily – due to increasing environmentally destructive activities), what other choices could a 'rational' person make? Nafis Sadik, then executive director of the United Nations Population Fund, makes this narrative quite explicit; given the choice, women will have smaller families. She writes:

> Many women, especially in developing countries, have few choices in life outside marriage and children. They tend to have large families because that is expected of them. Investing in women means widening their choice of strategies and reducing their dependence on children for status and support. Family planning is one of the most important investments because it represents the freedom from which other freedoms flow. (Sadik 1994: 209)

So, under the apparently emancipatory guise of liberal feminism, women (and men) in so-called developing nations are enticed to adopt managerial-capitalist modes of sexual subjectivity, as part of their path toward well-being. Indeed, when this insight is also viewed in light of the strong normativity of environmentalism, we see that under the banner of 'our common future', ecological discourses are co-opted to the task of producing women as self-disciplining, eco-capitalist subjects (Sadik suggests that women's more acute experiences of environmental degradation only confirm the necessity of their rational choice to limit child bearing). In my view, this is the key narrative: most environmental discourses on population are embedded in a normative sexuality that is intimately involved in capitalist penetration. Population management is a form of globalizing environmentality, and that environmentality is inextricably linked to capital.

Notable in this environmentality is the fact that population discourse, and even the feminisms that appear to be in dialogue with it, *mask* their status as normative sexualities that accompany liberal capitalism. As Foucault notes, 'power is tolerable only on condition that it mask a substantial part of itself. Its success is proportional to its ability to hide its own mechanisms' (Foucault 1976: 86). So it is no great surprise that it is through a series of 'disappearing tricks' that population discourse is made palatable. In emphasizing (particular kinds of) education, freedom, health care and standard of living, population discourse works to seduce, to entice, and to create; these modes of subjectivation rely on hiding their workings and the normative constraints that appear throughout them.

The first disappearing trick lies in the complete absence of any overt talk about sex whatsoever in most population discourse. Foucault speaks about the regulation of sexuality through its production in discourse (*scientia sexualis*), not its banishment from discourse. I consider the absence of overt talk about sex (*qua* sex) entirely consistent with this characterization, in so far as population discourse does not operate by repressing sex but by rendering it discursive in a particular way that conceals its location in the realm of sexual activity. Sexuality is reduced to heterosexual reproduction; reproduction is reduced to the rational behaviours of individuals in the context of complex expert negotiations around regional and global 'carrying capacity', a very particular discursive existence indeed.

The second disappearing trick lies in the submergence of the profound racism of population discourse in Western-derived assumptions about rational ecological behaviour. Population is a problem of the regulation of certain *kinds* of bodies, specifically exoticized, racialized bodies that are figured as unruly, uncontrolled, and incapable of submerging their desires to the common good of sustainability. The notion of reproductive choice is not only constituted according to a very particular definition of rational choice, but is also produced according to racist, colonialist assumptions about the self-regulatory abilities of *particular* bodies and hidden under an apparently self-explanatory 'common good' of sustainability in which all are to participate as willing subjects.

The final – and perhaps most complete – disappearing trick involves the assumption of heterosexuality that constitutes the entire discourse. Think of it this way: if the problem of population is simply one of 'too many people', then why not encourage a greater variety of non-heterosexual, non-reproductive sexual practices? The fact that this is completely unthinkable in the minds of most suggests that population discourse isn't about limiting numbers of people on the planet, but about instituting a form of ecological management through sexuality.

Conclusion: Sex, Nature and Resistance

All of these disappearances are part of an ecological disciplinary discourse: in the face of natural limits, the appropriate, rational action is self-control. The problematization of population as an (for some, 'the') ecological question translates 'natural limits' into 'sexual limits' in a way that renders invisible the views of nature underscoring the former, the views of bodies permeating the latter, and the racialized, gendered and heterosexualized power relations involved in both. That sexual asceticism is so strongly tied to ecological subjectivity makes it almost impossible to argue that there may be places where resistance to sexual regulation may be tied to resistance to ecological degradation. But that is where resistance must begin: in a non-fundamentalist environmental-sexual ethics.

As Éric Darier argues in the last chapter of this volume, 'if environmentalism is to retain its radical and critical features, it has to avoid becoming just another fundamentalism'. Certainly, the power effects of population discourse show what happens when 'nature', in the guise of natural limit, is understood as the template for human sexual conduct. The kind of sexual fundamentalism that appears at the core of population-talk bears a rather disconcerting resemblance to other profoundly conservative normative

(and frequently naturalized) sexualities. Sexuality is translated into
the erasure of sex as environmentalism includes yet another dimension into its 'just say no' campaigns. And this asceticism is particularly acute in the absence of a countervailing ethical sexual practice.
Thus, to borrow again from Darier, this suggests the need for an
'environmental ethics à la Foucault [that] implies constant self-
reflection, self-knowledge, self-examination, of transforming one's
life into an aesthetic of existence' in the realm of sexual *and*
environmental conduct.

For Darier, as for Foucault, 'resistance . . . is an illustration of
the self-critical affirmation of ways of relating to the world rather
than an instrumental strategy for a teleological purpose'. The
point is not to create a series of sexual norms to 'save the Earth',
but to engage in practices of critical self-reflection *against precisely such norms* – here especially those that create unproblematic,
'natural' linkages among sex, knowledge and nature – in order
to 'become something different from what we were made'. Resistance to eco-sexual normativity, then, begins in questioning
and discursive disruption, rather than in an easy acceptance of the
assumption that environmentalism requires 'saying no' to sex. It
begins in a process of discursive exposure: making visible the
workings of the racist, sexist and heterosexist inflections of population discourse, making clear the assumptions of a particular sort
of rational subjectivity that accompany discourses of 'appropriate' global ecological citizenship for individuals and nations alike.
It begins in a process of calling into question the 'naturalness' of
any sexual talk or practice, testing and shaking up the grounds of
both calcified and emergent articulations.

Tempting though it might be, resistance to eco-sexual normativity
is not a mere matter of 'just saying yes'. Nor is an ethics made
by finding or confessing one's 'true' sexuality beneath layers of
repression, environmentally induced or otherwise. It cannot be a
simple question of 'doing the right thing' according to an abstract
set of expert-derived principles. This uncertainty, this lack of a
strategic or normative ethics, makes the development of a collective response to eco-sexual normativity quite difficult. 'However,'
writes Darier, 'as any action is situated in a specific context of
power relations, it is possible to know if – strategically and at a
given time – a green act of resistance merely legitimizes the existing system of power relations or undermines it.' Although there
may be no easy answers, and although it may not be desirable to
replace an ascetic eco-sexual normativity with (say) a hedonistic

one, I do think that in this particular context a possible avenue for resistance is in the reassertion of an overt sense of 'polymorphous' pleasure into environmentalist discourses, toward a multiplicity of sexual and natural discursive articulations.

While it is clear that part of the success of population discourse is its mobilization of pleasure in the relationship between reducing reproduction and increasing living standard, it is also clear that this is a pleasure born of denial in the context of a series of other denials, a reduction of multiple possibilities to one. So what other pleasures are possible? I alluded above to a process of questioning reproductive heterosexual penetrative normativity as part of a strategy of resistance to the assumption that population control equates with the limitation of all sexual activity. In this case, both heterosexuality and ascetic ecological subjectivity are called into question, separately and in their 'natural' articulation. Such a questioning would create spaces for the exploration of others. Further, it might be possible to consider some contemporary Foucauldian-inspired queer analysis and politics – specifically that which tries to 'denature' sexual identity – as a site from which to incorporate a variety of *different* understandings of nature in sexual discourse. What might it be like to 'try on' different natures as part of a process of pleasurable, creative self-understanding? Or the reverse: what might it be like to 'try on' different sexualities in the interpretation of nature for ecological discourses (e.g. Sandilands 1994)? The point is not to arrive at some non-heterosexual normative practice, but to mobilize resistances to heterosexuality *with* resistances to eco-normativity as a way of using each to call into question the 'naturalness' of the other.

Of course, this kind of anti-normative questioning does not guarantee that the planet will be saved, in either the short or the long term. Such a quest would result in precisely the kind of eco-fundamentalism that has been generated by the articulation of ecological with population discourses. What this type of process of resistance does suggest is that space be made for the possibility of a genuinely ethical self-transformative practice as part of the point of the environmental movement itself. If environmentalism is to go beyond 'just saying no', if it is to lead to something other than a series of Draconian codes governing ever more intimate aspects of individuals' lives, then spaces for exploration must be allowed to flourish and proliferate. Polymorphous sexualities and multiple natures are thus at the heart of green resistances. Where population control, despite its claims to the contrary, fails to free humans and non-humans alike from normative constraints, self-questioning and disruption may be more promising.

Notes

1   As Barbara Duden notes, the term *population* lost its specific reference to human beings in the early nineteenth century; it can refer as much 'to mosquitoes as to humans', thus subordinating the lives of individuals (both human and non-human) to statistics. See Sachs 1993: 148.

2   It should be pointed out that a conclusive relationship between population (in and of itself) and poverty or health has never been shown.

3   There is some conflict in ecological circles about whether there are already too many human beings on the planet, as some wilderness advocates might argue, or whether there will be fairly soon, as might be the position of resource management types. Complex calculations of 'carrying capacity' aside, this confusion reinforces the idea that 'How many is too many?' is part of a discursive contestation about what nature is supposed to look like.

4   In a recent article on population, among other things, in *The Globe and Mail* of Toronto (Saturday 20 July 1996, D1) eco-crisis manager Thomas Homer-Dixon made this stance quite clear, stating that democracy might need to be sacrificed to ecology.

5   As Foucault notes, it is the so-called aberration that comes to define the norm. Thus, the ideal subject of population–environment discourse is only possible with the institution of the subject who needs to be controlled, the proverbial 'population pervert'.

6   Not all environmentalisms can be understood in this way. Some, such as deep ecology, are (arguably) anti-modern. In general, I am speaking about mainstream environmentalism, which some have chosen to call 'resource managerialism'. What is interesting to note, however, is that on the issue of population, even some deep ecologists seem content to accept population management strategies that derive from precisely the 'shallow' ecological discourses to which they otherwise object.

7   See e.g. the 'Women's Declaration on Population Policies in Preparation for the 1994 International Conference on Population and Development' (Mazur 1994: 267–72).

5

Ecological Modernization and Environmental Risk

Paul Rutherford

Introduction

Foucault did not develop his work on biopolitics into a consideration of environmental problems, but rather focused on the role of
the social sciences in producing the human subject through the
discursive practices of medicine, psychiatry and so on. Nor did he
consider in detail the way in which the *natural* sciences have
contributed to the problematization of nature and the subsequent
extension of the techniques of modern biopower in shaping the
contemporary social relation to nature. In chapter 2 above I discussed how Foucault's work on biopolitics and governmentality
can be developed to understand what Éric Darier has described as
the 'historico-epistemological conditions of emergence' of the environment as an object of public policy, and the associated 'environmental mobilisation of the population' through those policies
(Darier 1996a). Elsewhere I have considered Foucault's reluctance
to extend his analysis of power relations to encompass the natural
sciences, and in particular the way in which ecological science
acts to discipline and control the 'action environment' (including
the alignment of the physical environment) of social agents
(Rutherford 1994a).

In this chapter I consider this Foucauldian perspective on ecological problems in light of a discussion of the recent work of
German social theorists (Habermas, Eder, Beck and Luhmann)
who have sought to understand the connection between ecological
problems and the broader processes of societal modernization and
the ways in which the social relations with nature are influenced
by the link between power and knowledge in modern society.

Such an approach is justified on two main grounds. First, these German authors have produced some of the most significant works in contemporary social theory dealing with environmental questions. In sociology, in Europe but also elsewhere, the work of Beck is particularly influential. The second ground is that in developing the notions of biopolitics and governmentality, it becomes evident that Foucault's work engages many concerns similar to those raised by Nietzsche, Weber and the Frankfurt school.

Foucault's Relation to the Critical Tradition in Social Theory

Foucault described his intellectual project as involving the elaboration of 'a history of rationality' that was not based on the 'founding act of the rationalist subject' (Foucault 1983b: 198–201; 1984c; 1988e: 13). He saw this as part of a broader 'historical critique of reason', represented in France by the history of science of Bachelard and Canguilhem and in Germany by the 'Frankfurt School and Lukács, by way of Feuerbach, Marx, Nietzsche, and Max Weber' (Foucault, cited in Foucault 1983b; Gutting 1989: 9–12).

Dreyfus and Rabinow have suggested that Foucault inherited from Weber 'a concern with rationalisation and objectification as the essential trend . . . and most important problem' of modern society (Dreyfus and Rabinow 1982: 166).[1] Although Foucault and Weber shared common intellectual concerns (such as rationalization, power and discipline), there were nevertheless important differences between them. Thus, whereas Weber tended to view societal rationalization as a global, all-encompassing process, Foucault was concerned with rationality in a much more specific and relative sense, which denied any 'absolute form of rationality against which specific forms might be compared or evaluated' (Smart 1983: 126). In contrast to Weber, Foucault explicitly rejected casting rationalization in terms of any totalizing notion of modern society or culture, and as a consequence held open the possibility of resistance, whereas Weber succumbed to the fatalistic vision of the *iron cage* of bureaucratic domination and the spread of instrumental reason.[2]

Both Weber and Foucault dealt with questions of domination and discipline. Weber's concept of power emphasized the importance of the state and the intentionality of subjects, and saw power as negative and prohibitive. Foucault regarded power as something which not only constrained individuals but also *produced* the different modes of subjectivity and the social relations possible in any particular historical milieu. Importantly, both emphasized an understanding of societal rationalization as the disciplining of the body, the origins of which are traced to the institutional practices of the monastery and the army in medieval Europe.[3] Weber characterized the rational disciplining of the body as a process in which the 'natural rhythm' of humans as organisms is brought into 'line with the demands of the work procedure, (and) . . . is attuned to a new rhythm through the functional specialisation of muscles and through the creation of an optimal economy of physical effort' (Weber 1968: 1156). This has clear similarities to Foucault's description of *biopower*, or the 'anatomo-politics of the human body', as a form of power that begins to emerge in the seventeenth century and which is 'centered on the body as a machine', involving the disciplining of the body through 'the optimisation of its capacities' so as to produce a 'parallel increase of its usefulness and its docility, its integration into systems of efficient and economic controls' (Foucault 1976: 139). Like Weber, Foucault saw this new form of discipline as indispensable to the development of capitalism, which required the 'controlled insertion of bodies into the machinery of production and the adjustment of the phenomena of population to economic processes' (ibid. 141). Colin Gordon has suggested a link between Foucault's later work on governmentality (and neo-liberalism), and a growing interest in the significance of Weber's influence on recent intellectual history. In particular, he points to Foucault's claim that Weber provided a counter-focus, in social theory, to Marxism by suggesting a historical understanding of the present in terms of processes of rationalization which are 'multiple, specific and potentially discordant' (Gordon 1986: 79; 1987: 295–6).

The intellectual influence of Nietzsche and Weber on the Frankfurt school of critical theory, including Jürgen Habermas, has been significant. Horkheimer and Adorno, in their treatment of the *dialectic of enlightenment*, argued that Nietzsche was the first to recognize the existence of a nihilistic 'anti-life force' inherent within all rational thought. Their discussion of the domination of nature as a universal feature of instrumental reason draws heavily on the Nietzschean theme that knowledge operates as a tool of the 'will to power' in which the drive to predict and master nature serves the interests of *self-preservation* (Adorno and Horkheimer 1986). Similarly, key aspects of Weber's treatment of societal rationalization were appropriated by Adorno and Horkheimer in their analysis of the domination of reason by instrumental rationality and the rise of a bureaucratized, 'totally administered society'. Habermas too bases central elements of his understanding of societal rationalization and modernization on a particular reading of Weber, arguing that Weber's analysis fails to appreciate the 'selectivity', or differentiation, exhibited in the processes of rationalization. According to Habermas, Weber could not adequately explain the way in which, under conditions of capitalist modernization, instrumental rationality 'surges beyond the bounds' of the material reproduction of economy and state, distorting the communicative reason necessary to the 'symbolic reproduction of the life-world'. Hence, he argues that it is possible to overcome Weberian pessimism (the iron cage) once social theory understands that the 'colonisation' of life-world by instrumental rationality is a pathological distortion of the modernity, rather than its inevitable outcome. The progressive potential of modernity can be realized provided social theory appreciates the different analytical approaches appropriate to action within the separate social environments of life-world and system. The first requires a hermeneutic, or 'action-theoretic', approach, while the latter demands a systems theory (Habermas 1987: 303–1).

Similarities have also been drawn between the work of the early Frankfurt school and Foucault. Honneth, for example, points to several key features of critique common to Adorno and Foucault. According to Honneth, both Adorno and Foucault understood modernity as a process of technical or instrumental rationalization that, under the cloak of moral emancipation and progress, violently disciplines a 'pre-rational' dimension of the human body to produce the 'modern, forcefully unified individual' (Honneth 1986: 56–8). Each finds the root of modernity in the intellectual and political changes initiated by the European Enlightenment; each works on the view that knowledge assures domination behind the 'generalization of theoretical and moral validity claims' and the growth of legal and constitutional structures. On this view, both Adorno and Foucault understand instrumental rationality as expressing a tendency towards the totalitarian control of social life. Modernity, in other words, is characterized by the regulative capacity to 'intervene like total institutions in the life context of every single individual in order to make him a conforming member of society through discipline and control, manipulation and drilling'. Honneth, in agreement with Habermas (1985), thus sees Foucault as succumbing to a totalizing critique similar to that which deprives Adorno and Horkheimer of a rational basis for their critical social theory. While pointing to the different conceptions of subjectivity that lead to these similarities, he nevertheless claims that Foucault's social theory is in the end a 'version of the Dialectic of Enlightenment reduced to systems theory' (Honneth 1986: 58).[4]

Thomas McCarthy has also drawn out some broad affinities (as well as differences) between Foucault and the Frankfurt school, including Habermas. He argues that both Foucault and the Frankfurt school assert the 'primacy of the practical over the theoretical' by treating knowledge production as social practice and requiring that 'epistemic practices' be understood within their broader practical context. Foucault concludes from this the impossibility of knowledge or truth (at least in the human sciences[5]) that is outside of relations of power, hence capable of grounding a theory of the social totality, whereas the Frankfurt school does not give up the attempt to find a universalizing truth-function for reason in the progressive realization of a totalized concept of social emancipation (McCarthy 1990: 438–42). Following on from this, Foucault sees a pervasive complicity of human science expertise in modern forms of domination and discipline. Habermas, while critical of the role played by the social sciences and social-scientific expertise in societal rationalization, nevertheless seeks to distinguish between different forms of social enquiry in a way that does not regard them all as extensions of an instrumental rationality directed towards ever more effective forms of domination. Despite the differences between the two approaches to social theory, a key feature of each is the use of 'functional accounts of how and why purportedly rational practices came to be taken for granted'. Such accounts are central to critique inasmuch as they problematize and destabilize the apparently natural and necessary character of social and epistemic practices by demonstrating how these are in fact the product of 'contingent relations of force and an arbitrary closing off of alternatives' (ibid. 439–40).

The Modernizing Rationality of Ecological Movements: Eder *contra* Habermas

Environmental movements are often seen (particularly by themselves) as presenting an alternative understanding of environmental protection to that suggested by the highly expert, rationalized model of modern science. It is thus not uncommon for ecological movements to be seen as fundamentally anti-modernist. Habermas, for example, characterizes ecological issues as concerning 'the grammar of forms of life'. On this view, ecological problems arise within the life-world (the areas of cultural reproduction, social integration and socialization), but are provoked by the 'reification of communicative spheres of action' brought about by the intrusion of functional, 'system-steering' media of money and power (Habermas 1981: 33). He suggests that ecological conflicts and environmental movements should be understood as particularistic expressions of resistance to pressures towards such colonization of the life-world. He identifies the critique of economic growth and the 'self-destructive consequences of the growth in (social) complexity' as key unifying themes of the new social movements. However, while he sees ecological problems as reactions to specific, tangible, environmental problems, he also argues that ecological problems are 'largely abstract and require technical and economic solutions that must in turn be planned globally and implemented by administrative means' – that is, through instrumental rationality (ibid. 35). Here he also characterizes ecological concerns as expressions of resistance to the problems generated by the 'over complexity' of the societal system of functional integration. Hence ecological problems arise as systemic abstractions 'forced upon the life-world' which can be properly dealt with only within a life-world that is itself highly rationalized. At the same time, however, these systemic 'abstractions' cut across the boundaries between the different modes of action co-ordination in advanced industrial societies. Ecological conflicts and problems therefore 'arise at the seam between system and life-world'.

A consequence of approaching ecological conflicts and problems in this way is that they are seen as reflecting an unavoidable and unending *tension between communicatively derived cultural norms specifying the acceptable limits to human appropriation of the natural environment and the functionally defined, systemic imperatives of the material reproduction of society*. It is within this context that Habermas adopts a pessimistic view of the 'emancipatory' potential of new social movements, regarding any such potential as subverted and obscured by the failure of these movements to distinguish between the 'rationalisation of the life-world' and the 'increasing complexity of the social system', between the different developmental logics of life-world and system (ibid. 36–7).

This theme of ecological problems as systemically induced also plays a central role in the work of other important contemporary social theorists, particularly Niklas Luhmann and Ulrich Beck, whom I discuss further below. However before doing so, a further comment on the relationship of ecological movements to modernity may be useful. Ecological movements can be seen as reflecting a cultural rejection of technological modernity, and this can be variously evaluated, either positively (deep ecologists) or negatively (Habermas). It is undeniable that a theme common to much non-scientific ecological thinking is a marked ambivalence towards 'mainstream' or 'reductionist' science. There is no doubt that an earlier (i.e. pre-World War II) romantic nature conservation sentiment played an important role in the development of the counter-cultural side of contemporary environmentalism (Jamison and Eyerman 1994; Worster 1987a). Nevertheless, it is also true that since the 1970s environmental movements have tended to become more scientized (and globalized in outlook), and more inclined to embrace the potential positive uses of new 'clean' technologies (Buttel and Taylor 1992; Cramer et al. 1989). Without denying the importance of the counter-cultural element of much ecological discourse, it remains the case, as Steven Yearley argues, that environmental movements are profoundly anchored in modern science, even though the very epistemological and sociological nature of scientific knowledge production conspires to make such a reliance highly problematic, unstable and contested[6] (Yearley 1992: 529). Even those ecocentric or deep ecology theorists most suspicious of 'reductionist' science and instrumental reason frequently do not reject science *per se*, but, much to the annoyance of Habermas (1982), advocate a holistic 'new science' capable of a communicative, rather than a purely technical-instrumental, relation with nature (Eckersley 1992: 114–16; Fox 1990: 252–3; Mathews 1991: 48–50).

Klaus Eder has provided a useful way of viewing the relationship between these often contrasted elements of contemporary environmentalism: namely, a highly rationalized scientific ecology and a romantic, moral-cultural attitude towards nature. Eder identifies two competing cultural models of nature contributing to Western modernity. He sees these as expressing contradictory discourses: the *justice* perspective is the dominant cultural model of nature in the West, finding its expression in the instrumentalist-utilitarian tradition; while the *purity* perspective embodies a non-utilitarian, romantic attitude which rejects the reduction of nature to an object of theoretical reason. The 'cultural code' of modern Western society consists of both of these discourses, so that the history of modernity, including the social relation to nature, is to be understood as the product of the interrelationship between these two cultural discourses. The counter-tradition represented in the purity perspective is thus not, as Habermas claims, irrational or anti-modern, but a different form of rationality which seeks to define an *alternative modernity* (Eder 1990b: 28–37).

Whereas Habermas tends to focus narrowly on those features of the ecological movements that reflect this alternative purity perspective, Eder argues that *both* models of nature shape contemporary ecological movements. There is within such movements a much greater potential for ambivalence than is recognized by Habermas, so that, while environmental movements often draw on the romantic, counter-cultural tradition (as expressed in the moralism of deep ecology), they also draw on the utilitarian perspective with its focus on efficiency. Eder correctly suggests that in this way contemporary ecological thinking can be considered 'the most advanced version of the dominant utilitarian mind, a radicalisation of modern economic ideology.' (Eder 1990a: 75). Such an argument is consistent with Foucault's claim that modern political economy emerges in conjunction with biopolitics and its focus on what he calls the 'population–riches problem'. Indeed, contemporary ecological discourse is an articulation of biopolitics and its problematization of population in relation to resources.[7] As Donald Worster has argued, scientific ecology, which emerged in its modern form in the 1950s, understands nature in terms of a *bio-economic model*, and conceives of itself as 'the science of natural economics' (Worster 1987a: 311–13).

Eder claims that theorizing about modernity has largely centred on the political and economic reproduction of society, but that now the focus is shifting to include the problems of *ecological reproduction of society*. *Contra* Habermas, Eder argues that the problem of nature is not simply a technical problem of the functional integration of the material needs of the modern social system with its environment, but is also a *cultural problem*, in that it questions the moral dimensions of the notion of progress, which has itself begun to threaten the 'conditions of life' themselves (Eder 1990b: 40–2).

Eder therefore rejects the false idealization implied in Habermas's separation of life-world and system. While recognizing the validity of Habermas's concern for relating these 'two logics of social life', he argues that practical reasoning can never be separated from the context of social systemic factors (power and money) which it serves to reproduce (Eder 1988: 937–40). Habermas's overly rigid analytical separation of system and life-world, with its surrender of nature solely to the systemic realm of functional reason, according to Eder, underestimates the interpenetration of morality and technology in social life. What is more, it obscures the fact that Western culture is the product of the interaction of competing discourses on nature, of these two indissolubly linked notions of progress and modernity. Eder suggests that as the relation between society and nature is symbolically mediated, this necessitates reconstructing 'the theoretical idea of forces of production as a cultural category, as a specifically defined cultural form for appropriating nature. [We can] . . . see the basic forms of social life . . . as being determined by specific cultural definitions of that relation to nature' (Eder 1990a: 69). This approach to environmental discourse has the potential to help accomplish what Habermas has difficulty in doing: linking the problems of material reproduction at the system level with actions of ecological movements in a way that permits these to be understood as more than simply reactive skirmishes at the interface of system and life-world. It allows a more complex, sophisticated understanding of the ways in which *discourse* on ecological problems contributes to the historical production of contemporary society.

Ecological Hazards and Risk Society: Beck

Eder argues that the problematization of nature and progress is related to fundamental changes in social structure brought about by a global process of modernization and rationalization involving the emergence of post-industrial class conflicts. The main feature of this new type of society is thus social conflict centred on the 'problem of the exploitation of nature' and the pivotal role played by social and cultural movements in 'determining the direction of further "modernisation"' (Eder 1990b: 37–41). Ulrich Beck, in his influential writings on *risk society* also argues that the processes of global modernization have given rise to a phase of modernity characterized by a new *ecological field of conflict*. For Beck, late modernity is to be understood in terms of a systemically induced shift from problems of wealth distribution to those of risk distribution. Thus contemporary Western societies are less concerned with how to overcome scarcity than with how to limit and distribute the effects of a whole new category of systemically produced 'latent side effects' that are the unintended, unforeseen hazards caused by the success of science and technology in meeting the material production needs of Western societies (Beck 1992b: 19–22). The benefits of science and technology in utilizing nature are increasingly overshadowed by the political and economic costs of managing the hazards thereby generated, which now threaten the natural foundations of life.

As opposed to Habermas's view of ecological movements as primarily anti-modern, Beck sees them as the result of a growing critical-reflexive awareness of the risks produced by late modernity itself. This awareness can be attributed to the increasing *scientization* of risk and the expanding *commerce* in risks (ibid. 56). The scientization of risk undermines a strict separation of system and life-world, because risk is experienced in an already highly scientized life-world: that is, the perception of modern ecological hazards depends on 'a theoretical and hence a scientised consciousness, even in the everyday consciousness of risks' (ibid. 28). Because Beck sees the substantive production of risks as closely tied to the development of expert scientific knowledge, he focuses on the link between risk production and its 'cognitive agents'. The latter comprise not only those experts who produce scientific knowledge and its technological applications, but also those *counter-experts* (of the ecology movements, citizens' action groups, etc.) who produce critiques of environmental degradation, technology and so on. Advanced technological society thus displays a 'system-immanent' capacity to endanger its ecological conditions of existence while at the same time producing a self-referential 'questioning of itself through the multiplication and economic exploitation of hazards' (ibid. 56–7). The current concern about ecological problems derives from the existence of these *systemic contradictions* between the technological production and political administration of risks, which become an object of public concern through the activities of the 'counter-experts' of the ecology movement. Ecological conflicts challenge some of the key premises of industrial society, such as the value of progress and economic growth, as well as the character of scientific rationality itself. Beck suggests (as does Eder) that ecological conflicts thus 'take on the character of *doctrinal struggles* within *civilisation* over the proper road for modernity' (Beck 1992b: 40; Eder 1993: 103–12). At the same time, technologically induced risks create political and market opportunities, in terms of such things as pollution control technology and expanded demand for professional expertise in areas of environmental management, assessment and administration (Christoff 1996; Weale 1992).

These tensions lead to 'definitional struggles over the scale, degree and urgency of risks' (Beck 1992b: 46). On one level, hazards appear as the creation of an autonomous process resulting from a strictly instrumental use of technology in commodity production. However, hazards are defined and evaluated not privately at the level of the firm, but through a matrix of 'quasi-governmental power positions' incorporating debate among scientific experts, juridical interpretation in the courts, and comment in the mass media. The unintended consequences of putative private economic activities are transformed into socially defined risks through scientific contests fought out by 'intellectual strategies in intellectual milieux'. Thus the production and distribution of knowledge is central to the functioning of late modern society (Beck 1992a: 112–14).

Yet, while the definition of risks results from a series of more or less deliberate decisions (and is therefore social in character), it is not political in the sense of being defined by the decisions of formal political institutions. The Western political system is premissed on a differentiation of parliamentary politics from the '*non*-politics' of the techno-economic pursuit of interests through private investment decisions and scientific research agendas. But it is primarily in these areas that the decisions which produce ecological risks are made. It is in this sense that Beck speaks of social change as the *autonomized*, latent side-effect of scientific and technological decisions (Beck 1992b: 183–4). This is not a distortion of modernity, but rather the result of the success of rationalization and progress, and occurs in part through the equation of social with economic progress assumed by Western utilitarian culture. Risk society is thus shaped by two contradictory processes – the institutionalization of representative democracy and the legitimation of the supposed intrinsic value of progress in scientific and technical knowledge – which lead to far-reaching social changes under the guise of 'normalcy'. Scientific and economic development in risk society thus take on the status of a *sub-politics* which, while not subject to institutionalized political authorization and legitimation, nevertheless constantly produces and shapes ecological risks as the object of public discourse, over which governments are called to act (Beck 1992a: 114–15; 1992b: 186–7). This scientifically generated awareness of ecological and technological risks results in a thoroughgoing systemic transformation of politics in risk society, expressed in three key areas: the breakdown of the cultural consensus regarding the link between scientific-economic development and progress; increased demands for political control and accountability of processes that lie largely outside the public sphere; and the breakdown of the notion of a *political centre* capable of controlling the autonomous processes of technological-economic change, simultaneously (and paradoxically) accompanied by the extension of monitoring activity by the state to ever more intimate levels of industrial management.

Functional Differentiation of Society and Ecological Communication: Luhmann

The theme of the lack of a political 'centre' of contemporary Western society also plays a central role in the work of Niklas Luhmann. However, whereas Beck suggests that this leads to a 'reflexive modernity' with the potential to reinvent politics through the 'self-criticism of risk society' (Beck 1992b: 183–236; 1994: 1–55), Luhmann is far more pessimistic about the possibility of a rational co-ordination of societal responses to ecological problems (Sciulli 1994: 44). Like Beck, Luhmann does not situate ecological problems in nature, but within society. More specifically, he is concerned with developing a systems-theoretical understanding of the manner in which social systems become aware of, and communicate, the differences between themselves and their environment. The distinction between system and environment is one of two key concepts in Luhmann's systems theory. Here the concept of *environment* is understood at a very general level to refer to the context in which the 'operationally closed', self-referential, functional subsystems of society (the scientific, legal, political and economic systems, etc.) operate as self-reproducing entities. Luhmann defines these functional subsystems as *autopoietic* (a concept taken from the work of Maturana and Varela in theoretical biology), to indicate 'that the system is the product of its own activity (work), and not simply self-sufficient activity as such' (Sciulli 1994: 14). The autopoietic nature of functional subsystems is determined not by external environmental influences, but by the intrinsic primary goal of all such self-reproducing systems – 'the continuation of autopoeisis *without* any concern for the environment' (Luhmann 1989: 14, emphasis added).

A second pivotal concept for Luhmann's theory is the substitution of 'communication' for 'action' as the most basic operation of functional systems, in which communication becomes the medium through which self-referentiality is produced and sustained. Communication is the process whereby social systems constitute themselves by *observing* themselves. Hence, the environment for Luhmann is 'anything which social communication can refer to' (Miller 1994: 104).

When Luhmann does specifically address problems of ecology, his concern is to examine how modern societal subsystems react to these types of problems and to explain why 'society' has difficulty in perceiving and managing them appropriately (Luhmann 1989: 33–5). His approach to these questions is shaped by the view of modern society as an assemblage of highly differentiated functional subsystems, in which the *key problem is the lack of any central mechanism to control these subsystems*, other than the unco-ordinated reactions or autopoetic adjustments ('resonance') of each to the interference of the others (Sciulli 1994: 47). This is so because each of the subsystems is directed to performing a relatively limited social function: for example, the subsystem of economy is narrowly concerned with prices and payments, rather than with the broader environment. Luhmann argues that subsystems operate with a set of binary codes which specify the ways in which reality becomes the subject of communication. Codes specify values and counter-values (in law legal/illegal, in science true/false), and operate so as to exclude other possible ways of ordering reality (Luhmann 1989: 44–5). Subsystems react to their environments (which includes the other subsystems) only in the terms set out by these binary codes. Furthermore, because it is through such codes that systems self-referentially differentiate themselves from their environment, and because functional subsystems can discern and respond to environmental disturbances only in terms of their own internal codes and meanings, the possibility of resonance between different subsystems is severely limited. At a general societal level this means that resonance between different subsystems is restricted to what can be communicated across subsystems as meaningful; thus, 'each system has a different access to itself than to its environment which it can only construct internally' (Luhmann 1994: 14).

Several significant consequences flow from Luhmann's approach. First, talk of exposure to ecological risks is possible only where there is resonance, or reaction, by a social subsystem to events in its environment (which includes other subsystems). Given that systems can respond only in accordance with their own particular structures or codes, ecological risks can be perceived by society only as exclusively *internal* phenomena. Physical and biological 'objective facts' have no social effect (resonance) unless they are the subject of communication. Luhmann thus argues that society cannot communicate directly with its environment, but instead can 'only communicate *about* its environment' *within* itself (Luhmann 1989: 28–31). The key question that results from this, then, is how society structures the way it deals with environmental information. Here Luhmann points to an apparently insoluble paradox. Modern society, as a highly differentiated set of function subsystems, structures communication about itself through binary codes, so that resonance between society and its environment is always directed through one of the function subsystems and their associated programmes (scientific theories, legal rules, etc.). The differentiation of society is a result of its increasing complexity; yet the mechanisms for dealing with this complexity (function systems, coding, etc.) operate by *reducing information*, by *simplification* (Luhmann 1994: 18–19).

Here Luhmann is pointing to the reductive character of modern expert knowledge systems. He rejects those who (like Husserl) criticize modernity on the basis of its tendency towards a one-dimensional 'technicalisation (that) forgets the "lifeworld"' (ibid. 17). Such technicalization is a fundamental characteristic of modern science, and in a move similar to that adopted by Habermas, Luhmann dismisses the critique of science (and technology) on this basis as a futile exercise (Habermas 1982; Luhmann 1994: 18). In much the same way as Beck, Luhmann also rejects attempts to base solutions to ecological problems on some new form of environmental ethics (Beck 1992a; Luhmann 1989: xvii). Neither can a solution be found in science, for, as a function subsystem, it cannot provide 'meaningful' solutions that would be recognized within other subsystems (politics, law, etc.). Paradoxically, the complexity of modern society relies on the ability of science (and other subsystems) to reduce the complexity of the world through codification. Science and technology thus construct simplifications that are then 'experimentally' reinserted into the world as a 'simplification that works' (Luhmann 1994: 18), but only within their own subsystem domain.

Eder's criticism of Habermas's rigid separation of system and life-world applies with even greater force to Luhmann's systems theory. Similarly, the approach of Beck's work that makes it most useful, the elaboration of the connections between science and politics, is systematically discounted by Luhmann, and along with it, the ability of politics to offer any solutions to ecological problems. Habermas's relegation of ecological problems to the status of skirmishes at the interface between system and life-world is carried further by Luhmann, possibly even to the extent that such 'problems' amount to little more than system-generated 'noise' that is incapable of providing a meaningful basis for co-ordinated action across subsystems. In particular, Luhmann has little to say about the ways in which individuals and social groups may be involved in the complex interplay between the function subsystems and an increasingly complex environment.

Ecological Modernization

One potentially fruitful way of connecting the macro-sociological perspectives developed by theorists such as Beck and Eder with institutionalization of specific regulatory practices and policies is through the notion of *ecological modernization*. This term arises out of recent attempts to analyse the changes that occurred during the 1980s in the formulation and implementation of environmental policy in Western Europe – especially in Germany, The Netherlands, Austria and the Scandinavian states. Peter Christoff sees these changes as a response to the 'perceived limits of state regulatory intervention' in achieving improvement in environmental management, and involving a whole range of policy approaches and instruments aimed at the 'integrated management of "clean" production'. These 'institutional transformations' are seen as resulting in significant changes both in investment patterns and production techniques (particularly in manufacturing and energy production) and in the relationship between the state, industrial interests and environmental groups (Christoff 1996).

The catalyst for these changes can be found in what Christoff describes as the 'increasingly sophisticated forms of community understanding and political mobilisation around environmental issues'. Albert Weale argues that these changes can be understood as a response to the increasing fragility (and declining effectiveness), throughout the 1970s and early 1980s, of the earlier political and policy coalitions in which environmental movements and interests were involved (see Cramer et al. 1989). According to

Weale, it was from within the environmental movement that there emerged a new category of discourse (that of 'ecological modernization') which challenges the conventional view of an inherent conflict between environmental protection and economic growth *per se*. Instead, there is a reconceptualization of the relationship between economics and environmental imperatives, in which the maintenance of ecological health is increasingly seen as an *essential pre-condition for long-term economic development* (Weale 1992: 31). This change also formed the basis for the subsequent discourse on sustainable development that by the late 1980s had gained widespread international influence through the United Nations Conference on Environment and Development process. The UNCED report, *Our Common Future* (Brundtland 1987), provides a particularly clear statement of how this new political rationality is deeply embedded in the discourse on sustainable development.

The meaning of 'ecological modernization' is, as Christoff notes, open to a range of interpretations. At one end of the spectrum there is a narrowly technocratic understanding consistent with the 'traditional imperatives of capital' and the standard view of modernization. Here the adoption of clean production technologies and precautionary approaches to environmental protection in no way impede the dynamics of the international economic system. Indeed, these sorts of environmental measures often contribute directly to the increased *efficiency* and profitability of the technically advanced industrial sectors, while also promoting other benefits such as the rationalization of regulatory regimes across states, increasing certainty for investment planning, and facilitating international market penetration or dominance (Christoff 1996).

Further along the ecological modernization spectrum are applications of the environmental equivalent of the welfare state. Here the state and markets influence economic activity in ways which may not be directly favourable to the interests of particular corporate actors, but instead seek to use a variety of regulatory and economic instruments to force the incorporation of costs arising from environmental externalities. Associated with this is an emphasis on what Christoff describes as the 'transformative impact of environmental awareness', as a means of enhancing citizenship and democratic participation through a revitalization of civil society and the public sphere. Central to this is the suggestion (reminiscent of Beck) that the political issues raised by the ecological modernization go beyond economic, and even narrowly ecological, considerations. Thus Weale argues that ecological modernization results in a

> shift in focus reflected in the changing pattern of interest aggregation and interest articulation. Where once it was possible to contrast an economic feasibility coalition and a clean environment coalition, ecological modernisation suggests a plural and variegated set of interests, with competing and different interpretations of what values are at stake in matters of environmental policy. These changes ramify through the way that environmental policy is perceived and they include changes in strategies of regulation, emerging styles of public policy, alterations in patterns of international relations, a changing relationship between science and policy and ideological competition and debate. (Weale 1992: 32)

Nevertheless, much of this 'shift of focus' remains within a familiar utilitarian perspective. Counterposed to this, according to Christoff, is a more radical aspect to the ecological modernization discourse, expressing a form of *ecological critique* that challenges the more orthodox notions of industrial modernity, particularly the way in which it defines the social relation to nature in instrumental terms. Christoff's argument has some parallel with Eder's, in that he understands ecological critique as embracing both an 'emergent scientific understanding of ecological needs' and a 'normative (re)evaluation of Nature' which draws on a nineteenth-century romantic resistance to industrialization. Like Eder and Beck, he emphasizes that ecological critique is itself a product of 'simple modernity'. In effect, it is an immanent critique that 'makes radically problematic and contradictory the industrialising imperative which lies at the heart of modernisation by redefining the cultural and ecological limits to the instrumental domination of nature' (Christoff 1996:).

Conclusion: Political Rationalities and Ecological Discourses

Space does not permit a more detailed comparison between the theorists discussed above and Foucault. Nevertheless, a theme common to Beck and Eder in particular, but also to Habermas and Luhmann (albeit in a more theoretically abstract manner), is the problem of the social relation to nature in contemporary Western society, and the ways in which modern scientific knowledge and expertise shape the distribution of power. If the notions of biopolitics and governmentality are developed so as to examine the emergence of ecological discursive practices, Foucault's work can be seen to open up new perspectives on these concerns. As was argued at the beginning of this chapter, Foucault's interest in developing a historical critique of specific rationalities has much in common with the sociological tradition drawn on by authors such as Beck and Habermas. Given the shared concern to understand modern society as shaped by processes of rationalization, consideration of insights drawn from the works considered here may contribute to a more critical, sophisticated social-theoretical understanding of environmental problems.

Foucault's insistence that we understand particular relations of power and social institutions as the result of historically specific political rationalities, rather than as the result of some generalized or totalizing process of societal rationalization is an important corrective to this tendency in theorists such as Beck and particularly Habermas. Foucault's notion of biopolitics can be linked to contemporary scientific ecology as a mode of regulatory science; but this is not to suggest that contemporary environmental discourse is a unity, reflecting the triumph of technical or instrumental rationality in general. Instead, the more limited suggestion is made that systems ecology (and projects like the International Biological Programme) can be understood as a form of political (or governmental) rationality: that is, systems ecology is one such rationality among a plurality of rationalities, even within the domain of environmental discourse.

This approach, for example, when applied to Eder's work, suggests that what he calls the 'purity model' of nature has been until recently a marginalized rationality in Western culture. None the less, it has interacted historically with, and influenced, the expression of the dominant rationality, the justice model of nature. A roughly congruent move can be found in Beck's notion of a sub-politics when he argues that a risk society produces increased opportunities for shaping contemporary society from below. This results from the inclusion of groups and individuals previously not involved in 'the substantive technification and industrialisation process', such as social movements, counter-experts, and so on (Beck 1994: 23). Here we can see a clear similarity to Foucault, who argues that a power relation is an agonism, or 'permanent provocation'[8] (Foucault 1982: 222). In Foucault's view, power relationships are dynamic, and therefore always potentially unstable.

Consequently, under particular circumstances, even long-established states of domination may be subject to reversal. Hence, in Foucault's terms, Eder's purity model and some aspects of Beck's sub-polity can be seen as resistance to the dominant understandings of nature, what Foucault describes as 'an insurrection of subjugated knowledges', those 'naïve', 'disqualified', localized, non-scientific discourses which oppose the 'tyranny' of particular globalizing scientific disciplines (Foucault 1980h: 81–5). The point in making such a contrast is not to counterpose modern, rationalized knowledge to anti-modern, irrational forms of belief, which are thereby devalued and excluded. Rather, Foucault saw this as a practical genealogical task aimed at establishing 'a historical knowledge of struggles' which could be made use of tactically in contemporary political and social contests (ibid. 83).

However, a genealogy of environmental discourse cannot be concerned solely with the struggle between scientific and non-scientific rationalities. It would also need to encompass the competition within the discourse of scientific ecology itself (i.e. between systems and population ecology, community ecology, etc.), and to consider how these apparently esoteric, technical debates influence the historical formation of the regulatory sciences and ecological programmes of government.[9] Thus, the development of scientific ecology, particularly systems ecology, provided both a guiding political rationality and the technical apparatus of calculation and assessment that by the late 1960s began to make possible a form of regulatory science that was capable of governmentalizing society–environment relations, as argued in chapter 2.

The question can be asked as to whether the sorts of ecological biopolitics suggested here could have been different. At issue is the way in which specific forms of ecological governmentality have been institutionalized, and this is very much an empirical question. The role of the USA has been significant, inasmuch as it was there that saw the emergence of contemporary industrialized 'big science'. This was initially very much influenced by national characteristics. However, given the emerging transnational character of scientific research agendas (e.g. the International Biological Programme) and the hegemony of US science in the post-war period, we can discern a widespread (but by no means universal) internationalization of techniques (e.g. Environmental Impact Assessment) and ecological theories originating in the USA.[10] In these circumstances, the possibility of the emergence of an alternative understanding of environmental protection to the highly 'rationalized' model of scientific expertise represented in bodies like the Environment Protection Agency must be regarded as remote. The purity model of the social relation to nature was, and is, largely a subjugated knowledge. To counterpose these two cultural models as if they could be translated in a straightforward manner into clearly diverging institutional structures ignores the complexity of ties between the notions of modernity embodied in the two discourses. At the same time it underestimates, in Foucault's words, 'the effects of a power which the West since Medieval times has attributed to science and has reserved for those engaged in scientific discourse' (Foucault 1980h: 85). Indeed, modern biopolitics, with its focus on the administration of life in a corporeal, bodily sense, encompasses precisely all those political rationalities and governmental technologies which are intrinsically coupled to the growth of scientific knowledge and expertise. Meaningful discussion of the potential for alternative institutional approaches to environmental management (or care) must recognize that what is in question is an alternative set of power relations, in which the relative strategic positions of the purity and justice perspectives may be altered while none the less remaining inextricably linked. The degree to which such a reversal of strategic relations is possible in ecological matters is dependent, however, on the highly complex interaction of many social systemic factors – hence the importance of considering the sorts of system integration and coordination problems posed by the social theorists considered above.

The re-characterization of Foucault's notion of biopolitics in terms of ecological concerns focuses on the problem of governing the conduct of populations and their relations with the natural environment. At the same time, the political rationality of systems ecology articulates these objects of government in relation to the global ecosystem. Thus, while it is undoubtedly necessary to understand the micro-relations of power (local technical practices of laboratory and field-work, computer modelling, the production of regulatory standards and environmental assessment techniques, etc.) (Darier and Shackley 1998; Rutherford 1994a, 1994b) which contribute to management of ecological relations, it is equally important that this be linked to an analysis of biopolitics at the macro-level of entire populations and societies. Such a move is of course in keeping with Foucault's own theoretical development (Dean 1994a: 174–93). It is none the less true that Foucault's work (and that of his successors) has generally attempted to understand the practices of government within the context of particular national societies, a move motivated in part by an underlying concern with specific genealogies of power, as opposed to the universalizing tendencies of much traditional political and social theory.

While this motivation is to be endorsed, care should be taken not to over-emphasize the nation-state and national cultures at the expense of analysing the problematic of government in a way that gives appropriate weight to the global (or at least transnational) assemblages of forces and networks of authoritative judgement that shape contemporary social relations. Included in this would be consideration of the role of international non-governmental organizations, the link between science and international environmental policy (ozone depletion, climate change, etc.) as well as other international agencies (such as the World Bank). As Mitchell Dean has argued, the Foucauldian concern with the 'problematic of government is not so much a solution to the paradoxical nature of the state but a research agenda into the contingent trajectories by which the state assumes its present and changing form' (ibid. 181). As ecological problems demonstrate, that form is increasingly one in which national structures are overlaid by international patterns of governance which embody processes of both marketization and regulation, and which rely on expertise and knowledge that is to a significant degree denationalized (if not globalized). In the context of environmental problems, it is therefore important to try to unravel the relations between such denationalized scientific expertise, on the one hand, and on the other, the political rationalities and various governmental programmes for ecological management conceived in terms of a global, systemic interdependence between society and nature.

A persistent theme in much of the theoretical work considered in this chapter has been the tensions between the role played by highly rationalized, often technocratic, scientific expertise and that of counter-cultural, 'romantic', ecological movements. Authors such as Beck, Eder and Christoff have sought to locate these apparently contradictory tendencies as expressive of the tensions inherent in what Beck describes as late or 'reflexive' modernity. These apparently contradictory elements of environmental discourse can be understood in terms of Foucault's notion of governmental rationality, or governmentality. The recent work of Nikolas Rose and Peter Miller identifies three key characteristics of governmental rationalities. If the ecological modernization discourse is considered in the light of these three elements, we can move beyond the general assertion that both the utilitarian and the counter-cultural discourses are immanent in modernity, and instead begin to consider how and why these elements fit together in contemporary practices for governing the environment.

According to Rose and Miller (1992: 178–9), governmental (or political) rationalities are characteristically moral, epistemological and idiomatic. They are expressed in moral terms that elaborate the ideals and principles with which government should properly be concerned. Ecological governmentality is particularly concerned with questions of justice and equity – questions such as inter-generational equity, the relation between development and environmental protection, and the relations between needs of human society and biotic rights of non-human nature. Thus a significant element in the environmental debate is the concern to develop an environmental ethics. Governmental rationalities also have an epistemological character; they are articulated in terms of a specific knowledge of the objects and problems to be addressed (ibid. 179–82). This epistemology is in large part derived from scientific ecology, which, as I have argued in chapter 2, represents an essentially economic model of nature. Thus it is scientific ecology that provides the authoritative accounts of the sorts of entities which government must manage: ecosystems, global climatic and atmospheric processes, habitat and species diversity, population and carrying capacity, and so forth. Finally, all governmental rationalities are expressed in their own distinctive idiom, which functions as an intellectual means for making reality 'thinkable in such a way that it is amenable to political deliberations' (ibid. 179). Hence the relationship of society to the natural environment is conceived in terms of the language of security and risk; ecological hazards and insecurity must be addressed by putting in place behaviours that minimize risk. The idiom of ecological rationality is paradigmatically represented by the *precautionary principle*, which reverses the onus of scientific proof to insist that practices and actions cannot be deemed safe simply because the evidence of potential environmental harm is not certain.

Rose and Miller argue that government in the sense used by Foucault (i.e. 'the conduct of conduct')[11] is a *problematizing* activity in which the 'articulation of government has been bound to the constant identification of the difficulties and failures of government' (ibid. 181–3). Ecological governmentality is such a rationality inasmuch as it continuously seeks to improve the techniques for managing environmental problems. At the same time, it also problematizes the social relation to nature at a basic ontological level. In many respects ecological thought reflects the fundamental philosophical dilemma of the *dialectic of enlightenment* in which modernity, with its dependence on rational-instrumental, scientific knowledge, embodies a self-destructive social relation to nature. As I have argued, such a theme is common not only to much recent social theory dealing with the ecological problem, but also to Foucault. The works of Foucault, and others since his death, on governmentality provide a useful, historically concrete framework for analysis that, while cognizant of the macro-sociological dimension of ecological biopolitics, also focuses attention on understanding specific, *localized* governmental programmes and technologies involved in governing the social relation to nature. The work of Rose and Miller in particular emphasizes that *programmes of government* emerge as means of establishing 'translatability between the moralities, epistemologies and idioms of political power, and the government of a specific problem space, (which) establishes a mutuality between what is desirable and what can be made possible through the calculated activities of political forces' (ibid. 182). An important task for Foucault scholars who seek to understand the relations of power and knowledge in contemporary ecological discourse is the application of these insights to work on an environmental 'history of the present'. Such work would involve the meticulous, empirical study of the three dimensions of governmental rationalities and the ways in which these are shaped by the dynamic interactions of scientific knowledge and expertise, ecological movements, state-based regulatory activities, and the influence of global forces of marketization.

Notes

1 While Foucault clearly located his work within the same broad problematic as Weber, he insisted that post-war French philosophical thought 'knew absolutely nothing – or only vaguely, only very indirectly – about the current of Weberian thought' (see Foucault 1983b: 200).

2 Colin Gordon, however, argues that 'Weber is as innocent as Foucault of the so-called Weberianism that adopts a uniform, monolithic conception of historical phenomena of rationalization' (see Gordon 1987: 293–4). Brian Turner suggests that while Smart's characterization of Weber is justified, it is important to note that Weber did

argue against postulating 'general laws of social development', and to that extent Weber's work 'lacked internal consistency' (Turner 1987: 232–3).

3 Turner argues that while Weber's main focus is on the changes in knowledge and consciousness brought about by rationalization and the development of capitalism, this perspective also incorporates a 'general process whereby the body ceases to be a feature of religious culture and is incorporated via medicalization into a topic within scientific discourse'. Thus there is a shift to 'regulation of the body and of populations' (Turner 1987: 224–6). See also Miller 1987: 5–9.

4 Elsewhere Honneth argues that the usefulness of Habermas's differentiation of spheres of social action (symbolic and material) is undermined by the move (Habermas 1987) to a systems theory approach dominated by a technocratically conceived understanding of two fundamentally different modes of action co-ordination. Thus, Honneth claims, despite his criticism of Horkheimer and Adorno, Habermas fails to extricate his own theoretical project from the technocratic diagnosis of modernity laid out in *Dialectic of Enlightenment*. See Honneth 1991; N. Smith 1993).

5 Foucault claims that while the nascent natural sciences were 'historically rooted' in investigatory practices of disciplinary power, they were able to detach themselves from this 'politico-juridical model' of power (Foucault 1975: 224–7). For more detailed discussion of this see Rutherford 1994a, 1994b.

6 See also ch. 2 above.

7 See preceding note; also Rutherford 1994a, 1994b.

8 Gordon translates this as meaning a 'contest in which the opponents develop a strategy of reaction and of mutual taunting' (1991: 46).

9 For some excellent historical studies of the conflicts within scientific ecology in the post-World War II period, see Palliadino 1991; Mitman 1988; Taylor 1988.

10 For detailed discussion of the influence of US science on the growth of contemporary ecological theories, see Golley 1993; Jamison 1993; McIntosh 1985). For detailed consideration of the political institutionalization of environmental protection in the USA, see Jasanoff 1990 and Harris and Milkis 1989.

11 There are in fact several ways in which Foucault uses the term 'government'. For a detailed discussion, see Hindess 1996.

Part II

Environmentalities

6

Environmentality as Green Governmentality

Timothy W. Luke

In the USA, playing off stereotypes of 'the environmentalist', ranging from the limousine liberal to the Sierra Club backpacker to Earth First! monkey-wrenchers, 'wise use' anti-environmentalism feeds on the self-evidence of mass media coverage on the environment. Because elitist do-gooders and wacko tree-sitters allegedly agitate to trade off people's jobs against the survival of spotted owls, snail darters, or desert tortoises, the Wise Use/Property Rights movement in the USA pumps up these images from the six o'clock news as its essential credo: environmental protection is costing jobs and undermining the American economy. Therefore, it is right to have moved, as one of its key organizers, Ron Arnold, puts it, to declare a 'holy war against the new pagans who worship trees and sacrifice people' (Helvarg 1994: 12). The self-evidence of radical fringe environmentalists abridging fundamental property rights to realize their foolish pagan fantasies of resource non-use, as depicted in any network television send-up of such eco-subversives, gives ordinary Americans *causus belli* to retaliate in the name of economic rationality and sound governance.

Following Michel Foucault, this study comes out against the self-evidence of the six o'clock news to breach the Wise Use/Property Rights movement's invocation of such historical constants, obvious prerogatives or basic rights as their justification for anti-environmentalism. Rather than seeing mainstream or radical environmentalism so self-evidently as a distemper of foolish resource non-use when it comes to nature, this study provisionally suggests that most environmentalist movements now operate as a basic manifestation of governmentality. Indeed, this 'green governmentality', which the Wise Use/Property Rights movement occasionally decries, would seem to be the latest phase in a solid series of statist practices beginning in the eighteenth century. Thus, this analysis is 'a breach of self-evidence', and particularly 'of those self-evidences on which our knowledges, acquiescences, and practices rest' (Foucault, in Burchell et al. 1991: 76), during a time in which the US Speaker of the House and the entire 104th Congress act as if they are Ron Arnold's closest allies in the holy war against environmental protection.

As it is discursively constructed by contemporary technoscience, the art of government now finds 'the principles of its rationality' and 'the specific reality of the state' (Foucault 1991a: 97), like the policy programmes of sustainable development, balanced growth or ecological harmony for its many constituent populations of human and non-human beings, in the systemic requirements of ecology. Government comes into its own when it has the welfare of a population, the improvement of its condition, the increase of its wealth, longevity, health and so on, as its object. And ecology gives rational governments all of life's biodiversity to reformat as 'endangered populations', needing various state ministrations as objects of managerial control ignorant of what is being done to them as part and parcel of 'a range of absolute new tactics and techniques'(ibid. 100). Ecology simply crystallizes the latest phase of the 'three movements: government, population, political economy, which constitute . . . a solid series, one which even today has assuredly not been dissolved' (ibid. 102) in the formations of green governmentality.

This chapter, then, collects together fragments of rhetoric with shards of practice to probe a few green twists in the logic of governmentality. Over the past generation, the time–space compression of postmodern living has brought the bio-power of the entire planet, not merely that of human beings, under the strategic ambit of state power. The environment, particularly the goals of its protection in terms of 'safety' or 'security', has become a key theme of many political operations, economic interventions and ideological campaigns to raise public standards of collective morality, personal responsibility and collective vigour. Therefore, this brief discussion follows Foucault by exploring how green governmentality in the United States operates as 'a whole series of different tactics that combined in varying proportions the objective of disciplining the body and that of regulating populations' (Foucault 1976: 146).

These interconnections become even more intriguing in the aftermath of the Cold War. Having won the long twilight struggle against Communist totalitarianism, the United States is governed by leaders who now see 'Earth in the balance', arguing that global ecologies incarnate what is best and worst in the human spirit. On the one hand, economists, industrialists and political leaders increasingly tend to represent the strategic terrain of the post-1991 world system as one on which all nations must compete ruthlessly to control the future development of the world economy by developing new technologies, dominating more markets, and exploiting every national economic asset. However, the phenomenon of 'failed states', ranging from basket cases like Rwanda, Somalia or Angola to crippled entities like Ukraine, Afghanistan or Kazakhstan, is often attributed to the severe environmental frictions associated with rapid economic growth (Kaplan 1996). Consequently, environmental protection issues, ranging from resource conservation to sustainable development to ecosystem restoration, are getting greater consideration in the name of creating jobs, maintaining growth, or advancing technological development.

Therefore, the policy agendas of American superpower must serve the nation and the planet by functioning as an 'environmental protection agency' on a global scale, since so many of today's transnational security threats are, according to the Clinton/Gore administration, ecological in nature. To explore these curious wrinkles in the order of things, this study retraces how a new ordering of things has emerged out of some odd linkages between sustainability theories, resource managerialist practices, diplomatic communiqués and polemical writings as they operate in the normalizing tactics of America's current-day green governmentality. This normalization project is a vast undertaking, and not all of its implications have yet revealed themselves at this juncture. In this chapter, then, I hope to explore a handful of elective affinities which emerged together after the Cold War in combinations of sustainability discourses, US foreign policy and green capitalism, in order to elucidate what might be seen as green governmentality.

Geo-Power in Geo-Economics/Geopolitics

A political, economic and technical incitement to talk about ecology, environments, or nature first surfaced in the 1960s, but it has become far more pronounced in the 1990s. Not much of this talk takes the form of general theory, because its practices have instead been steered toward analysis, stock-taking and classification in quantitative, causal and humanistic studies. The project of 'sustainability', whether one speaks of sustainable development, growth or use in relation to Earth's ecologies, embodies this new responsibility for the life processes in the American state's rationalized harmonization of political economy with global ecology as a form of green geopolitics. Taking 'ecology' into account creates discourses on 'the environment' that derive not only from morality, but from rationality as well. Indeed, as humanity faced 'the limits of growth', and heard 'the population bomb' ticking away, ecologies and environments became more than something to be judged morally; they became things the state must administer. Ecology, then, has evolved into 'a public potential; it called for management procedures; it had to be taken charge of by analytical discourses', as it was recognized in its environmentalized manifestations to be 'a police matter' – 'not the repression of disorder, but an ordered maximization of collective and individual forces' (Foucault 1976: 24–5). After 1992, this geopolitics has assumed many intriguingly green forms.

Discourses of 'geo-economics', as they have been expounded by Robert Reich (1991), Lester Thurow (1992), Edward Luttwak (1993) and others (Kennedy 1993; McLaughlin 1993; Oates 1989), as well as rearticulations of geopolitics in an ecological register, as they have been developed by President Bill Clinton or Vice-President Al Gore (1992), both express new understandings of the Earth's economic and political importance as a site for the orderly maximization of many material resources. Geo-economics, for example, transforms through military metaphors and strategic analogies what hitherto were regarded as purely economic concerns into national security issues of wise resource use and sovereign property rights. Government manipulation of trade policy, state support of major corporations, or public aid for retraining labour all become vital instruments for 'the continuation of the ancient rivalry of the nations by new industrial means' (Luttwak 1993: 34).[1] The relative success or failure of national economies in head-to-head global competition is taken by geo-economics as the definitive register of any one nation-state's waxing or waning international power, as well as its rising or falling industrial competitiveness, technological vitality and economic prowess. In this context, many believe that ecological considerations can be ignored, or at best given only meaningless symbolic responses, in the quest to mobilize as many of the Earth's material resources as possible. In the ongoing struggle over economic competitiveness, environmental resistance can even be recast as a type of civil disobedience, which endangers national security, expresses unpatriotic sentiments, or embodies treasonous acts.

Geo-economic strategies have been a feature of public discourse for at least two decades. The oil crises of the 1970s first recentred elite and popular thinking about the tie between national economic productivity, natural resources and nationalistic competitiveness within a global economy. After 25 years of Cold War conflict, in which virtually everything was organized around conducting an East/West struggle between two military blocs centred on nuclear deterrence, geopolitical manoeuvring and ideological confrontation, many nation-states were caught short by the oil shocks of 1971, 1973 and 1979. For geo-economics, however, Japan's response to this 'oil shokku' during the 1970s was highly prescient, inasmuch as the Japanese state allegedly refined its geo-economic strategizing: defining economic production as power creation, market building as empire creation, technological innovation as strategic initiative, natural resource extraction as national necessity, and labour docility as patriotic discipline. Macro-economics is here seen as war conducted by other means, and all natural resources, then, become strategic geo-power assets to be mobilized, not only for growth and wealth production, but also for market domination and power creation. To resist growth is not only to oppose economic prosperity, it is to subvert the political future, national interest and collective security of the nation-state.

Arguing that 'whoever controls world resources controls the world in a way that mere occupation of territory cannot match', Barnet, for example, asked, first, if natural resource scarcities were real, and second, if economic control over natural resources was changing the global balance of power (Barnet 1980: 17). After surveying the struggles to manipulate access to geo-power assets like oil, minerals, water and food resources, he saw a new geo-economic challenge as nation-states were being forced to satisfy the rising material expectations of their populations in a much more interdependent world system (ibid. 310–16). Ironically, the rhetorical pitch of Reich, Thurow and Luttwak in the geo-economics debate of the 1990s mostly sticks with these terms of analysis. Partly a response to global economic competition, and partly a response to global ecological scarcities, today's geo-economic reading of the Earth's political economy constructs the attainment of national economic growth, security and prosperity as a zero-sum game. Having more material wealth or economic growth in one place, like a particular nation-state, means not having it in other places – namely, rival foreign nations. It also assumes that material scarcity is a continual constraint; hence, all resources, everywhere and at any time, must be subject to exploitation.

Geo-economics accepts the prevailing form of mass market consumerism as it presently exists, defines its rationalizing managerial benefits as the public ends that advanced economies ought to seek, and then affirms the need for hard discipline in elaborate programmes of productivism, only now couched within rhetorics of highly politicized national competition, as the means for sustaining mass market consumer life-styles in nations like the United States. Creating economic growth, and producing more of it than other equally aggressive developed and developing countries, is the *sine qua non* of 'national security' in the 1990s. As Richard Darman, President Bush's chief of OMB declared after Earth Day in 1990, 'Americans did not fight and win the wars of the twentieth century to make the world safe for green vegetables' (Sale 1993: 77). However, not everyone sees environmentalism in this age of geo-economics as tantamount to subversion of an entire way of life tied to using increased levels of natural resources to accelerate economic growth. These geo-economic readings have also sparked new discourses of social responsibility into life, such as the green geopolitics of the Clinton administration with its intriguing codes of ecological reflexivity.

This presidential commitment to deploying American power as an environmental protection agency has waxed and waned over the past quarter-century, but in 1995 President Clinton made this sort of green geopolitics an integral part of his global doctrine of 'engagement'. Indeed, 'to reassert America's leadership in the post-Cold War world', and in moving 'from the industrial to the information age, from the Cold War world to the global village', President Clinton asserted:

> We know that abroad we have the responsibility to advance freedom and democracy – to advance prosperity and the preservation of our planet . . . in a world where the dividing line between domestic and foreign policy is increasingly blurred . . . Our personal, family, and national future is affected by our policies on the environment at home and abroad. The common good at home is simply not separate from our efforts to advance the common good around the world. They must be one and the same if we are to be truly secure in the world of the 21st century. (Clinton 1995)

So it is through acting as an agency of environmental protection on a global scale that the United States sees itself reasserting its world leadership after the Cold War. As the world's leader, in turn, America stipulates that it cannot advance economic prosperity and ecological preservation without erasing the dividing lines between domestic and foreign policy. In the blur of the coming Information Age and its global villages, the United States cannot separate America's common good from the common goods of the larger world. To be truly secure in the twentieth century, each American's personal, family and national stake in their collective future must be served through the nation's environmental policies. Secretary of State Warren Christopher confirmed President Clinton's engagement with the environment through domestic statecraft and diplomatic action thus: 'protecting our fragile environment also has profound long-range importance for our country, and in 1996 we will strive to fully integrate our environmental goals into our diplomacy – something that has never been done before' (Christopher 1996b: 12).

Because 'the nations of the world look to America as a source of principled and reliable leadership', new leading principles and reliable sources for this authority need to be discovered (ibid. 9). And, to a certain extent, they can be derived from a tactics of normalization rooted within the codes of geo-power, eco-knowledge and enviro-discipline. From President Nixon's national launch of an American Environmental Protection Agency to President Clinton's global engagement of America as the world's leading agency of environmental protection, one can see the growing importance of a green governmentality in the state's efforts to steer, manage and legitimate all of its various policies.

Repudiating 'the end of history' thesis, Secretary of State Christopher announced at a major address hosted by the John F. Kennedy School of Government at Harvard University that the Unites States must cope instead with 'history in fast-forward', since it now faces 'threats from which no border can shield us – terrorism, proliferation, crime, and damage to the environment' (ibid. 11). Such 'new transnational security threats' endanger 'all of us in our interdependent world' (ibid. 12), so the United States will step forward in the post-Cold War era to combat these threats as an integral part of its anti-isolationist policies. As it runs headlong ahead on fast-forward, the United States now pledges through its Secretary of State to reduce greenhouse gases, ratify biodiversity conventions, and approve the Law of the Sea. Even so, President

Clinton, Vice-President Al Gore, and Secretary Christopher also recognize 'how we can make greater use of environmental initiatives to promote larger strategic and economic goals . . . helping our environmental industrial sector capture a larger share of a $400-billion global market' (ibid.).

Consequently, Secretary Christopher directed the staffs of Global Affairs, Policy Planning and the New Bureau of Oceans, International Environment and Scientific Affairs to identify environmental, population and resource issues which affected key US interests during February 1996. Along with naming a new Assistant Secretary for Oceans, International Environment and Scientific Affairs, Christopher also ordered that each American embassy now have an environmental senior officer, and that all bureau and mission planning have an environmental element in their agenda (1996a). As he told the House International Relations Committee, in 1996 things would change at the State Department, because he was 'fully integrating environmental goals into our daily diplomacy for the first time', and 'making greater use of environmental initiatives to promote our larger strategic and economic goals' (1996c: 160).

These efforts to link economic growth with ecological responsibility, however, are stated most obviously in Vice-President Gore's environmental musings. To ground his green geopolitics, Gore argues that 'the task of restoring the natural balance of the Earth's ecological system' could reaffirm America's long-standing 'interest in social justice, democratic government, and free market economics' (Gore 1992: 270). The geo-powers unlocked by this official ecology might even be seen as bringing 'a renewed dedication to what Jefferson believed were not merely American but universal inalienable rights: life, liberty, and the pursuit of happiness' (ibid.). At another level, however, Gore takes his own spiritual-religious opposition to geo-economics to new heights, arguing that America's new strategic goals after the Cold War must re-establish 'a natural and healthy relationship between human beings and the earth', replacing the brutal exploitation of nature with an 'environmentalism of the spirit' (ibid. 218, 238).

He asserts confidently that industrial civilization, like all highly organized cultures, depends upon 'a web of stories' to explain what it is, where it is going, and why it exists. Capitalism's existing stories, however, are riddled with the geo-economic themes of instrumental rationality, mindless growth and possessive individualism. Hence, 'new stories about the meaning and purpose of human civilization' must be devised (ibid. 216). To tell his new story, however, Gore casts all those advanced industrial societies, which are still hooked on geo-economics, as 'dysfunctional civilization'. On his diagnosis, their dysfunctionality has many origins: big science, instrumental rationality, capitalistic greed, industrial alienation and growth mania. None the less, its most basic cause is that worsening addiction to mass consumption. Because allegedly 'we' (meaning everyone in advanced industrial society) have lost our direct everyday connections to the natural world, we are all 'addicted to the consumption of the earth itself' (ibid. 220). Lonely, empty and obsessive, Gore argues, Americans attempt to fill this void with the inauthentic surrogates of more consumer goods. Thus, we become biosphere abusers. He does not, like the deep ecology community, call for us to face down the addiction by going cold turkey at the mall or by returning to a wild nature. Like all addicted individuals or any dysfunctional family, he argues, we are in denial. Still, we must, and fortunately can, heal ourselves. Indeed, there is an easy way out of dysfunctionality through responsible stewardship of nature.

Gore argues that such absolutions 'can heal the wound and free the victim from further enslavement' (ibid. 236–7). In healing talk of self-condemnation, then, Gore finds the easy therapy for redeeming both nature and humanity from industrial geo-economics. Sensing the mass public's anxious need for such rough-and-ready redemption, he labels us all 'dysfunctional deviants', identifies the causes of our common neuroses, and provides the talking cure needed to realize our collective salvation: namely, 'the new story of what it means to be a steward of the earth' (ibid. 237).

Gore's new story, in turn, blames geo-economics upon the old stories of materialism, instrumentalism and empiricism allegedly given to us by Bacon, Descartes and Galileo. For redemption, he turns to new pantheistic tales for a curative ontology, eschewing old-fashioned scientific narrative in favour of New Age re-enchantment: 'it is my own belief that the image of God can be seen in every corner of creation, even in us, but only faintly. By gathering in the mind's eye all of creation, one can perceive the image of the Creator vividly' (ibid. 265). Gore is no medieval mystic or woo-woo tree-hugger, seeking to glimpse God with the unaided eye of pure ecological faith. On the contrary, his New Age epiphany is hi-tech: God in his mind's eye can be seen very vividly as a hologram. Just as 'when one looks not at a small portion but at the entire hologram', there are 'thousands of tiny, faint images' that come together 'in the eye of the beholder as a single large, vivid image', so too are 'the myriad slight strands from earth's web of life – woven so distinctively into our essence – that make up the "resistance pattern" that reflects the image of God, faintly. By experiencing nature in its fullest – our own and that of all creation – with our senses and with our spiritual imagination, we can glimpse, bright shining as the sun, the infinite image of God' (ibid.).

Having gathered all creation into his mind's eye, Gore's spiritual imagination projects an environmental hologram whose bits encode a well-known story in their multi-dimensional patterns. This is a moral equivalent of war. Here, Gore's new story of Earth stewardship takes an odd turn as he identifies the need for a Global Marshall Plan to launch sustainable development as the basis of his green geopolitics. In that historic programme, as Gore notes, several nations joined together 'to reorganise an entire region of the world and change its way of life' (ibid. 296). Like the Marshall Plan, Gore's new Global Marshall Plan must (strangely for a design dedicated to environmental spiritual renewal) 'focus on strategic goals and emphasise actions and programs that are likely to remove the bottlenecks presently inhibiting the healthy functioning of the global economy . . . to serve human needs and promote sustained economic progress' (ibid. 297). Here, Gore's new story of stewardship of the Earth gets to its punchline. The green geopolitics of his Global Marshall Plan provides a global agenda for advancing a Strategic Environmental Initiative. Adopting strategic environmentalizing initiatives as the central organizing principle 'means embarking on an all-out effort to use every policy and program, every law and institution, every treaty and alliance, every tactic and strategy, every plan and course of action – to use, in short, every means to halt the destruction of the environment and to preserve and nurture our ecological system' (ibid. 274). Geo-economics is a predatory nationalistic attempt to monopolize material wealth for only a few in a handful of nation-states. Like President Clinton's theory of 'engagement', a green geopolitics would recognize that our 'ecological system' is the global business environment, as well as the world's natural environment. Both will be destroyed if we allow unchecked growth, mindless consumption, dysfunctional development and obsessive accumulation to continue. Both can be saved, however, if we plan on a global scale for environmentally appropriate growth, mindful consumption, sustainable development and careful accumulation guided by an ethic of environmental stewardship.

Gore's blur of domestic and foreign policies then flows into a six-point course of action that necessitates (1) stabilizing the world population, (2) deploying appropriate technologies, (3) devising techniques of ecological accounting to audit the production of all economic 'goods' and ecological 'bads', (4) imposing new regulatory frameworks to make the plan a success, (5) re-educating the global populace about environmental necessities, and, finally, (6) establishing models of sustainable development. Because there are no other institutional entities – the UN, OECD or NATO – with the muscle for performing the heavy lifting needed to manage the global environment, according to Gore, 'the responsibility for taking the initiative, for innovating, catalysing, and leading such an effort, falls disproportionately on the United States' (ibid. 304). At the end of the Cold War, we cannot simply show the interventionist central bureaucracies of the state the door; nor can we allow them to remobilize society around geo-economic programmes of mindless material development. On the contrary, we must bring the state back in. Only now, the bureaucrats will be mindful of what could be called 'the e-factor', or 'ecology' as efficiency and economy (Makower 1993: 56).

The centrality of 'the e-factor' in some current strategies for maintaining the environment and the economy is well illustrated by Japan's 1990 sustainable development programme, which launched a 100-year plan for developing new high-technology solutions to the sustainability challenge. In part a stroke of symbolic politics for the festivities associated with 1990's Earth Day celebrations, and in part just another turn of national technology policy, Tokyo's initiative established the Research Institute of Innovative Technology for the Earth (ibid.). This planned pursuit of ecological leadership, in turn, follows the remarkable increases in overall industrial efficiency attained in Japan as a by-product of its response to the 1973 oil crisis. For every unit of GNP, Japan now uses only 50 per cent of the energy and raw materials consumed in the United States (ibid.). And this level of manufacturing efficiency already gives Japanese producers a 5 per cent cost advantage over American firms on a number of their products (ibid. 56–7).

Japan's policy also indicates how sustainable development can be turned away from the ends of preserving nature and toward the goals of advancing national and corporate economic growth. It begins to approach what Vice-President Gore means by 'stewardship' as it transforms environmental sustainability into a multipronged programme for corporate culture revitalization, national efficiency maximization, and ecological regulation management in the 1990s. Sustaining nature will be an important by-product, but its immediate goals meet transnational security threats by maintaining national competitiveness and making environmental innovations. Ecological sustainability is remoulded as an economic growth ideology, and Vice-President Gore sounds the alarm about the Japanese challenge on the environmental front to American business and society:

> in almost every area of technology relevant to the environmental crisis, Japan is boldly taking the lead. What is maddening to many Americans . . . is that almost all of the key discoveries that led to these new technologies were made in the United States and then ignored by industry and government alike. (Gore 1992: 335)

Japan, then, is eating America's lunch at the ecological products counter just as it has done before at the consumer goods, steel, electronics goods, automobile and optical goods tables. 'But', as Gore asserts, 'all is not yet lost: what appears as still another example of a serious deficiency in America's ability to compete may actually be an ideal opportunity for the United States to address a pervasive and persistent structural problem in its approach to economic competition' (ibid.).

Sustaining nature by preserving ecosystems in this green geo-politics now becomes just one more goal among many in a new Strategic Environmental Initiative, focused on 'the development of environmentally appropriate technologies' (ibid.). Unsustainable development is largely caused, Gore suggests, by older, inappropriate, anti-environmental technologies. A global initiative is needed to find substitutes for them, and the United States must lead this campaign to heal its economy and, of course, the environment. Gore says the right things about changing our economic assumptions about mindless consumption, but his bottom line for sustainable development is found in sustaining American business, industry and science. The Strategic Environmental Initiative is primarily strategic, and only secondarily environmental, as it seeks to centre America on a new collective economic purpose which

> will demand the kind of determined effort that made the Apollo Program so productive and inspiring. The new program could reinvigorate our ability to excel at applied as well as basic research, spur gains in productivity, lead to innovations, breakthroughs, and spin offs in other fields of enquiry, and reestablish the United States as the world's leader in applied technology. (Ibid. 337)

As the world's leading capitalist economy, Gore concludes, 'the United States has a special obligation to discover effective ways of using the power of market forces to help save the global environment' (ibid. 347).

In the final analysis, ecologically sustainable development, as Makower observes, boils down to a new form of economic rationality. It is 'a search for the lowest-cost method of reducing the greatest amount of pollution' in the turnover of production processes (Makower 1993: 57). Almost magically, sustainable development can become primarily an economic, not merely an environmental, calculation. The initiatives taken by businesses to prevent pollution, reduce waste, and maximize energy efficiencies are to be supported. But even in taking these steps, businesses are reaffirming most of the existing premises of technology utilization, managerial centralization, and profit generation now driving advanced corporate capitalism.

This manoeuvre is done not just to preserve Nature, mollify green consumers, or respect Mother Earth; it is also done to enhance corporate profits, national productivity and state power, because 'the e-factor' is not merely ecology – it also is efficiency, excellence, education, empowerment, enforcement *and* economics. As long as implementing ecological changes in business means implementing an alternative array of instrumentally rational policies, like finding lower-cost methods of energy use, supply management, labour utilization, corporate communication, product generation or pollution abatement, sustainable green development maintains the economy. Gore's new stewardship through sustainable development may not be strictly ecological, but it strives to cultivate the image, at least, of being environmentally responsible (Piasecki and Asmus 1990). This compromise allows one to work 'deliberately and carefully, with an aim toward long-term cultural change, always with an eye toward the bottom line, lest you get frustrated and discouraged in the process', so that these 'environmentally responsible businesses can be both possible and profitable' (Makower 1993: 228).

Eco-Knowledge as Theory/Practice

Geo-power in green geopolitics counters the logic of geo-economic industrialism by moving liberal welfare states on to an ecological footing, redeputizing some of their administrative personnel as

bureaucratic greens. Because most consumers are willing participants in a dysfunctional geo-economic civilization not yet subject to
full-blown green governance, they must be forced to be functional
in accord with the regulatory goals of geo-environmentalizing
bureaucracies. Entirely new identities built around new collective
ends, like survival or sustainability, can be elaborated by systems
of eco-knowledge.

Inasmuch as economic and governmental techniques are a central focus of political struggle today, the complex interactions of
populations with their surroundings in political economies and
ecologies are forcing states to develop eco-knowledge in order to
redefine what is within their competence. Eco-knowledge codes
indicate that, to survive now, it is not enough for states merely
to maintain legal jurisdiction over their allegedly sovereign territories. As new limits to growth constantly are being discovered,
states are forced to guarantee their populations' productivity in
every environmental setting encompassed by the global political
economy (e.g. Hardin 1993).

Governmental discourses must methodically mobilize particular
assumptions, codes and procedures to enforce specific understandings of the economy and society. Yet, as geo-powered ecological
ethics about Earth in the balance will show, eco-knowledges work
just fine at performing these same tasks. Indeed, they can generate
new administrative 'truths' or managerial 'knowledges' that will
denominate codes of power with significant reserves of popular
legitimacy. Inasmuch as they classify, organize and legitimate larger
understandings of ecological reality, such discourses can authorize
or invalidate the options for constructing particular institutions,
practices or concepts in society at large. They simultaneously frame
the emergence of new collective subjectivities – global ecologies
as dynamic bio-economic systems – and collections of subjects –
individuals as bio-economic units in such global systems – to protect
the environment. Still, as the Wise Use/Property Rights movement
reveals, one must remember how extensively the meanings of ecological subjectivity are still being contested on the Left and the
Right. Ecological subjectivity can be expressed in small-scale experiments by autonomous human beings following their own local
political agendas in many bio-regional communities, or it may be
retooled in vast statist programmes for interacting within Global
Marshall Plans, depending upon which interpretations are empowered where (Foucault 1976: 143–4). Whether traditional
geo-economic or newer geopolitic discourses, articulated in the

Clinton/Gore register of green engagement with transnational security threats and sustainable prosperity projects, prevail is still to be determined by the political struggles of the 1990s. None the less, sustainable development discourses remain a key form of eco-knowledge on this embattled terrain.

Sustainable development discourse emerged at a historically particular juncture in recent history: the early 1970s. At this time, the popular fascination with ecology after the first Earth Day celebrations in 1970, the elite preoccupation with resource scarcities in the midst of OPEC's manipulation of oil prices and supplies during 1971–3, and the apparent abatement of superpower competition in US/USSR *détente* around 1972–5 allowed new global agendas to be advanced above and beyond Cold War debates fixed upon East/West rivalry. In these more North/South-centred discussions, questions were raised about the survivability of contemporary industrial civilization in light of tremendous material waste in the overdeveloped North's economies of affluence, as well as pressing material shortages arising out of the underdeveloped South's population explosions. Even though they are crudely formulated, these preoccupations are captured in *The Limits to Growth* report of The Club of Rome in 1972. Not anticipating any social learning or systemic shocks that might change behaviour, *The Limits to Growth* experts concluded:

> If the present growth trends in world population, industrialisation, pollution, food production, and resource depletion continue unchanged, the limits to growth on this planet will be reached sometime within the next one hundred years. The most probable result will be a rather sudden and uncontrollable decline in both population and industrial capacity. (Meadows et al. 1972: 27)

Such conclusions, despite all of their methodological murkiness, drew attention. Sustainable development is one response to 'the limits to growth' phenomenon, but it assumes that the limits to growth are quite flexible. Indeed, sustainable growth is anticipated by envisioning the creation of a much more complex global system with many contradictory trends working simultaneously in favour of conservation and waste, ecological care and anti-environmental neglect, social change and institutional inertia (e.g. Brown et al. 1995). The advocates of sustainable development, in turn, want to problematize these tendencies, while presenting new tactics and values to mitigate or eliminate them.

The concept of sustainability grew in popularity during the 1980s with the publication of the World Conservation Strategy (IUCN 1980). This programme asserted that the sound maintenance of the world's ecology could be sustained only if three objectives were met, namely: 'the utilisation of good cropland for crops rather than cattle raising, the ecologically sound management of crops, and the protection of watershed forests' (Redclift 1987: 21). Even now, however, few objectives identified by sustainable development theory are being effectively realized, in either developed or developing countries, because 'the environment' and 'development' have been treated for so long as two poles of an unbreakable antimony. As the World Commission on Environment and Development (also known as the Brundtland Commission) noted in its 1987 report, economic growth advocates are often not terribly interested in seeing more environmental regulations, and the 'standard agenda' of policy making for many environmental groups suffers from many errors and biases, including the following.

> First, it is usually the effects of environmental problems that are addressed in public documents, as we have seen. Second, environmental issues are usually separated from development issues and frequently pigeon-holed under 'conservation'. Third, the Commission complains that critical issues, such as acid rain or pollution, are usually discussed in isolation, rather as if solutions to these problems can be found in discrete areas of policy. Fourth, the Commission criticises what it sees as a narrow view of environmental policy, which relegates the 'environment' to a secondary status – it is 'added on' to other, more important development issues. (Brundtland 1985, cited in Redclift 1987: 14)

In addition to changing economic growth strategies in the North, the goal of sustainable development discourses was to find a successful strategy for underdeveloped Second, Third and Fourth World countries to attain economic growth.

Given these goals, the definition of sustainable development advanced by the World Commission on Environment and Development in its 1987 report, *Our Common Future*, remains very instructive:

> Humanity has the ability to make development sustainable – to ensure that it meets the needs of the present without compromising the ability of future generations to meet their own needs. The

concept of sustainable development does imply limits – not absolute limits but limitations imposed by the present state of technology and social organisation on environmental resources and by the ability of the biosphere to absorb the effects of human activities . . . technology and social organisation can be both managed and improved to make way for a new era of economic growth. (Brundtland 1987: 8)

With this declaration, one group of environmental experts, in answering a call by the General Assembly of the United Nations, used their special investigative powers to refocus the power/knowledge nexus in environmental affairs. As its chairperson, Gro Harlem Brundtland declares in the report's foreword:

[T]he environment does not exist as a sphere separate from human actions, ambitions, and needs, and attempts to define it in isolation from human concerns have given the very word 'environment' a connotation of naiveté in some political circles . . . but the 'environment' is where we all live; and 'development' is what we all do in attempting to improve our lot within that abode. The two are inseparable. (Ibid. ix)

In the eco-knowledge shared by the Brundtland Commission, the environment is not merely the realm of 'nature' somehow separate, distinct and autonomous from 'humanity'. Rather, the environment is where 'we all' (humanity) actually 'live', and development is what 'we all do' (human activities, designs, organizations) to 'improve our lot' (material satisfactions of human needs) within that abode (nature) (ibid.). Environment and development, then, are inseparable. Deep ecologists, eco-feminists, Buddhist economists, bio-regionalists, and other nature preservationists might well argue that material simplicity, or perhaps even poverty, is morally desirable for the Earth to survive. The Commission's eco-knowledge, to the contrary, holds that 'widespread poverty is no longer inevitable. Poverty is not only an evil in itself, but sustainable development requires meeting the basic needs of all and extending to all the opportunity to fulfill their aspirations for a better life. A world in which poverty is endemic will always be prone to ecological and other catastrophes' (ibid. 8). Humanity must not choose to live in the poor-house, opting not to improve its economic lot to preserve the Earth. Such moves would be evil themselves; the world must instead, ironically, become more, not less, economically developed to escape ecological disasters.

In advancing this agenda, the Brundtland Commission expresses a central logic for eco-knowledge needed by any environmental protection agency; it assumes that everything it stipulates can be known – how to define aspirations for a better life, what constitute basic needs, when to manage economic growth, why to improve technology, where to organize environmental resources, who is to judge the ability of of biosphere to absorb human pressures – is known, or is, at least, knowable. And since these eco-knowledges exist, all that existing state regimes need to do is to mobilize the moral-political will needed to operationalize this knowledge about how geo-power works: forcing the rich to become frugal, transferring resources to the poor, enhancing citizen participation in collective decision making, slowing population growth everywhere, creating harmony between the ecology and the economy of the environment where humanity lives. Like any national environmental protection agency, the World Commission concludes, sustainable development will never be reducible to a steady state or harmonious balance, '[b]ut rather a process of change in which the exploitation of resources, the direction of investments, the orientation of technological development, and institutional change are made consistent with future as well as present needs . . . in the final analysis, sustainable development must rest on political will' (ibid. 9).

The institutional gaps in political will, which now prevent this kind of change, are legion. Because existing national governments are slow to respond, selfishly nationalistic in their response, financially incapable of responding, or unable to compel those responsible for ecological damage to respond to their directives, new international bodies, like the World Commission on Environment and Development, must somehow intervene.

Nevertheless, what is 'eco-knowledge'? How does it come to be known, and by whom, and about what? Is sustainable development discourse anything more than an eco-knowledge of/by/for the modern capitalist mode of production, which became fully transnational in scope and impact only during the 1960s. As the geo-power talk of the Clinton administration illustrates, it is the sustainability of this capitalist order, working finally on a truly transnational scale, which now preoccupies sustainable development. A joint declaration of the International Union for the Conservation of Nature, the United Nations Environmental Programme, and the World Wildlife Fund in 1991 defined sustainable development as 'improving the quality of human life while living within the carrying capacity of the supporting ecosystems' (IUCN 1991). This sort of statement, however, only shows how discourse can acquire strange articulations in the talk of non-governmental organization (NGO) environmental experts. Earth in this frame is reduced to 'the supporting ecosystems of human life'. It has some apparently determinable 'carrying capacity' with certain upper limits, and these are to be set by techno-economic interventions aimed at improving 'the quality of human life'. But, the geological time-scale being evoked here also spurs one to ask: all or some humans' lives, what kind of quality, which improvements, living now within what carrying capacity, which supporting ecosystems? Lest we be chronocentric, how do we know that early Neolithic communities, late Pleistocene hunter clans, or the first Meso-potamian cities are not what ought to be sustainably developed, since they obviously lived most of the time within their ecosys-temic limits? Already, ideological constructs like 'quality of life', 'standards of living' and 'improving human life' are poking through discursive tropes to channel the identification of nature as an ecological support system or carrying capacity which may need continuous improvement.

One must wonder about eco-knowledge as 'sustainable devel-opment'. Its articulation already begs its own definition inasmuch as its first term always remains tacit. Some take sustainable devel-opment to mean ecologically sustainable. Others just as rightly see it as economically sustainable, technologically sustainable or politically sustainable. Chambers of commerce and ministries of industry in the 1990s glibly adopt sustainable development dis-course as their own: this dam, that factory, these highways, those power lines must be built to sustain, not nature, but job creation, population growth, industrial output or service delivery. Such ele-ments improve human life and enhance its ecosystems' carrying capacities. This construction, however, clashes with ecological inter-pretations in which humans allegedly are seeking 'social and mater-ial progress within the constraints of sustainable resource use and environmental management'; and, as a result, 'renewable resources (plants, trees, animals and soil) will be used no faster than they are generated; non-renewable resources (such as fossil fuels and metals) will be used no faster than acceptable substitutes can be found; and pollutants will be generated no faster than can be absorbed and neutralised by the environment' (McMichael 1993: 309).

As a social goal, sustainability is fraught with unresolved questions. Sustainable for how long: a generation, one century, a millennium, ten millennia? Sustainable at what level of human appropriation: individual households, local villages, major cities, entire nations, global economies? Sustainable for whom: all humans alive now, all humans that will ever live, all living beings living at this time, all living beings that will ever live? Sustainable under what conditions: contemporary transnational capitalism, low-impact Neolithic hunter-and-gather societies, some future space-faring global empire? Sustainable development of what: personal income, social complexity, gross national product, material frugality, individual consumption, ecological biodiversity? For the most part, few of these questions are even being adequately conceptualized, much less thoroughly addressed in the debates over sustainable development.

To begin with, eco-knowledges often look to a planetary scale for answers. How much more can human beings sustainably take from nature? One can appraise this sustainability issue roughly in terms of human impact on the planet's biosphere. Vitousek and colleagues look at the biosphere's net product of photosynthesis, seeing net primary production (NPP) as all energy transformed via photosynthesis by primary producers (photosynthesizing life-forms) minus energy they use to reproduce themselves (Vitousek et al. 1986). By the mid-1980s, human beings were consuming 40 per cent of terrestrial NPP, and 25 per cent of total NPP (including marine, aquatic and terrestrial sources). These figures, in turn, reflect not only levels of direct resource utilization, but also levels of indirect resource degradation due to anthropogenic causes (ibid.). Two more doublings of human population, again assuming only a 1980s level of resource use, would mathematically exhaust all NPP needed by all other life-forms (ibid.). While this event may be one or two generations away, and it would obviously be the ultimate catastrophe of sustainability, it seems apparent that we are already at a critical juncture of sustainability. Rich communities and powerful states still have the clout to buy and/or force their way past some of the material constraints: this is 'the e-factor' for Clinton and Gore. But there are millions living in deforested, desertified, eroded and salinated zones of Africa, Latin America, Asia and Europe – Rwandans, Sudanese, Chadians, Bolivians, Brazilians, Belizians, Cambodians, Bengalis, Kashimiris, Ukrainians, Russians, Armenians – already suffering from ecologically unsustainable development in their territorial spaces. Soon, unless nature is preserved, will everyone be a Rwandan, will every place be in Aralsk, will everything be Love Canal? This is Secretary of State Christopher's transnational security threat, so now the CIA, DIA, State Department and Defense Department are developing 'early warning systems' to detect environmental catastrophes (e.g. Greenhouse 1995).

Yet, eco-knowledge of nature is tenuous. By what rules can the environment be somehow gauged as normal or at least subjected to normalizing criteria that will reveal year-in, year-out predictable levels of rain, soil creation, timber growth, fish population, agricultural output or human settlement. Once these factors have been identified and tracked, ecological monitors may watch such variables, and maybe manage the global ecosystem. But other scientific analyses indicate that there may be incredible variations in all these ecological factors from year to year or decade by decade. Nature may well be far more chaotic, much less predictable, and not as normal as many scientists hitherto have believed. As a result, technocratic efforts to capture its energies as geo-power in normalizing models, which artlessly assume levels of docile predictability and stable replicability in ecological dynamics, may reduce any Strategic Environmental Initiative to administer nature to complete meaninglessness.

In some sectors or at a few sites, ecologically more rational participation in some global commodity chains may well occur as a by-product of sustainable development. Over-logged tropical forests might be saved for biodiversity-seeking genetic engineers; over-fished reefs could be shifted over to eco-tourist hotel destinations; over-grazed prairies may see bison return as a meat industry animal. In the time–space compression of postmodern informational capitalism, many businesses are more than willing to feed these delusions with images of environmentally responsible trade, green industrialization, or ecologically sustainable commerce, in order to create fresh markets for new products.

None the less, do these policies contribute to ecologically sustainable development? or do they simply shift commodity production from one fast track to another slower one, while increasing opportunities for more local people to gain additional income to buy more commodities that further accelerate transnational environmental degradation? or do they empower a new group of outside experts following doctrines of engagement to intervene in local communities and cultures so that their geo-power may serve Global Marshall Plans, not unlike how it occurred over and over again during Cold War-era experiments at inducing agricultural development, industrial development, community development, social development and technological development? Now that the Cold War is over, as the Clinton/Gore green geopolitics suggests, does the environment simply substitute for Communism as a source and site of strategic contestation, justifying rich/powerful/industrial states' intervention in poor/weak/agricultural regions to serve the interests of outsiders who want to control how forests, rivers, farms or wildlife are used?

Enviro-Discipline at Work

The ideas advanced by various exponents of sustainable development discourse are intriguing. And, perhaps if they were implemented in the spirit that their originators intended, the ecological situation of the Earth might improve. Yet, even after two decades of heeding the theory and practice of such eco-knowledge, sustainable development mostly has not happened, and it most likely will not happen, even though its advocates continue to be celebrated as visionaries. Encircled by grids of ecological alarm, sustainability discourse tells us that today's allegedly unsustainable environments need to be disassembled, recombined and subjected to the disciplinary designs of expert management. Enveloped in such enviro-disciplinary frames, any environment could be redirected to fulfil the ends of other economic scripts, managerial directives and administrative writs denominated in sustainability values. Sustainability, then, engenders its own forms of 'environmentality', which would embed alternative instrumental rationalities beyond those of pure market calculation in the policing of ecological spaces.

Initially, one can argue that the modern regime of bio-power formation described by Foucault was not especially attentive to the role of nature in the equations of biopolitics (Foucault 1976: 138–42). The controlled tactic of inserting human bodies into the machineries of industrial and agricultural production as part and parcel of strategically adjusting the growth of human populations to the development of industrial capitalism, however, did generate systems of bio-power. Under such regimes, power/knowledge systems bring 'life and its mechanisms into the realm of explicit calculations', making the manifold disciplines of knowledge and discourses of power into new sorts of productive agency as part of the 'transformation of human life' (ibid. 145). Once this threshold was crossed, social experts began to recognize how the environmental interactions of human economics, politics and technologies continually put all human beings' existence as living beings in question.

Foucault divides the environmental realm into two separate but interpenetrating spheres of action: the biological and the historical. For most of human history, the biological dimension, or forces of nature acting through disease and famine, dominated human existence, with the ever present menace of death. Developments in agricultural technologies, as well as hygiene and health techniques, however, gradually provided some relief from starvation and plague by the end of the eighteenth century. As a result, the historical dimension began to grow in importance, as 'the development of the different fields of knowledge concerned with life in general, the improvement of agricultural techniques, and the observations and measures relative to man's life and survival contributed to this relaxation: a relative control over life averted some of the imminent risks of death' (ibid. 142). The historical then began to envelop, circumscribe or surround the biological, creating interlocking disciplinary expanses for 'the environmental'. And these environmentalized settings quickly came to dominate all forms of concrete human reality: 'in the space of movement thus conquered, and broadening and organising that space, methods of power and knowledge assumed responsibility for the life processes and undertook to control and modify them' (ibid.). While Foucault does not explicitly define these spaces, methods and knowledges as 'environmental', these enviro-disciplinary manoeuvres are the origin of many aspects of environmentalization. As biological life is refracted through economic, political and technological existence, 'the facts of life' pass into fields of control for any discipline of eco-knowledge and spheres of intervention for the management of geo-power.

Foucault recognized how these shifts implicitly raised 'ecological issues' to the extent that they disrupted and redistributed the understandings provided by the classical episteme for defining human interactions with nature. Living became environmentalized as humans, or 'a specific living being, and specifically related to other living beings' (ibid. 143), began to articulate their historical and biological life in profoundly new ways from within artificial cities and mechanical modes of production. Environmentalization arose from 'this dual position of life that placed it at the same time outside history, in its biological environment, and inside human historicity, penetrated by the latter's techniques of knowledge and power' (ibid.). Strangely, even as he makes this linkage,

Foucault does not develop these ecological insights, suggesting that 'there is no need to lay further stress on the proliferation of political technologies that ensued, investing the body, health, modes of subsistence and habitation, living conditions, the whole space of existence' (ibid. 143–4).

Even so, Foucault here found the conjunction needed for 'the environment' to emerge as an eco-knowledge formation and/or a cluster of eco-power tactics for an enviro-discipline. As human beings begin consciously to wager their life as a species on the products of their biopolitical strategies and technological systems, a few recognize that they are also wagering the lives of other, or all, species as well. While Foucault regards this shift as just one of many lacunae in his analysis, everything changes as human bio-power systems interweave their operations in the biological environment, penetrating the workings of many ecosystems with the techniques of knowledge and power. Once human power/knowledge formations become the foundation of industrial society's economic development, they also become a major factor in all terrestrial life-forms' continued physical survival. Eco-knowledge about geo-power thus becomes through enviro-disciplines a strategic technology that reinvests human bodies – their means of health, modes of subsistence, and styles of habitation integrating the whole space of existence – with bio-historical significance. It then reframes them within their bio-physical environments, which are now also filled with various animal and plant bodies positioned in geo-physical settings, as essential elements in managing the health of any human ecosystem's carrying capacity.

As Foucault portrays the arts of government, they are essentially concerned with how to introduce rational economy in the management of things into the political practices of the state. Government becomes in the eighteenth century the designation of a 'level of reality, a field of intervention, through a series of complex processes' in which 'government is the right disposition of things' (Foucault 1991a: 93). It evolves as an elaborate social formation, or 'a triangle, sovereignty-discipline-government, which has as its primary target the population and as its essential mechanism the apparatuses of security' (ibid. 102). Most significantly, Foucault sees state authorities mobilizing governmentality to bring about 'the emergence of population as a datum, as a field of intervention and as an objective of governmental techniques, and the process which isolates the economy as a specific sector of reality' (ibid.), so that now 'the population is the object that government must take into account in all its observations and *savoirs*, in order to be able to govern effectively in a rational and conscious manner' (ibid. 100). The networks of continuous, multiple, complex interaction between populations (their increase, longevity, health, etc.), territory (its expanse, resources, control, etc.) and wealth (its creation, productivity, distribution, etc.) are sites of governmentalizing rationality to manage the productive interaction of these forces.[2]

Individuals and groups are enmeshed within the tactics and strategies of more complex forms of power, whose institutions, procedures, analyses and techniques loosely manage mass populations and their surroundings in a highly politicized symbolic and material economy. While it is still an inexact set of bearings, Foucault asserts that 'it is the tactics of government which make possible the continual definition and redefinition of what is within the competence of the state and what is not, the public versus the private, and so on; thus the state can only be understood in its survival and its limits on the basis of the general tactics of governmentality' (ibid. 103).

Because governmental techniques are always the central focus of political struggle and contestation, the interactions of populations with their natural surroundings in highly politicized economies compel regimes to constantly redefine what is within their competence throughout the modernizing process (Luke 1994a, 1994b). To survive in the fast capitalist world of the 1990s, it is not enough for territorial states merely to maintain legal jurisdiction over their allegedly sovereign territories – a fact that geo-economics aggressively celebrates. As ecological limits to growth are either discovered or defined in sustainability discourses, states are forced to make good upon an almost impossible obligation: namely, guaranteeing their populations' fecundity and productivity in the total setting of a global political economy by becoming 'environmental protection agencies'. To develop these protected environments and their increasing populations, as the Clinton/Gore vision of green governmentality shows, economic growth must not be limited, but rather become sustainable (Brown et al. 1991).

Enviro-discipline, then, must methodically mobilize particular assumptions, codes and procedures to enforce specific understandings of the economy and society. They generate eco-knowledges, like those embedded in notions of sustainability or development, that also constitute significant reserves of legitimacy and effectiveness.[3] Inasmuch as they classify, organize, and vet larger understandings of reality, such discourses can authorize or invalidate the possibilities for constructing particular institutions, practices or goods in society at large. They simultaneously frame the emergence of collective subjectivities – nations as dynamic populations – and collections of subjects – individuals as units in such nations (Luke 1993a). The parameters of enviro-discipline, in turn, can be re-evaluated as 'the element in which are articulated the effects of a certain type of power and the reference of a certain type of knowledge, the machinery by which the power relations give rise to a possible corpus of knowledge, and knowledge extends and reinforces the effects of this power' (Foucault 1975: 29). In green governmentality, the disciplinary articulations of sustainability and development centre on establishing and enforcing 'the right disposition of things' between humans and their environment.

The application of enviro-discipline expresses the authority of eco-knowledgeable, geo-powered forces to police the fitness of all biological organisms and the health of their natural environments. Master concepts, like 'survival' or 'sustainability' for species and their habitats, empower these masterful conceptualizers to inscribe the biological/cultural/economic order of the Earth's many territories as an elaborate array of environments, requiring continuous enviro-discipline to guarantee ecological fitness. The survival agenda, as Oates argues, 'applies simultaneously to individuals, populations, communities, and ecosystems; and it applies simultaneously to the present and the future' (Oates 1989: 148).

When approached through this mind-set, the planet Earth becomes an immense engine, or the human race's 'ecological life-support system', which has 'with only occasional localised failures' provided 'services upon which human society depends consistently and without charge' (Cairns 1995). As this environmentalized engine, the Earth then generates 'ecosystem services', or those derivative products and functions of natural systems that human societies perceive as valuable (Westmen 1978). This complex is what must survive; human life will continue if such survival-promoting services continue. They include the generation of soils, the regeneration of plant nutrients, capture of solar energy, conversion of solar energy into biomass, accumulation/purification/distribution of water, control of pests, provision of a genetic library, maintenance of breathable air, control of micro- and macro-climates, pollination of plants, diversification of animal species, development of buffering mechanisms in catastrophes and aesthetic enrichment (Cairns 1995). As an environmental engine, the planet's ecology requires eco-engineers to guide its sustainable use, and systems of green governmentality must be adduced to monitor and manage the system of systems which produce all these robust services. Just as the sustained use of technology 'requires that it be maintained, updated and changed periodically', so too does the 'sustainable use of the planet require that we not destroy our ecological capital, such as old-growth forests, streams and rivers (with their associated biota), and other natural amenities' (ibid. 3). Survival is the key value.

This command to go anywhere at anytime to defend the cause of survival may direct enviro-discipline to pursue other equally problematic values on a global level with the full force of state power and positive science: namely, stability, diversity and interdependence. A powerful nation-state is no longer empowered simply to defend its territory to protect its population. As Clinton and Gore claim, it must now also identify and police the surroundings in all of its many operational environments, to guarantee ecological stability, biological diversity and environmental interdependence. Because some states are more sustainable than others, their survival imperatives may become guide-lines for environmental colonialism. In order to survive, the state may choose to impose the status of a green belt, forest preserve, nature reservation or environmental refuge upon other societies as part of its Strategic Environmental Initiatives.

To serve and protect the values of the ecosystem, Oates claims that the ecological ethic of stability as 'a steady state' will not result in 'stagnation'. Such an outcome would, of course, offend the growth fixations of consumers and citizens living in liberal capitalist democracies. On the contrary, he believes that it would mean 'directing growth and change in nondestructive ways, generated within the standing pattern that supports life' (Oates 1989: 152). But who directs growth and change for whom? Is there a standing pattern that directs life? Does anyone really know enough about it to direct growth in accord with it? In practice, Global Marshall Planners in Washington could use ecological criteria to impose their sustainable development of economic growth at home as they also force an ecological steady state upon others abroad. If India's hundred millions stay on foot or bicycles, then Germany's tens of millions would stay in their cars. If Indonesia keeps growing trees, then Japan can keep consuming lumber. And if Brazil's ranchers keep turning rain forest into cattle ranges, then America's suburbanites will get their cheeseburgers.

Obviously, an enviro-disciplinary 'steadying state', designed
and managed by green bureaucrats, will be needed to enforce
environmentalized stable states of dynamic ecological equilibrium,
which Oates identifies as the *sine qua non* of stability. Ironically,
then, this green governmentality, as it stabilizes everyone's fitness
and health, should restructure 'populations and growth' by planning for sustainable patterns in timber harvesting, oil production,
agricultural output, land use and consumer marketing, to contain
but not end the growth fetishism of mass consumption capitalism. Oates concurs with Gore that all geo-economic national markets run on a paradox: 'whatever is achieved instantly becomes
inadequate when measured against the ethic of continual consumption. Satisfaction only creates dissatisfaction, in an accelerat-
ing cycle. "More" is an unrealisable goal' (ibid. 155). Since these
consumerist values cause more and more damage, the ecological
strategies of enviro-discipline countries must enforce a new social
commitment to their opposites: namely, the willing acceptance of
'less' as the moral basis for new ecological values on a social and
an individual level. For survival's sake, 'the ethical consciousness
of earth's human population must therefore be as ecologically
well regulated as the size of the earth's population' (ibid. 154).

Protecting the whole, in the practices of enviro-discipline, might
also follow the strange credo of *biophilia*, or love of life, in a
framework of *biocentrism*, or placing earth–life–nature beyond
anthropocentrism at the core of green thought and bureaucratic
practice. If environments are to be protected, then all the life
within them would, of course, anchor the practical forms of human
engagement with the world. Yet, this emotional commitment
to 'Life', or life seen as the super-organism of all life on Earth,
might entail condemning large groups of humanity in acts of clear
misanthropy by containing, destroying or limiting traditional forms
of human living to guarantee ecological survival. It is not that
enviro-disciplinarians love their lives less, but that they love all
other animal and plant life more – so they must reason as they
prevent all human communities from developing to enhance environmental survivability. This contradiction actually makes sense,
because it places limits on geo-economic excesses whenever the
survivalist steady state operatives see everyday policies threatening non-human life's survival and stability. 'Where survival of the
whole seems threatened', Oates concludes, 'as in issues of extinction and pollution, then the basic ethos of protecting the whole
predominates' (ibid. 192).

Conclusion

Foucault is correct about the modern state. It is not 'an entity which was developed above individuals, ignoring what they are and even their very existence', because it has indeed evolved 'as a very sophisticated structure, in which individuals can be integrated, under one condition: that this individuality would be shaped in a new form, and submitted to a set of very specific patterns' (Foucault 1982: 214–15). Producing discourses of ecological living, articulating designs of sustainable development, and propagating definitions of environmental literacy for contemporary individuals simply adds new twists to the 'very specific patterns' by which the state formation constitutes 'a modern matrix of individualisation' (ibid. 215). The regime of bio-power, in turn, operates through ethical systems of identity as much as it does in the policy machinations of governmental bureaus within any discretely bordered territory. Ecology merely echoes the effects from 'one of the great innovations in the techniques of power in the eighteenth century': namely, 'the emergence of "population" as an economic and political problem' (Foucault 1976: 25).

Once demography emerges as a science of statist administration, its statistical attitudes can diffuse into the numerical surveillance of nature, or Earth and its non-human inhabitants, as well as the study of culture, or society and its human members.[4] Government and now, most importantly, statist ecology preoccupy themselves with 'the conduct of conduct'. Previously, the ethical concerns of family, community and nation guided how conduct was to be conducted; but at this juncture, environment emerges as a ground for normalizing individual behaviour. Environments are spaces under police supervision, expert management or technocratic control; hence, by taking environmentalistic agendas into the heart of state policy, one finds the ultimate meaning of the police state fulfilled. If the police, as they bind and observe space, are empowered to watch over religion, morals, health, supplies, roads, town buildings, public safety, liberal arts, trade, factories, labour supplies and the poor, then why not add ecology – or the interactions of organisms and their surroundings to the police zones of the state? Here, the conduct of any person's environmental conduct becomes the initial limit on others' ecological enjoyments; so too does the conduct of the social body's conduct require that the state always be an effective 'environmental protection agency'.

The ecological domain is the ultimate domain of being, with the most critical forms of life that states must now produce, protect and police in eliciting bio-power: it is the centre of their enviro-discipline, eco-knowledge, geo-power (Luke 1994a, 1994b).

Mobilizing biological power, then, accelerated after the 1970s, along with global fast capitalism. Ecology became that formalized disciplinary mode of paying systematic 'attention to the processes of life ... to invest life through and through' (Foucault 1976: 139), in order to transform all living things into biological populations, so to develop transnational commerce. The tremendous explosion of material prosperity on a global scale after 1973 would not have been possible without ecology to guide 'the controlled insertion of bodies into the machinery of production and the adjustment of the phenomena of population to economic processes' (ibid. 141). An anatomo-politics of all plants and animals emerges out of ecology, through which environmentalizing resource managerialists acquire 'the methods of power capable of optimising forces, aptitudes, and life in general without at the same time making them more difficult to govern' (ibid.).

To move another step beyond Foucault's vision of human bio-power, adjustment of the accumulation of environmentalized plants and animals to that of capital is necessary to check unsustainable growth. Yet, in becoming an essential sub-assembly for transnational economic development, ecological techniques of power rationalize conjoining 'the growth of human groups to the expansion of productive forces and the differential allocation of profit', inasmuch as population ecology, environmental science and range management are now, in part, 'the exercise of bio-power in its many forms and modes of application' (ibid.). Indeed, a postmodern condition is perhaps reached when the life of all species is now wagered in all of humanity's economic and political strategies. Ecology emerges out of bio-history, circulating within 'the space for movement thus conquered, and broadening and organising that space, methods of power and knowledge' needed for enviro-disciplinary interventions as the state 'assumed responsibility for the life processes and undertook to control and modify them' (ibid. 101).

This chapter has explored only one path through the order of things embedded in contemporary mainstream environmentalism. Ultimately, it suggests that we cannot adequately understand governmentality in present-day regimes, like the United States of America, without seeing how many of its tactics, calculi or institutions assume 'environmentalized' modes of operation as part and parcel of ordinary practices of governance. Strategic Environmental Initiatives are now standard operating procedures. To preserve the political economy of high-technology production, many offices of the American state must function as 'environmental protection agencies', inasmuch as they continue to fuse a politics of national security with an economics of continual growth, to sustain existing industrial ecologies of mass consumption with the wise use of nature through private property rights. Conservationist ethics, resource managerialism and green rhetorics, then, congeal as an unusually cohesive power/knowledge formation, whose actions are an integral element of this order's regime of normalization.

Notes

1   James Fallows (1989) pursues a similar line of argument.
2   The statistical surveillance regime of states, as Foucault maintains, emerges alongside monarchical absolutism during the late seventeenth century. Intellectual disciplines, ranging from geography and cartography to statistics and civil engineering, are mobilized to inventory and organize the wealth of populations in territories by the state. For additional discussion, see Burchell et al. 1991: 1–48. A very useful example of sustainability thinking conjoined with professional-technical environmentality can be found in Trzyna 1995.
3   For a typical expression of sustainability discourse as a legitimation code, see Young 1990.
4   For more elaboration of why state power must guarantee environmental security, see Myers 1993.

7

Art and Foucauldian Heterotopias

Thomas Heyd

Introduction

An invisible grid with aboriginal boulder structures at its crossing
points is laid over the Northern Plains of North America. These
structures are aesthetically interesting arrangements of glacial
boulders that often call to mind wheels, and have been called
'medicine wheels'.

In the following I describe these structures and explain the
difficulties involved in their interpretation. In the process of clari-
fying their meaning for contemporary non-natives, I propose that
they be considered as art. In this connection, I briefly discuss,
Michel Foucault's paper 'Of Other Spaces' and the notion of
'heterotopia', and propose that these aboriginal boulder structures function as heterotopias. That is, in so far as these structures
are exquisitely suited to their places, they effectively question, and
even interrogate, all other sites located in the natural environment
of the Northern Plains.

Foucault introduces the expression 'heterotopia' in a little-known
text called 'Of Other Spaces', a translation of 'Des Espaces autres'
published in *Architecture-Mouvement-Continuité* in 1984, and
based on a lecture on architectural studies given in March 1967
(Foucault 1986). Although this paper is not pivotal in Foucault's
corpus, I suggest that its approach is consistent with his other works,
inasmuch as the notion of heterotopias developed there represents
resistance in the face of apparently overwhelming homogenization. I claim that, in so far as these boulder structures are heterotopias, Foucault's conception can facilitate a new understanding
of them as well as of contemporary industrial interventions in
the land.

Plains Boulder Structures: Medicine Wheels

'Medicine wheel' is the name given, since the late 1800s, to a kind of boulder structure found in the Northern Plains of North America. The name has been applied in a generic manner to boulder structures that are relatively similar to the Bighorn Wheel on Medicine Mountain in the American state of Wyoming, in distinction to smaller, less complex stone circle structures such as those often called 'teepee rings'. Significantly, the name 'wheel', although used in contemporary classification, is misleading if considered as an indication of the image that its original builders may have had, because wheels were probably unknown in the Americas before the arrival of Europeans.

Medicine wheels, furthermore, are usually not completely circular; instead of radial symmetry, some of these structures have a tendency towards bilateral symmetry – a feature common to all the vertebrates that were known to the Plains Indians (Wilson 1981: 346–7). After a careful survey of the diverse structures usually called 'medicine wheels', John H. Brumley has offered the following definition:

> All medicine wheels consist of a combination of at least two of the following three primary components: (a) a prominent centrally located stone cairn of varying size; (b) one or more concentric stone rings of generally, circular shape; and/or (c) two or more stone lines radiating outward from a central origin point, central cairn or the margins of a stone ring. (Brumley 1988: 3)[1]

Medicine wheels are often situated on knolls overlooking the prairie, and are mostly found in Alberta and Saskatchewan (both in Canada), and less frequently in Montana and northern Wyoming. The majority are probably accretional, having achieved their present shapes through additions over a long period of time. Although some medicine wheels are of very recent origin – at least one is from this century – others are of great age; the original installation of the Majorville wheel in southern Alberta, for example, seems to date back 5,000 years.

There is great diversity of form among the 67 structures examined by Brumley. Although generally not discussed in these terms, medicine wheels often have considerable aesthetic interest. Some of them are shaped like turtles, many resemble nerve-cells, and some seem fashioned on the model of sea-urchins. Much as in non-figurative painting, values such as rhythm in the patterns and spatial relations among the various elements contribute to their aesthetic effect.

Considerable effort has been exerted to determine the meaning and function of these structures. In some cases it has been possible to learn of the meaning they hold for the First Nations people of the area. We know, for example, that the medicine wheel of Steel (his full name was Ski-matsis: that is, Fire Steel), a great Blood warrior, was built on the Blood Indian Reserve in southern Alberta as a memorial in 1940 (Dempsey 1956). Moreover, reports from native consultants indicate that the Bighorn Wheel may have been used for vision quests (Wilson 1981: 337–8). None the less, the great age of many of these structures, and the fact that there is considerable uncertainty about the identity of the inhabitants of North American prairies at various points in historic and prehistoric times (Forbis 1963), leaves the determination of the original meaning and function of the structures quite unsettled.

The hypotheses posited range from the supposition that the wheels served as 'stone age calendars' to the view that they had a role in the periodic thirst dance, also called sun dance.[2] It is, of course, quite possible that, given the variety of peoples with quite diverse cultures who may have participated in the installation and use of these structures, each wheel may have had multiple functions (Wilson 1981: 336).[3]

The combined picture created by the testimony of contemporary native people about the meaning of these structures for them and by archeological research about their original functions certainly contributes to the appreciation of these installations as meaningfully inscribed, culturally structured entities; it saves us from the ethnocentric supposition that the Northern Plains were cultural wastelands, patiently awaiting their violent branding by contemporary, maximum-yield, industrial ranching and farming practices. None the less, neither native nor archeological accounts fully plumb the significance of these sites for contemporary non-native peoples in the region. Without reflection, such accounts, moreover, are absorbed much too easily by the dominant culture as entertaining but emasculated folklore. I propose that, from the point of view of non-native Canadian and US culture, these structures should be considered as art.

Plains Boulder Structures: Art

Prehistoric pictographs and petroglyphs generally are referred to as 'rock art', despite the general reluctance of archeologists to engage themselves in their interpretation.[4] For example, while urging, in a recent paper, a certain degree of caution in the interpretation of the petroglyphs and pictographs found at Writing-On-Stone in southern Alberta, Martin P. R. Magne and Michael Klassen (1991) freely and repeatedly referred to these cultural manifestations in terms of 'rock art'. Similarly, in a recent paper on southern African pictographs J. F. Thackeray (1990) frequently refers to the manifestations in question as 'rock art'. Thackeray even notes that '[t]he art has been referred to as "The San artistic achievement"', without finding it necessary to raise the question as to whether these cultural manifestations should be called 'art' (Thackeray 1990: 139).

It seems that the appropriateness of calling prehistoric cultural manifestations 'art' becomes subject to examination only when something other than pictographs and petroglyphs is under consideration. Paul S. C. Taçon (1991), for example, does consider the legitimacy of calling certain prehistoric, Australian stone tools 'art'. He notes that the reluctance to consider these items as art arises partially from the lack of 'a cross-cultural, non-biased definition of art' (Taçon 1991: 192). Without claiming to develop limiting criteria for art, he suggests, none the less, that 'many forms of stone tools produced over the past 6000 years in western Arnhem Land' (Northern Territory, Australia) be considered as art, because these tools 'have both aesthetic and symbolic value which influenced their manufacture' (ibid. 194).

The literature dealing with the definition of art is large (Davies 1991; Sparshott 1982). Prima facie the range of options among limiting criteria is great. For instance, some only admit as artworks items created with the intention of making art; others require an art-making tradition as a prerequisite for something to be a candidate artwork. Presumably, if one settled on a particular definition, one could reach a decision about whether the boulder structures called medicine wheels should be considered art. Given the ongoing debate regarding the nature of art, having to settle that question would take us too far afield from our purpose. Here I would like to side-step that debate and limit myself to the observation that, given their aesthetic qualities and their potential for symbolic interpretation, there is as much reason to consider medicine wheels 'boulder art' as there is to call pictographs and petroglyphs 'rock art'. Medicine wheels, moreover, share crucial family resemblances with certain contemporary artworks in the category 'earthworks' or 'land art', which lends further credibility to the proposal that medicine wheels be considered art.

Michael Heizer, Robert Smithson, Walter de Maria and Richard Long have made artworks that in various respects resemble medicine wheels. Heizer's Five Conic Displacements, Double Negative and Complex One, de Maria's Lightning Field, as well as Smithson's Spiral Jetty and Amarillo Ramp, are all located in remote, relatively inaccessible locations in the American south-west. Like medicine wheels, these works introduce marks into the landscape which turn the surrounding land and sky into an all-encompassing stage and mute audience. Some earthworks have more affinities with medicine wheels than others, though. As has been noted in the art-historical literature, works such as Heizer's and Smithson's are best seen as extensions of minimalism and conceptual art.

Notably, when asked about the role of landscape in his decision to move out of his New York studio into the Nevada desert, Heizer replied that he had 'no interest in landscape in terms of art . . . American landscape art is one thing, but my work doesn't have anything to do with that, it has to do with materials. I went to those places for material' (Heizer and Brown 1984: 11). Indeed, Complex One, the monumental Nevada earthwork resembling Mayan pyramids, has been fitted with a 'plaza', located in an excavated depression, intended to delete from view the surrounding mountain ranges.

Richard Long's land art, by contrast, seeks integration with the place in which it is situated. Besides considering his programmed walks as art (sometimes he walks straight lines over hills and creeks; sometimes he walks all the roads within a certain perimeter), he also builds stone circles and stone lines in remote locations. He says of these structures: 'These works are made of the place, they are a re-arrangement of it and in time will be re-absorbed by it' (Long 1986: 236). Like Heizer's works, his stone circles and stone lines depend on local materials; but unlike Heizer's works, Long's land art also achieves its standing from the character of the pre-existing place. Long does not attempt to separate his pieces from the rest of the place, as Heizer does by excavating and building obstacles to a clear view. Long builds his pieces with the help of, and into, the place. In Long's works one indeed finds strong resemblances to medicine wheels, which are also made from the materials of the place, and which seem to be carefully located so as to suit the pre-existing place.

My argument so far has been that it is reasonable to consider medicine wheels as art. Recently, however, the interpretation by non-native people of native or tribal artefacts as art has been subjected to severe critique (Clifford 1988). For example, with regard to the New York Museum of Modern Art exhibition ' "Primitivism" in Twentieth-Century Art' it has been argued that the categorization of native or tribal artefacts as art is equivalent to a co-optation of non-European cultures. The co-optation occurs through a process of decontextualization that 'transforms cultural objects into contentless forms that can be recontextualised by another culture' (Traugott 1992: 42). James Clifford points out that '[s]ince 1900 non-Western objects have generally been classified either as primitive art or ethnographic specimens' (Clifford 1988: 198). Either form of 'cultural salvage' fragments the integrity of the artefacts in question.

The problem at hand seems to be related to the problem of 'Understanding a Primitive Society' debated nearly 30 years ago by Peter Winch (1970) and Alasdair MacIntyre (1970). The issue in that debate concerned the manner in which the anthropologist is to proceed if, once she has understood something in the host culture's terms, she hopes to make it understood in her home culture's terms. If, as is likely, there are concepts in one culture that the other one fails to have, then some kind of 'salvage' operation seems inevitable. This is why it may have been tempting to understand tribal artefacts 'either as primitive art or ethnographic specimens'. The issue of interpretation (and 'salvage'), however, cannot be avoided once the existence of artefacts from other cultures has been recognized. Clifford suggests that a non-ethnocentric approach may consist in giving equal importance to the contextual meaning that such artefacts have within the host's, and the interpreter's cultural milieu.

Applied to our encounter with these boulder structures, Clifford's suggestion implies that one should pursue both the contemporary native and the original native meanings of these structures, and also their significance to contemporary non-native peoples. The native meanings may be established through consultation with First Nations people and through the assessment of the archeological records. I propose that, for a first approximation to the contemporary non-native significance of these structures, the exemplary integration in the landscape of these structures (which contrasts so notably with most of the interventions in land of contemporary industrial, exploitation-oriented users) should be taken into account.

I suggest that full recognition of these structures' integration into the land may be facilitated by our recognition of them as art. On the one hand, recognition as art should counteract the obfuscating tendency to view these structures merely as quaint 'mysteries', and, on the other hand, undermine the temptation to view them in a sterile manner as objects of merely 'empirical' scientific investigation.

Plains Boulder Structures: Heterotopias

'Of Other Spaces'

Michel Foucault is primarily known for his work on the intersections of power, knowledge and subjectivity. Very little of his work directly addresses the notion of space (but see Foucault 1980f, 1984e). When questioned on this matter, Foucault at times turned almost hostile to wards his interlocutors, although he later admitted that these issues were quite relevant to his work (Foucault 1980f).

The role of space in the distribution of power becomes a topic for Foucault mostly in the context of the panopticon, Jeremy Bentham's architectural invention which makes possible the complete surveillance of inmate populations (Foucault 1980b). Foucault resists, however, suggestions that the architectural or geographical arrangement of space may (pre)determine effects such as the oppression or liberation of individuals. At most, he concedes that spatial arrangements may be considered co-determinants of any perceived conditions; rather, he emphasizes that practices and institutions should occupy the central place in the analyses of society (Foucault 1984e). Given this situation, the text 'Of Other Spaces' stands out, since it directly focuses on space and place (Foucault 1986).

The connection between 'Of Other Spaces' and Foucault's other writings may not be apparent at first, since it is not directly concerned with the topics of power, knowledge or subjectivity. None the less, 'Of Other Spaces' obliquely contributes to Foucault's arguments for the residual potential for resistance inherent in every situation, even in the face of apparently overwhelming – explicit or tacit – structures of control. This is evident from the fact that

Foucault's initial conclusion, that 'the anxiety of our era has to do fundamentally with space', is followed by his claim that 'despite all the techniques of appropriating space, despite the whole network of knowledge to delimit or formalise it, contemporary space is perhaps still not entirely desanctified' (ibid. 23), where 'desanctification' refers to the normalization or homogenization of space.

Foucault's discussion of not-yet-desanctified space might suggest some kind of quasi-romantic allegiance to a 'formerly better time'. But such a conception is vigorously rejected by Foucault elsewhere (Foucault 1984e: 249). A reading of this text more consistent with his other texts, however, is that he conceives of these 'disturbing' differentiations of space (i.e. un-'desanctified' space) as ruptures or discontinuities that constitute counter-examples to the supposition that the fabric of power and knowledge is seamless. It is in this context that Foucault introduces and discusses the notion of heterotopia – literally 'other place'.

Heterotopias

Desanctification of space comes down to a reductive conceptualization of inherently significant places into sites merely 'defined by relations of proximity between points or elements; formally we can describe these relations as series, trees, or grids' (Foucault 1986: 23). Indeed, the notion of place is becoming largely lost in a society that actively supports the proliferation of establishments such as identical-looking fast food outlets, gas bars and malls, and that (dis-?)orients itself to a large extent by images from anywhere, which in turn are reproduced anywhere else, on ubiquitous television screens. Foucault supposes, however, that

> perhaps our life is still governed by a certain number of oppositions that remain inviolable, that our institutions and practices have not yet dared to break down. These are oppositions that we regard as simple givens: for example between private space and public space, between family space and social space, between cultural space and useful space, between the space of leisure and that of work. (Ibid.)

Moreover, in Foucault's view '[t]he space in which we live . . . is also, in itself, a heterogeneous space. . . . we live inside a set of relations that delineates sites which are irreducible to one another and absolutely not superimposable on one another' (ibid.). The heterogeneity of space may be described according to the relations between sites; hence, he suggests that one may speak of places of transportation, places of temporary relaxation, and so on.

Foucault uses the term 'heterotopia' to indicate a kind of place somewhat similar to those called 'utopias'.[5] Heterotopias and utopias share 'the curious property of being in relation with all other sites, but in such a way as to suspect, neutralise, or invert the set of relations that they happen to designate, mirror, or reflect' (ibid.). Whereas '[u]topias are sites with no real place', heterotopias 'do exist and . . . are formed in the very founding of society – [they] are something like counter-sites, a kind of effectively enacted utopia in which the real sites, all the other real sites which can be found within the culture, are simultaneously represented, contested and inverted' (ibid.).

Foucault gives a list of six 'principles', or typical features, of heterotopias. Heterotopias (1) are probably constituted by all cultures (though they exhibit varied forms); (2) over time may serve various functions within a given society; (3) are 'capable of juxtaposing in a single real place several spaces, several sites that are in themselves incompatible' (ibid. 25); (4) 'are most often linked to slices in time' – that is, to breaks in the perception of ordinary time; (5) 'presuppose a system of opening and closing that both isolates them and makes them penetrable' (ibid.); and (6) have a function, lying between two poles, with respect to all other spaces:

> Either their role is to create a space of illusion that exposes every real space, all the sites inside of which human life is partitioned, as still more illusory. . . . Or else, on the contrary, their role is to create a space that is other, another real space, as perfect, as meticulous, as well arranged as ours is messy, ill constructed, and jumbled. (Ibid. 27)

In contemporary societies the theatre, the cinema, the garden, the museum, the library and the barracks, among other things, function as heterotopias. The cinema, for example, literally creates illusions that may make us question our apprehension of supposedly real spaces. By contrast, museums and gardens create real spaces that in their 'perfect' order of things may cause dislocations in, and reconsiderations of, our perception of ordinary spaces. Furthermore, it would seem that certain artworks are also examples of heterotopias.

Cubist paintings, such as Picasso's *Demoiselles d'Avignon*, may create illusions that denounce as illusory our apprehension of real space in terms of orderly, frontally perceived single images (as Renaissance perspective had suggested). Alternatively, rigorously planned Renaissance city squares are real spaces that in their designed perfection recall and highlight the messy, ill-constructed spaces in which most of us actually live. In other words, heterotopias serve as places of disturbance; their existence unsettles the regular categorizations of our living space.

Boulder structures

Aboriginal medicine wheel boulder structures may be seen as heterotopias – that is, as counter-sites – because, although they are located in the 'productive' spaces of industrial agriculture of the prairies, they 'suspect' and interrogate those spaces and the concomitant, violently interventionist practices. These boulder structures juxtapose incompatible sites by bringing together a perspective on land of its original inhabitants and a perspective on land of its present exploitation-oriented users. In so far as the origin of these sites points to times receding indefinitely far into the past, reflection on them constitutes a slice or break in the ordinary perception of time. In so far as they remain recalcitrant to interpretation, they make evident that 'opening' knowledge may be required for their comprehension; in fact, their cryptic nature makes them places 'outside of all places' (ibid. 24).

In their resistance to interpretation, these boulder structures return our gaze to the prairies, turned into denatured, overgrazed cattle pastures, and to the once verdant river valleys, turned into flooded, mega-project water reservoirs. In so far as medicine wheels are structures built not against the land, as are most of our contemporary users' interventions in the prairie landscape, but with and into the land, they constitute 'a kind of effectively enacted utopia'.

Notes

1 But see Nikiforuk 1992: 54, which quotes Michael Wilson as saying that Brumley's definition 'leaves out a whole variety of closely related stone spokes, circles and simple cairns'.

2 It is to be noted that deconstructionist theory has thrown into question the very idea that the intentionality of the builders and users of prehistoric sites is something stable that can be found or reconstructed: see e.g. Davis 1992. See also Wilson (1981: 336), who notes that 'we cannot dig up ideas'. We may assume, however, that we are on relatively safe ground as long as we seek only functions of items, not intentions of individuals.

3 See also Bednarik (1991–2: 14), who argues that 'the older rock arts were . . . integrated into [newer] belief systems, [and] reinterpreted'.

4 But see e.g. Tilley (1991), who is willing to interpret them. Regarding the willingness to speak of 'Ancient Amerindian Art', and to call 'artists' those who fashioned paintings, sculptures, etc. in the early Americas, see e.g. Kubler 1991.

5 Recently the term 'heterotopia' has been popularized by Vattimo (1992). He uses it in a different sense, however. Vattimo traces what he sees as a transition from the idea of utopia to the idea of heterotopia as the movement from monolithic to pluralistic conceptions of the good life and the good society.

8

Nature Writing as Self-Technology

Sylvia Bowerbank

> In caring for the earth and its creatures we must also learn to care
> for ourselves, because taming nature with respect and love means
> taming ourselves as well.
>
> – Cronon (1993)

Since Nietzsche, no one has done more than Michel Foucault to
unmask the modern soul. In his *Genealogy of Morals*, Nietzsche
asks: 'Would anyone care to learn something about the way in
which ideals are manufactured? Does anyone have the nerve?'
(1956: 180). In the same spirit of relentless critique, Foucault's
later writings take up the task of writing a genealogy of ethics. He
interrogates the past, not in order to rehearse once more a history
of beliefs, but to reconstruct a history of real practices. In the
process, he develops a theoretical framework for understanding
the production of the subject as an effect of 'practical rationality
governed by a conscious goal' (Foucault 1984e: 255; Cook 1993).
He analyses technologies of the self and their interactions with the
other technologies of practical reason: technologies of production,
of sign systems and of power. 'Technologies of the self', as Foucault
defines them, 'permit individuals to effect by their own means or
with the help of others a certain number of operations on their
own bodies and souls, thoughts, conduct, and way of being, so
as to transform themselves in order to attain a certain state of
happiness, purity, wisdom, perfection, or immortality' (1988c: 18).
Across the historical board, cultivation of the self is a painstaking
labour of self-vigilance, assessment, correction and transformation. In 'On the Genealogy of Ethics', Foucault points out that
technologies of the self have been deliberately elaborated for at

least 2,000 years, though not necessarily in exactly the same way. The history of the cultivation of the self, therefore, provides a 'general and very rich framework' for interpreting all auto-biographical texts, all the 'so-called literature of the self' (1984d: 369). Taking this cue from Foucault, in this essay I analyse recent nature writings in order to understand the practices used to define and to change the self in light of ecological principles. Given the subtle, often hidden linkages between self and social technologies, a critique, based on the historical constitution of the subject, needs to be brought to bear on new self-technologies advanced in the name of ecological responsibility and well-being. Of particular interest here is the nature journal, the notebook deployed to construct and to narrativize green subjectivity.

During the past decade, an increased proliferation of nature writings has marked the emergence of an important cultural phenomenon, at least in North America. According to John A. Murray, editor of *New Nature's Voices*, several thousand titles of nature writings are listed in *Books in Print*, and even more are being published (1992: xxiv).[1] At the same time, both the reading and writing of nature are increasingly taught in the classroom as ecological practices.[2] Mitchell Thomashow, like many other educators, recommends keeping 'an ecological identity journal' as a way of nourishing oneself as an active environmentalist (1995: 15). Countless people are keeping private nature journals, describing and puzzling out the meaning of their wild encounters with desert and tundra, with wolverine and bear.[3] Certainly, it seems, writing about such wilderness experiences is becoming almost as meaningful as having them.

What, then, is to be understood by all this recent activity of nature writing? Why do so many summer canoeists bear their water-logged journals down Canada's French River? What kind of subject production do these practices suggest? And, more generally, how are personal nature writings linked to public discourses of environmental knowledge and policy making? By convention, according to Finch and Elder, nature writing as a literary form is characterized by a 'filtering' of the experience of nature 'through an individual sensibility' (1990: 26). It requires that the writer not only reproduce direct knowledge of a specific environment, but also exhibit a personal acquisition of natural wisdom. As Barry Lopez writes in *Arctic Dreams*: 'The land urges us to come around to an understanding of ourselves' (1986: 247). As this essay argues, contemporary nature writing, at its most innovative, is now taking on a more politicized, urgent edge. It is being used strategically to inscribe new self-technologies for establishing, monitoring and sustaining an individual's ecological commitments and habits. Thus, the study of these ecological testimonies and their public effects may prove very instructive indeed. Given that the key words used in these writings – 'subject', 'nature' and 'ecology' – are all notoriously difficult, contested terms, certain questions need to be kept in mind. What construction of 'nature' is being inscribed? What notion of 'ecology' is being assumed or advocated? What 'subject' is inscribing and speaking for nature and ecology?

Foucault's historical writings uncover the often obscure linkages between technologies of the self and technologies of domination, for example, in Western systems of punishment, psychology and sexuality. In light of Foucault's critique of earlier constitutions of the self, as John Rajchman points out, 'the job of thought' is to undertake 'an unceasing questioning of historical bestowals of identity' (1992: 222). The bestowal of green identity is no exception. In 'The Greening of the Self', Joanna Macy claims that a great historical shift is now taking place: the modern construct of the subject – 'the prison-self of separate ego' – is being cast off and a new green subject is awakening to its true affiliation with the earth:

> The conventional notion of the self ... is being undermined ... is being unhinged, peeled off. It is being replaced by wider constructs of identity and self-interest – by what you might call the ecological self or the eco-self, coextensive with other beings and the life of our planet. It is what I will call 'the greening of the self'. (Macy 1991: 184)

In Macy's description, the process of greening occurs as a somewhat mysterious, almost spontaneous development in which the self-directed modern subject is being replaced by a receptive subject caught up in a moment of change: 'Oh, the sweetness of being able to realise: I am my experience. I am this breathing. I am this moment, and it is changing, continually arising in the fountain of life' (ibid. 190). Macy's understanding of the greening of the self is based on a sharp demarcation between a modern self (as a construct, a metaphor and a falsehood) and a green self which is unproblematically a true and natural self. Macy is certainly not alone in this way of thinking: As Max Oelschlaeger writes, 'The modern concept of the subject – Man-who-would-manage-the-planet' is often seen as a mere artifice, a veneer, a contingency, 'a cultural accretion that overlays a wild nature, a first nature' (1994: 134). In the greening process, claims Joanna Macy, 'you become more yourself' (1991: 189).

To consider the greening of the self in light of Foucault's body of writings is to understand the process as a complex, deliberate and perhaps ironic historical labour. In his essay 'Practising Criticism', Foucault argues that deep transformations must take place in a 'free atmosphere' of critique. Thus, far from denying the potential for liberating change, Foucault's method of making 'facile gestures difficult' makes real change possible (1988f: 155). Joanna Macy's description of the greening of the self not only assumes a rhapsodic recovery of a true self, but also obscures the connections between the modern and the would-be green subject. Yet, it is that very modern subject that invents and undertakes appropriate self-technologies for the greening process. 'To be modern', writes Foucault, 'is to take oneself as a complex and difficult elaboration' (1984h: 41). It is Macy who chooses to adapt Buddhist practice and systems theory to her own project of the greening of the self. As Chaloupka and Cawley argue, the subject undertaking self-transformation in the name of nature is the same self-improving, driven and resourceful modern subject we know so well: 'Carrying our communicating, disciplined selves out to a wilderness escape, we find functions and roles, even there. We find assignments, too; we are there to relax, to recuperate, to report back that nature still exists, that it still teaches lessons' (Chaloupka and Cawley 1993: 15).

In Foucault's work, the subject is defined historically and is disciplined by its own self-constituting practices. This way of constructing subjectivity reconceptualizes the production, in this case, of a green subject into a historical development of appropriate self-technologies. In 'An Aesthetics of Existence', Foucault makes this telling comment: 'I believe . . . that the subject is constituted through practices of subjection, or in a more autonomous way, through practices of liberation, of liberty, as in Antiquity on the basis, of course, of a number of rules, styles, inventions to be found in the cultural environment' (1988a: 51–2). Thus, by making the constitution of the subject a matter of deploying appropriate self-technologies, Foucault's writings open up the possibility of what John Rajchman calls 'a practical freedom'. It is a freedom 'not of action, nor of intentions or desires, but of a choice of a mode of being' (1992: 219).

In general, as I argue elsewhere, the term 'greening' refers to the voluntary process of transforming the fundamental political and social systems, as well as the personal habits and sensibilities, of the peoples of industrialized societies in light of emerging ecological knowledges (Bowerbank 1995: 443). Greening is 'a voluntary process', because its practitioners deliberately seek appropriate technologies – whether material, symbolic, social or self-technologies – in order to effect fundamental change. As Raymond Williams points out in *Keywords*, the common usage of the word *ecology* now extends well beyond its strict scientific meaning (i.e. 'the study of the relations of plants and animals with each other and with their habitat') to include 'a central concern with human relations to the physical world as the *necessary basis for social and economic policy*' (Williams 1976: 111, my emphasis). The use of the term *greening* pushes this 'concern' a step further by deliberately conceptualizing *ecology* as an ongoing labour. Thus, greening moves ecology into the realm of practical reason; ideals can be transformed into activities. Accordingly, Mitchell Thomashow, for example, constructs the self-transformative process as 'ecological identity *work*': 'Ecological identity work yields a rich substrate . . . which allows people to bring their perceptions of nature to the foreground of awareness and to orient their actions based on their ecological world view' (Thomashow 1995: 23).

Here I will examine some of the practices that constitute green subjectivity. I do so in light of the question raised so chillingly by Foucault's writings: do disciplinary practices have the potential for a positive, as well as a self-sacrificing, effect on the subject?

Mitchell Thomashow's *Ecological Identity: Becoming a Reflexive Environmentalist* (1995) is a good place to begin, because it explicitly names and normalizes many of the self-technologies articulated in nature writings. Thomashow and his students do not just sit in the classroom reading the writings of Henry Thoreau, John Muir or Rachel Carson; they carry out 'ecological identity work' on themselves by means of such activities as natural history excursions, disturbed-place recollections, catalogues of personal property, sense-of-place maps and ecological identity journals. Written in a generous, inventive spirit, *Ecological Identity* is, in many ways, an admirable book, but it demonstrates little concern that the practices it recommends have long histories as disciplinary practices. To illustrate the need for critique, as well as invention, I shall analyse one of the activities devised by Thomashow to aid himself and his students (and now his readers) in their ecological identity work. The particular activity I want to focus on is one Thomashow calls the 'eco-confessional', in which the practitioner tells a personal story of ecological irresponsibility (1995: 153). Obviously, the relevance of Foucault's historical work on the confession is immediately suggested. The confession was, and remains, as Foucault shows, 'one of the West's most highly valued techniques for producing truth' (Foucault 1976: 59).

In a lengthy section of *Ecological Identity*, Thomashow confesses to an ecological crime: some years ago, while on vacation on a remote island off the Maine coast, he threw two large garbage bags, filled with disposable nappies, into the 'pristine waters' of the Gulf of Maine (1995: 152–60). There were extenuating circumstances: the house his family had rented was rustic, and therefore without electricity and hot water; washing had to be done by hand, making it difficult to use cloth nappies for his infant daughter. Thomashow knew that if they were going to use 'disposables', they should carry them back to the mainland when they left the island. There was no garbage pick-up or recycling on the island. Even so, knowing that other people made a habit of throwing their garbage into the ocean, in the end, against his better judgement, he chose what seemed the 'easy and lazy method' of disposal:

> I was hoping for a windy day, so the bag would quickly float out to sea and then become submerged so it couldn't be seen. But the ocean was unusually calm the day of our departure. . . . Several minutes later, seagulls pecked open the bags, scavenging my daughter's fecal matter. Before long, dozens of diapers were floating across this beautiful harbour, forming a white path of plastic waste. They were like white buoys on the water, meandering in the calm harbour, slowly spreading out, marking a trail of neglect. (Ibid. 153)

What is remarkable about Thomashow's reconstruction of this incident is that his motivations and actions are interrogated and elaborated in scrupulous detail. Tremendous labour is put into confessing. His sense of culpability is intensified precisely because of his high degree of ecological literacy, and because of his affection for the island's familiar, spectacular landscape. His annual visits, he writes, are 'intrinsic to my ecological identity' (ibid.). His rationale for confessing is both therapeutic and pedagogical. On the one hand, he gives evidence against himself in order to raise the issue of personal blame for ecological deterioration. At the same time, he invites his students to write their own eco-confessional narratives in order to personalize the environmental crisis. The effect of their confessions, he says, is that they suddenly realize that 'it is their culture, legacy, habits, and lifestyle that is at fault. This mess is their responsibility too' (ibid. 157). *Mea culpa.*

Thomashow does show some twinges of uneasiness regarding possible negative effects of the confessional mode; however, he claims that if his students are mature and don't take themselves too seriously, the activity will lead not to depression and guilt, but to compassion and action. After all, he writes, '[t]he purpose is not flagellation, but insight' (ibid. 153). If the intention is good, it seems, the practice itself need not be scrutinized. Yet, the confession is well entrenched in Western culture as a disciplinary mode of self-reformation. It has a history, as they say. In Thomashow's narrative of scrupulous self-examination, the disciplinary pattern of the confession is instantly recognizable, especially by those of us raised as Catholics or familiar with Foucault's work. While it is true that nowadays the confession as a ritualized discourse has lost most of its formality and localization, it continues to be reproduced in all sorts of modern settings in which we voluntarily keep detailed dossiers on ourselves. 'The obligation to confess is now relayed through so many different points, is so deeply ingrained in us,' writes Foucault, 'that we no longer perceive it as the effect of a power that constrains us' (1976: 60). Throughout his eco-confessional narrative, Thomashow structures his experience as both a private and a public event. In the original incident of the nappy dumping, Thomashow tried to hide his dirty deed. At the same time, he knew that community complicity would allow him to get away with the dumping of *anonymous* bags in the ocean. Once the nappies were floating in the harbour (as everyone knew, no one else had an infant on the island), the game was up. Nature had retaliated, in the guise of the sea-gulls, exposing the evidence and making Thomashow into a public spectacle. He was forced to own up. Most important, as he presents it, confessing does him good – no doubt as it has done many others in the past. Foucault's words surely would not be misplaced here: in a confession, 'the expression alone, independently of its external consequences, produces intrinsic modifications in the person who articulates it: it exonerates, redeems, and purifies him; it unburdens him of his wrongs, liberates him, and promises him salvation' (Foucault 1976: 62).

Both in the classroom and in his book, Thomashow teaches eco-confession unproblematically as a beneficial social practice. Surprisingly, for such an experienced teacher, Thomashow does not seem to worry about the power dynamics of a classroom in which students are asked to confess their ecological sins. In his narrative re-enactment of the original deed, Thomashow not only reinscribes the details of his sloth, shame and hypocrisy, but also ritualizes his self-interrogating process as an ecological practice with the potential to transform guilt into individual healing and social action. Thomashow's eco-confessional reproduces a structure of feeling that is already well established in ecological consciousness. An old Pogo cartoon put it quite simply: 'We have caught sight of the enemy and they is us.' Thomashow claims that the eco-confessional can be the first step toward the production of better alternatives (1995: 158). Maybe so. The greening of the self does entail the self-imposition of ecologically sound habits and attitudes, but how does the eco-confession contribute effectively to that end? It is questionable whether a guilty conscience necessarily leads to reformed habits. Ladell McWhorter argues that guilt itself is a form of power which protects the guilty: 'Guilt is one of the modern managerial self's manoeuvres of self-defence. . . . Guilt is a standard defence against the call for change as it takes root within us' (McWhorter 1992: 7–8). Before confessing our ecological sins, then, we need to understand the nature and history of the self-technology we employ. As Foucault writes with considerable scorn:

> One has to be completely taken in by this internal ruse of confession . . . to believe that all these voices which have spoken so long in our civilisation – repeating the formidable injunction to tell what one is and what one does, what one recollects and what one has forgotten, what one is thinking and what one thinks he is not thinking – are speaking to us of freedom. An immense labor to which the West has submitted generations in order to produce . . . men's subjection, their constitution as subjects in both senses of the word. (Foucault 1976: 60)

The efficacy and desirability of the eco-confession, as well as other techniques of the production of 'ecological identity', cannot be taken for granted. Mindful of the generations of people who have undertaken to improve human nature using similar techniques and have not, so far, achieved desirable results, we need to be cautious about our self-constituting practices. At the very least, the question needs to be raised: after centuries of association with technologies of dominance, can technologies of the self from the past – such as confession – be rehabilitated in a different era to achieve eco-logical well-being?

I now consider two interconnected practices used in the constitution of the green subject: the wilderness retreat and the nature journal, in its various private and published forms. Both these self-technologies have long histories as disciplinary practices which must be taken into account by the green practitioner. Politicized by urgent environmental concerns, the nature journal in the 1990s is clearly an advantageous site for taking up the task of cultivating a new green subjectivity. The keeping of a journal on oneself has been used since ancient times as an exercise by which, as Foucault writes, the self trains the self (Foucault 1984d: 364). Like other journals, the nature journal is an exercise book for self-transformation: one takes stock, monitors, observes, regulates, reformulates and reorients the self. The very act of keeping a journal 'effects subtle changes in the keeper' (Hinchman 1991: 138). The journal also provides a storehouse for the raw materials to be used in one's self-fashioning projects: one jots down agreeable or provocative quotations, accumulates memories of encounters with wild animals and birds, examines one's feelings and behaviour, and translates one's desires into activities. Whether intended for publication or not, nature writings record the author's struggles and accomplishments in harmonious self-composure. Thus, when Alan Drengson recently reflected on his 45 years of working to attune himself to his sacred place, the Olympic Peninsula, he took stock of his progress: 'Am I still an exotic being naturalised or have I become an indigenous dweller on the land?' (1994: 83).

In order to negotiate and to narrativize green identity, contemporary nature writing uses a distinctive narrative mode, which I would characterize as 'eco-pastoral'. 'Pastoral' is used here in the specialized sense of a book written to cure the soul, as in St Gregory's *Cura Pastoralis*. As Foucault writes, the pastoral mode constructs its preferred way of living 'under the theme of the care of oneself' (1984a: 45). The prefix *eco*, as Raymond Williams points out, clarifies, the fact that the discourse (*logos*) of 'ecology' is rooted in habitat (*eco*) (1976: 110–11). In eco-pastoral texts, the care of the self is reconfigured to make care of place essential to its meaning. The abstract principle of caring for the earth is localized and distributed among manageable projects undertaken in specific, personally meaningful places. However private, nature writings are much more than sites of pure subjectivity. Although nature writers may write alone, for personal benefit, the habit of good government over their affections is calculated to manifest itself in the public performance of ecologically sound behaviour. Thus, eco-pastoral writings are not just expressions of solitary or free feelings; they struggle towards a collective change in values and behaviour. In Foucault's terms, they constitute 'a true social practice' (1984a: 51). Understood as a collective phenomenon, eco-pastoral writings create a new cultural repertoire of appropriate emotions and habits, articulated in light of the ecological knowledge that is only now being constructed at the material and social levels. Good relations with nature are translated into a myriad of appropriate feelings and activities, subtly connected to the creation, maintenance and justification of the practitioner's superior ecological consciousness and stewardship.

The most common practice of self-care narrated in nature writings is the account of a wilderness retreat. Considered the foremost 'practice of the wild', to use Gary Snyder's (1990) apt phrase, wandering in the wilderness is a self-technology used to inculcate in oneself elective connectivity to non-human nature. The retreat from the world (into the desert, the forest or the country) is, of course, a well-established self-technology in Western history and, as such, it carries considerable cultural baggage, both good and bad. How could it be otherwise? In general, the wilderness retreat is a form of self-training undertaken, in various past cultures, to liberate oneself from the luxuries and corruptions of society. In *The Care of Self*, the third volume of *The History of Sexuality*, Foucault analyses the retreat as one of the techniques of self-governance undertaken by certain cultivated men – such as Marcus Aurelius, Epictetus and Seneca – of the first two centuries of the Roman Empire, a period which Foucault calls 'a kind of golden age in the cultivation of the self' (1984a: 45). It was a time when these few men – 'bearers of culture', as Foucault calls them – converted their Stoical philosophical preoccupations into 'a whole set of occupations', into the *labour* of the care of the self. The retreat, in particular, was an austere practice whereby the practitioner submitted to a state of 'fancied poverty' (to use Seneca's phrase); the practice included sleeping on straw, abstaining from food and drink, or eating only poor quality of food, in order to achieve superior detachment from the desires and vicissitudes of the world (ibid. 60).

The wilderness retreat, in the late twentieth century, has certain resemblances to earlier modes of austere retreat, as well as important differences. A wilderness retreat is often undertaken as a strategic withdrawal from distracting luxuries in order to cultivate a more 'natural' and necessary way of being. In fact, the quality and authenticity of the experience are measured by its degree of detachment from modern conveniences – that is, by its degree of voluntary hardship. The wilderness sojourner elects to live (temporarily) under a self-imposed regimen of constraints, privations, prohibitions and prescriptions. Even as the spirit soars in the presence of the wilderness, the body is made to carry all its necessities on its back, to sleep on the ground, to eat hard tack, muesli and glop, and to suffer the assaults of mosquitoes, black flies and tent-destroying bears, as well as the indignities of rash, diarrhoea, blisters and dampness to the bone. I intend no parody or exaggeration here, but merely describe my own practice. Well might a cynic say, with Foucault: indeed 'the soul is the prison of the body' (Foucault 1975: 30). Yet, as one wanders, the joys of the wild are manifold: the body falls into a new rhythm; the subject is at large; change is afoot. And why should one rejoicing in wild and free wanderings abandon a rhapsodic mode for a sobering self-critical mode?

The nature journal as a self-technology deliberately cultivates a certain structure of feeling, a reciprocity between the narrating subject and wild nature. Based on his study of Thoreau's practice, Scott Slovic shows that a nature journal is kept in order to line up one's 'internal rhythms with those of external nature', and to maximize those moments when the processes of the mind 'coincide intermittently with those of the natural world' (Slovic 1992: 6, 22). Nature writing is a distinctive form of testimony in which the subject bears witness to mutuality between the subject and self-willing nature. An intense moment of ecstatic mutuality with wild otherness is structured as an epiphany, as a rhetorical and spiritual high point in the text. It is a convention that is easy to poke fun at. In 'A Light Green Baroque', D. L. Rawlings critiques the artifice and the hypocrisy of the practice:

> The structural epiphany involves a kind of luminous hindsight: Sitting at the desk with PowerBook, herb tea, and a stack of index cards, one suddenly realises that upon reaching that farthest, highest peak, instead of eating a sandwich one in fact saw God. Bad writers botch this, but the good ones always get away with it, mostly because (as in hardcore porn) we want them to. (Rawlings 1996: 12)

But, as Rawlings admits, poststructuralist nature writers, such as himself, have not yet found appropriate rhetorical structures for the profound feeling of coextension with wild nature; they merely plug in, what Rawlings calls, a 'negative epiphany':

> Having reached the peak, we're guardedly ecstatic about not seeing God. . . . The negative epiphany demonstrates one's, *uhhh* . . . difficult, irresolute, yet also wildly, apperceptive grace, vis-à-vis the inescapable, meta-obdurate *lithicity* of . . . *ummm*: our sub/pre/post (or perhaps, in the broadest terms) *anti*-linguistic earth. (Ibid.)

Nature writing has a sense of itself as 'nature's genre', to use Lawrence Buell's phrase (1995: 397). Often, the concept of 'nature' that is inscribed is supposedly outside culture. Accordingly, the practice of the wild is constituted as a *via negativa*, a casting off of all things modern in order to enable one to become a true subject of nature's will. Terry Tempest Williams begins her story 'The Bowl' with a classic opening to a wilderness retreat: in order to save her soul, the individual flees decisively and absolutely from the city of destruction:

> There was a woman who left the city, left her husband, and her children, left everything behind to retrieve her soul. She came to the desert after seeing her gaunt face in the mirror, the pallor that comes when everything is going out and nothing is coming in. She had noticed for the first time the furrows under her eyes that had been eroded by tears. She did not know the woman in the mirror. She took off her apron, folded it neatly in the drawer, left a note for her family, and closed the door behind her. (Williams 1992a: 218)

In such narratives of the wild self, all civilized structures are, rhetorically speaking, cast off. Material technologies are cast off: if you want to get in touch with the 'beguiling nooks and crannies' of the earth, writes Wendell Berry, 'you will have to get out of your space vehicle, out of your car, off your horse, and walk over the ground' (1995: 698). House and home are cast off. To live suitably, Sue Hubbell writes: 'I slept outdoors . . . because I could not bear to go in. I wonder if I am becoming feral' (1986: 194–5). Ultimately, all cultural accretions must go. In *Arctic Dreams*, Barry Lopez's practice of wild reciprocity – at its narrative height on the tip of Saint Lawrence Island on the Bering Sea – leads him to abandon even the English language. Not knowing the local Eskimo language, as he says, he improvises an indigenous language, starting from scratch, by resorting to the elemental gestures of breathing and bowing:

> I took to bowing on these evening walks. I would bow slightly with my hands in my pockets, towards the birds and the evidence of life in their nests – because of their fecundity, unexpected in this remote region, and because of the serene arctic light that came down over the land like breath, like breathing. . . . I bowed. (Lopez 1986: xx)

> I bowed to what knows *no* deliberating legislature or parliament, *no* religion, *no* competing theories of economics, and expression of allegiance with the mystery of life. (Lopez ibid. 414; my emphasis)

With the same double gesture of negating and bowing, Lopez sheds the modern managerial self: 'I held the bow until my back ached, and my mind was emptied of its categories and designs, its plans and speculations' (ibid. 414). Even such an environmentally committed and well-crafted book as Lopez's *Arctic Dreams* not only avoids critique of its own practice, but excludes problematic details that would inevitably provoke such a critique. In an astute review of *Arctic Dreams*, Edward Hoagland criticizes Lopez for two important gaps in his text. First, Lopez leaves out what 'he must have seen' of the malaise and suffering of the people of the Arctic, the 'stress-chewed, haunted-looking, self-dramatising white men and furious, sometimes suicidal or homicidal Eskimos' that inhabit the stark landscape. Second, Lopez is silent regarding the compromising material and social realities that support his own successful practice as an environmental writer:

> Mr. Lopez appears to have travelled extravagantly . . . [but] he seldom specifies how much or with whose help. The Arctic is ferociously expensive and difficult to travel in, and even if a freelance writer were able to hire an airplane to go beyond where the mail planes reach, many landing sites are controlled by oil and mining companies or government agencies, so that he is likely to find himself wheedling rides above the Arctic Circle with oilmen or research scientists after having been vetted wittily for his political opinions beforehand by clever public-relations officials. (Hoagland 1986: 3)

These strategic omissions are typical of the way in which the conventional structures of nature writing disguise the narrating subject's dependencies and connections to modern society. 'The trouble with wilderness', as William Cronon writes in his superb essay of that title, is that it lets us pretend that we are not subjects of modern culture: 'we benefit from the intricate and all too invisible networks with which it shelters us, all the while pretending that these things are not an essential part of who we are' (1995: 81).

To frame the wilderness retreat within the history of the constitution of the subject no doubt goes against the grain of many of its privileged practitioners, myself included. One desires to know oneself as something other that a subject of technique. The wilderness is, accordingly, often constructed as a place free from man's schemes for mastery, a place where nature is following its own will. In fact, in its etymological roots, the word 'wilderness' refers to self-willing land (Vest 1985). In narrative accounts of the practice of the wild, the wilderness is briefly made to speak its will or, at least, to have its way with the narrating subject. This is how Terry Tempest Williams describes her solitary wanderings on the salt lands north of Great Salt Lake:

> I am never entirely at ease because I am aware of its will. Its mood can change in minutes. The heat alone reflecting off the salt is enough to drive me mad, but it is the glare that immobilises me. Without sunglasses, I am blinded. My eyes quickly burn on Salt Well Flats. It occurs to me that I will return home with my green irises bleached white. If I return at all. (Williams 1992b: 148)

The wilderness is also constituted as an open space where the subject is released into an alternative economy of freedom; the subject can, therefore, exercise and expand its self into what is referred to variously as 'the ecological self', or 'the transpersonal self' (Drengson 1994; Fox 1990). In response to 'the spontaneous power of nature', it is supposed that the subject can change, not through its own manipulations, but 'through the reciprocal communal activities of myriad beings within the physical realities of the place' (Drengson 1994: 76). As William Cronon writes, 'Wilderness is the place where, symbolically at least, we try to withhold our power to dominate' (1995: 87).

In 'Wings of the Eagle', Marie Wilson of the Gitksan-Wet'suwet'en tribe of British Columbia makes a startling comment about the practice of wilderness retreat: 'The environmentalists want these beautiful places kept in a state of perfection: to not touch it, rather to keep it pure. So that we can leave our jobs and for two weeks we can venture in wilderness and enjoy this ship in a bottle' (Wilson 1989: 217). This comment reveals the sharp difference between what wilderness trippers imagine they are doing (following indigenous ways of living on the land, however briefly) and their *actual practice* – dropping by for two weeks (or two months) to enjoy 'this ship in a bottle'. Those two weeks in the wilderness may be more precious to us than the other fifty; however, given our daily practices, do they constitute who we really are as subjects? As Marie Wilson says, 'I have had the awful feeling that when we are finished dealing with the courts and our land claims, we will then have to battle the environmentalists and they will not understand why' (ibid.). Right from the beginning of Euro-American settlement, the seemingly oppositional practices of the wild – expansionary conquest and reverential sojourns – have coexisted in a strange symbiosis. The wilderness retreat, at least as it has been practised, is a luxury product of the very culture the practitioner learns to despise.

To say this is not to suggest that we abandon the wilderness retreat or the nature journal as green practices. It is to acknowledge how arduous and inconclusive even our best efforts at greening are. Why should this discourage us? Quick fixes and big transformations – in the name of an 'ecological world order' – are no doubt dangerous and undesirable (Ferry 1995). What Foucault writes of recent little improvements in the quality of Western culture applies equally well to environmental matters: 'I prefer even these partial transformations that have been made in the correlation of historical analysis and the practical attitude, to the programs for a new man that the worst political systems have repeated throughout the twentieth century' (1984b: 46–7).

In Foucault's terms, deep transformations of the self, as of material and social reality, can take place only in a free atmosphere of criticism. Transformation and critique, far from being contrary modes, work together toward slow, authentic change. As Foucault argues, a 'permanent reactivation' of critique is, at present, our only procedure for determining 'what is not or is no longer indispensable for the constitution of ourselves as autonomous subjects' (ibid. 42–3). Seen in the light of Foucault's work, the self-cultivation of the green subject is a long, difficult historical endeavour with an uncertain result. The greening of the subject becomes a case of 'working on our limits'; it is 'a patient labor giving form to our impatience for liberty' (ibid. 50). To understand the positive implications of Foucault's writings is to be encouraged by these ironic words.

Notes

1 Other anthologies of nature writing published in the 1990s include Anderson 1991; Burks 1994; Finch and Elder 1990; Willers 1991.

2 Since the publication of Waage 1985, there has been tremendous expansion in this field; two very recent anthologies intended for classroom use are Anderson and Runciman 1995 and Ross 1995. See also Glotfelty 1993.

3 Hannah Hinchman's popular *A Life in Hand: Creating the Illuminated Journal* (1991) packages two texts together: the first is Hinchman's own nature journal, the second a blank book, inviting readers to go forth and create their own nature journals.

Part III
Resistances

9

Nature as Dangerous Space

Peter Quigley

We hold these truths to be self-evident.

– *Nature's Nation*

You rapturously pose as deriving your law from nature, you want something quite the reverse of that, you strange actors and self-deceivers.

– Nietzsche

Custom is a second nature, which destroys the first one. But what is nature? Why is custom not natural? I greatly fear that nature may in itself be but a first custom, as custom is a second nature.

– Pascal

I took a walk through the woods today, cherishing the pinion, juniper and ponderosa of the high chaparral, angered at the systemic attack being levelled against this community that nurtures us and exudes health and energy. I also began to reflect upon the fact that the academic environmental community has, of late, been struggling with the challenges posed by poststructural thinking. As much as I would like to once again embrace a unified sense of 'nature', that sacred fount of wisdom, joy and life, a 1960s sense of purpose and alternative life-style, a rallying point of righteous opposition to power, I can in no way deny the problematic state that such concepts have fallen prey to, and the degree to which it seems increasingly impossible 'to go home' to such ideas. Terry Eagleton once suggested that these jaded perturbations are the result of the collapse of the radical movement of the 1960s, of a bitter turn inward after Paris 1968. Others, writing in a less politically committed American scene, see the wallowing in ambiguity as the product of jaded boomers, middle age, First World affluent cynics and global capitalism. My position is that there is more vigour and less retreat in poststructural theory than those nostalgic for unquestioned assumptions and causes credit it with. Its essential insight regarding nature, and the point of departure for this chapter, is summarized by Eagleton:

> Ideology seeks to convert culture into nature, and the 'natural' sign is one of its weapons. Saluting a flag, or agreeing that Western democracy represents the true meaning of the word 'freedom', become the most obvious, spontaneous responses in the world. Ideology, in this sense, is a kind of contemporary mythology, a realm which has purged itself of ambiguity and alternative possibility. (Eagleton 1983: 135)

The Sophists bear witness to the fact that undermining sacred, transparent, foundational common sense has a long and noble tradition. All kinds of mannerists, impressionists, surrealists, Gongorists and anarchists are vindicated under the sign of the postmodern and the poststructural. These movements are always reminding us of perspective – critical perspective – where classical techniques tend towards the transparently seductive. And what concept is more ripe and appropriate for such questioning than 'the natural'? More recently in the field of language and social science, this tradition of problematizing perspective has been extended by, among others, Nietzsche, Barthes, Derrida and Foucault. As much as I wish it were otherwise, the fact is that after poststructuralism, it is impossible to take a term like nature at face value; it is impossible not to see the fissures of contradiction and the fault-lines of history that criss-cross the term. In short, it is impossible not to see human bias and self-reflexive anthropocentrism in the term. As Chaloupka and Cawley have recently stated, 'nature, like everything else we talk about, is first and foremost an artifact of language . . . It can be anything but direct and literal' (Chaloupka and Cawley 1993: 5). The academic environmental community in the USA has done a poor job of responding to the challenge of poststructuralism. In articles, books and conferences, the eco-lit community, in the USA at least, continues to side-step (in fact takes on reactionary postures) the power of the essential questions posed by poststructural thinking.

In this chapter I plan to show how a vital and politically vigorous poststructural nature is possible – is, in fact, crucial – for the politics of environmentalism, if not also for the intellectual culture of the USA. I also plan to discuss the various ways in which the eco-lit critical community is refusing to theorize from the poststructural perspective, as well as how this same community is labouring under a horribly distorted sense of what, for example, a Foucauldian intervention into nature means.

Recent texts, articles and conferences have demonstrated that there is, in much environmental discourse, a reactionary response to poststructural thinking and a rearguard attempt to sweep away its sceptical and progressive potential. At a recent conference, 'The Ends of Nature', at Kansas State, in addition to a few presentations that examined narratives of female bodies and foetuses, an issue handled particularly well by Carol Stabile, there was a general tendency to scoff at, deflect and generally seek consensus regarding the mischievous nuisances created by that unknowing urbanite, and European import, poststructuralism.

Bolstered by examples of eviscerated versions of poststructural practice,[1] many participants seemed confident that such assaults were exhausted, and exposed, and that those who indulged in such approaches didn't get it, were harming the cause, and were basically fouling the good work done by *true* nature lovers. The keynote speaker, Carol Stabile, offers some energy for this approach in her featured text, *Feminism and the Technological Fix* (1994). There she castigates a monolithically characterized poststructuralism (we get no indication of variety) for its lack of politics, its reduction of the social to language, and its capitulating ambiguity.

Challenging Marxism

It is interesting that, like romantic ecologists, some Marxists too are 'fighting back', or resisting the position which claims that there is no privileged position. Throughout her work is a resistance to the social being construed as the linguistic, to ignoring the 'material circumstances surrounding . . . production', the 'fragmentation of consciousness' (Stabile 1994: 148), 'political passivity' (ibid. 151) and non-representation (ibid. 140). No mention is made of critics like Michael Ryan (1982) or Mark Poster (1987) who have examined the Marxist qualities inherent in deconstruction, or Linda Hutcheon (1989) who takes on this negative definition of the postmodern: 'This misconception shows the danger of defining the postmodern in terms of (French or American)

anti-representational late modernism, as so many do . . . there is no
dissolution of representation; but there is a problematising of it'
(Hutcheon 1989: 50). Without taking on the arguments that have
complicated a Marxist materialist position, Stabile asserts this
foundational position against the perceived weaknesses of poststructural ambiguities. Tagged on to this is the assertion that too
many avant-garde movements have been so 'in form only' (Stabile
1994: 145), suggesting the ability to deep-read the times from a
privileged perspective.

Another recent Marxist approach to environmental issues also
finds poststructural/modernism wanting. Arran Gare's *Postmodernism and the Environmental Crisis* (1995) puts forth what
might be considered the most lucid litany of problems plaguing
Western civilization in particular, and global life in general: the
demise of a stable economy, the demise of a stable social or psychological base, the wholesale attack on the environment, the rise
of a trash culture, especially in the USA, and so forth. Most of
these complaints, accurate as they may be, are thinly veiled stock
concerns of traditional Marxism. The desire for unity, the fear of
the masses and their popular tastes, the desire for coherence and
order, all hover around an apparent concern for the environment.

Interestingly enough, this critique is carried on with the aid of
poststructural analyses, even though the thrust of Gare's text is
dismissive of poststructuralism on account of its lack of political
force. In the 'Introduction', for example, we are told that poststructural thinkers 'are totally inadequate as guides for political
action' (Gare 1995: 2). Nevertheless, he admits that poststructural
critiques

> have furthered the analyses revealing the drive to domination . . . and
> thereby have helped to legitimate discourses, suppressed by the
> dominant discourses of science and by Marxism, which are not
> oriented towards domination of the world and which accord more
> with a way of dwelling within the world which lets things be. They
> have also gone beyond language as such to investigate the institu-
> tional context of discourses. (Ibid. 90–1)

For all of this, Gare is not satisfied with poststructural theory.
Primarily, the cause of his dissatisfaction seems to be the poststructural questioning of *reason*, which removes the ground from
which Gare can orchestrate a more *realistic*, to his way of thinking, way of living. All through his text he laments the lack of
unity, the fragmentation, brought on by poststructural thought.

Certainly, this is one of the oldest Marxist complaints about capitalism: the fact that it destroys some imagined sense of seamless,
homogenous social and psychological reality. He is concerned
with poststructuralism's concern with language instead of real
things presumably, because this fuels the consumption of images.
Once again one sees the Marxist concern with alienation, reification
and fetishization. The problem with this analysis, as with traditional Marxism, is the haunting sense of the positing of unmediated
realities. Gare does not pause to consider that poststructuralists
like Baudrillard do not applaud the world of images;[2] they simply
suggest that it is where we are, and, further, that we are implicated, and there isn't a firm or disinterested position from which to
start. And, of course, Gare wants to *do* something. His impatience with the complications that poststructuralism has thrown
into the zealousness of the righteous opposition is everywhere
apparent. He calls for a '*realistic* alternative' (ibid. 32). He laments
that '*[o]riginal* artists . . . are no longer necessary, or even useful'
(ibid. 32). He decries the loss of 'grand narratives', '*genuine* praxis'
and '*action*' (ibid. 33). 'Once *originality* was regarded as important' (ibid. 29). 'Most improvements', the reader learns, 'have been
brought about by the pressure of *direct action*' (ibid. 78, my
emphasis). All these terms come from the confidence of the Enlightenment position. Later he calls for a return to thinking in totalit-
ies and nationalism, of all things. With the confidence of an
old historical materialism, Gare suggests that the current direction
of things – that is, the dominance of global capitalism – is
'irrational', and has 'the tendency to undermine the conditions of
its own existence' (ibid. 80).[3] Insinuating that the localized focus
of poststructural discourse is inadequate to the task, he feels it is
legitimate to assert the need for totalizing narratives. Gare seems
to have missed the discussion regarding how poststructural theory
is quite interested and capable of moving back and forth between
the local and the global. As Andrew Ross pointed out:

> The comforts provided by the totalising, explanatory power of
> Marxist categories are no longer enough to help us make sense of
> the fragmented and various ways in which people live and negoti-
> ate the everyday life of consumer explanation or without signific-
> ance. On the contrary, it is to say that such an explanation cannot
> in itself account for the complex ideological processes through
> which our various local insertions into the global economy are
> represented and reproduced. (Ross 1988: xv)

Here Ross is addressing and answering, in 1988, the concerns that Gare seems to have just discovered in 1995 concerning poststructural method. Ross makes it quite clear that the aim of a political poststructuralism is not an amputated, myopic examination of only what is immediate. And, of course, the issue of whether poststructuralism is ultimately a subversive challenge to capitalism or whether it capitulates in the demise of any opposition to capitalism has been argued for some time.

Although Gare berates current theory for its lack of seriousness, its play and its willingness to embrace contradiction and complexity, this seems hardly to take the power and complexity of the current state of affairs quite seriously enough. In other words, postmodern methodology seems to be constructing itself in a new way to meet a set of new situations. Finally, therefore, Gare offers a rearguard turn towards the brave days of modernism and reason, when 'passionate engagement' was embraced by '*individuals* who refused to compromise their convictions' (Gare 1995: 34). Postmodernists are, on the other hand, those who value the 'cool detachment of cynical opportunists' (ibid.). First of all, it is typical of Gare to treat postmodernism as a monolithic block. Secondly, characterizing postmodernists this way, a technique that amounts to name calling, in no way solves the problem regarding scepticism that postmodernists have thrown before us. In short, the desire for rationality, coherence, brave comrades, a noble cause uncomplicated by complicity, doctrinaire convictions, does not obligate philosophy, or current historical conditions, to deliver them. It is clear that Gare is critical of what he sees as the celebration of disorientation, 'the absence of any fixed reference points, the impossibility of representing the world . . . the absence of authenticity' (ibid.). Not liking some of these possible characterizations of postmodernism does not make them any less compelling. Instead of engaging these issues, Gare pursues a nostalgic trajectory towards reason, discipline and truth. He, in fact, sounds curiously conservative, and not the proponent of a reformed, 'radicalised Marxism' (ibid. 100) he wishes to be. He complains that the new social movements (which he incorrectly labels as poststructural and postmodern) have allowed for the depersonalizing of the social, for the loss of a unique identity, an *individual* as he stated above: 'In the postmodern period personal identity has become fluid' (ibid. 19). There are two issues here. First, postmodernism is often confused as both the creator of a condition and a reaction to a condition; it is often treated in the same essay as being both. (2) Gare, like Jameson and Marxists in general, cannot let go of the notion that there was some pre-ideological harmony, some solid self and solid reality that existed before capitalism melted all that was solid. In this spirit, Gare decries the emergence of a 'popular culture' that 'changes so quickly' (ibid. 29) and has also caused a crisis in the humanities, where one can no longer 'privilege one form of writing over another' (ibid. 23). Postmodernism simply points up the idea that a longing for a golden age is inferred by these criticisms, and also suggests that nostalgia for a past or, worse, a demand for a past that is gone, is irrational. In addition, poststructuralism relentlessly undermines the attempt to order narratives in a hierarchical arrangement.

Gare sounds conservative in other ways. He laments, with Daniel Bell, changes that modified the Protestant work ethic. Movement away from small town conformity, made possible by cars and other technological developments, as well as television's ability to create a mass audience, have 'dissolved local cultures and created a common culture committed to social and personal transformation' (ibid. 15). This interest in transformation is the fluidity he laments above. Gare really seems to show his conservative Marxist colours in the next line. 'The virtues endorsed by Protestantism had no place within this common culture which was concerned not with how to *work* and *achieve*, but how to *spend* and *enjoy*' (ibid.). Tainted by this direction, the New Left failed because it advocated 'a life of hedonism and self-indulgence' (ibid. 17, my emphasis). As in previously cited comments regarding a fluid, irrational, irresponsible self, Gare shows himself to be quite sure about what poststructuralism and modern society lack. In the end, he wants a return to a vigorous nationalism and grand narratives. How such narratives come about and by what authority is left vague.

Although the text is a marvellous vehicle for focusing a discussion on the way in which Marxism, postmodernism and the environment are intellectually interrelated, it is typical of many texts I consider here which strive to dismiss poststructuralism without adhering to and flowing with the radical paradigm it offers. The messenger, it seems, is often blamed. In addition, Gare's simplification of the nature of power and struggle is evident in his last chapter, which describes the new, nationalistic world order. What this approach fails to consider is the sense that the solutions he offers, updated though they may be, are considered by poststructuralists to be things of the past, and they have the feeling of the past about them.

Revealing is the connection between what he fails to quote from one of my articles which he cites and the direction he points to at the end of his text. Gare cites my article, 'Rethinking Resistance' (Quigley 1995), pointing to its concern with the way current resistance movements have failed. In other words, he took the part of the article that supported his thesis that essentialist postmodern movements provide the seed of their own undoing. What he ignores in this article, and in poststructural theory, is the degree to which poststructural theory can provide political guidance. Gare believes that the self, history and other 'substantial elements' must be put back into the game before significant steps *forward* can be taken. In my article, drawing on Nietzsche, LeGuin, Mouffe, Derrida and others, I suggest that forward action means working through the difficulties presented by poststructuralism, not shoving them aside. Indeed, I suggest that poststructuralism provided a view of the future that sees Gare's 'derealisation' and 'disorientation' as opportunity and challenge. I proposed that these were but the initial reactions to a new theoretical horizon. It is possible, I argued, to imagine a society that was non-exploitive, non-aggressive, non-discriminating, without recourse to grand narratives, foundations (albeit regional ones), political indoctrination and nationalism, all of which are indicated by Gare's proposal.[4]

It is further revealing that, after quoting from my piece, Gare goes on to champion Jim Cheney, the target of my article. Either Gare didn't finish my piece, didn't think it significant, chose not to include the concerns I raised about Cheney's 'Postmodern Narrative', or found the anarchist trajectory of my take on poststructuralism distracting. It is, nevertheless, interesting how reference to my article immediately precedes Cheney in Gare's discussion, but my criticisms are omitted. Cheney is important to Gare's argument,[5] because he claims to allow difference and narrative coherence to exist simultaneously, a feature of Gare's reformed Marxism and his sense of the new nationalism: 'Nationalism can then be redefined as the commitment by a regional community, through the stories by which it defines itself, to justice within the region, where justice is *understood* as the *appropriate*' (Gare 1995: 152, my emphasis). The heavily qualified conditionals go on from here. In short, Gare uses Cheney's local narratives on a larger scale, and runs into the same problems I identified regarding Cheney. First is the issue of an untheorized vision of how power shapes these new narratives and nation-states. Second is still the issue of what is being said in these narratives and how such discourses are passed on, especially if fluid transformations are to be eschewed. The concern which Foucault brings up about discourse and institutional power structures is dismissed here, for these are, apparently, reasonable, good narratives, not subordinating, deceptive ones. Cheney, like Gare, advocates a kind of special discourse that percolates out of a particular region. The humans of that region become, as a result of a kind of listening, stewards of that region. My article takes issue with the apparent mysticism that translates itself into prescribed social practice: a good Marxist response, one might say. Finally, Gare's use of Cheney strikes me as an unsuitable resolution of the issues raised by poststructural theory. Gare's attraction to originality, regionality, reason and the unified individual all drive him towards a less than satisfying response to the problems put forward by poststructuralism and the postmodern world. An anarchist sense of justice – in other words, a postmodern one – would not insist on new narratives, but would come from the humility and gentleness which result from a deconstruction of power, knowledge and authority. As I will argue later, nature, understood from a poststructural perspective, can offer such a political atmosphere. It is clear that Gare's attempt to link postmodern philosophy with New Age eco movements is shaky at best. The postmodern may accept New Age movements, but to identify the postmodern with the New Age, as Gare does, is tricky.

Challenging Mysticism

At the heart of the postmodern/poststructural is a rejection of unmediated foundations. In *States of Grace: The Recovery of Meaning in the Postmodern Age* (1991), for example, Charlene Spretnak both dismisses and appropriates the postmodern for her own spiritually vague trajectory. By casting vague aspersions on poststructural methodology, she moves quickly towards appropriating the term 'ecological postmodernism' for her own argument.

I agree with her claim that there is a reconstructive energy residing within the initial deconstructive energy of poststructural thinking. Spretnak's ecological postmodernism moves beyond, she says, the 'nihilistic disintegration of all values' (Spretnak 1991: 19). However, her move is to fill out the terms of her spiritual rhetoric of mystic interconnectedness by suggesting that her spiritual mysticism is a kind of postmodernism. In fact, the attack on various theories by poststructuralism opens up the spiritual space for Spretnak: 'Our cultural interpretations of reality . . . are sorely impoverished if they operate in isolation from the larger context' (ibid. 20). Which larger context? The larger context is the inter-connectedness suggested by postmodernism. The larger context gains validity by asserting that there has been a 'widespread, cross-cultural occurrence of the perception of interconnectedness' (ibid. 18). The *interest in* and *construction of* this larger context are not objects for scrutiny. How one *perceives* and *knows* this larger context remains fuzzy, of course, and the theoretical justification for seeing postmodernism in this is similarly undocumented.

Two more examples will have to serve as testimony to the problems here. Spretnak dramatizes the weaknesses she sees in postmodern thought by doing *gentle* battle with a graduate student who is polluted by sceptical language theory. In her spiritual journey she confesses that she 'sometimes encounters this attitude' (ibid. 16). When the student offers his sense of the postmodern, she writes, 'I glanced quickly around the circle and met the eyes of the two professors with whom I spent the afternoon. Those split-second glances confirmed what each of us knew' (ibid.). What seems most apparent here is the simple dynamic of power struc-tures forming to meet the face of ironic opposition. The 'glance', far from the spiritual union suggested by the 'circle', is more like a conspiracy, a hanging party. With confidence and power and arrogance gained from the 'glance', she constructs herself, with the approval of those who invited her to speak at the college, as the wise sage. In retort to the student's Foucauldian view of an opposition that emerges and then submerges, Spretnak is correct-ive in a sagely fashion: ' "No", I replied *gently*. "That's not at all what we're about" ' (ibid., my emphasis).

The clearest demonstration of the weakness in methodology that wants to insist on interconnectedness and mutual unspoken awareness Pies in the following sentence: 'Although most decon-structive postmodernists consider "nature", the "cosmos", and the "health of the biosphere" to be merely "socially produced" concepts, a collective awareness has gradually taken shape . . . such that we can no longer deny the pervasive force of a suicidal disorientation' (ibid. 14). This *non sequitur* actually serves as an argument! Although postmodern/poststructural theorists have taken the position that experience is mediated, Spretnak says, it is immaterial, because some people, collective awareness at a lunch table, simply want things to be otherwise. This 'argument' does not attempt to demonstrate the limits or problems associated with poststructural thought; it is just asserted that 'collective' thinking disregards it. This definition of 'collective awareness' is exactly what constitutes racism, hangings, Auschwitz, gang rape and homophobia, and is a technical discussion that those in pursuit of their goal frequently don't slow down for. Spretnak actually claims that it is theories like poststructuralism that bring about the destructive forces that modern society exhibits, as it 'devour[s] the sense of grounded, responsible being' (ibid. 15) needed for the apprehension of 'truth, beauty, a love of life' (ibid.). Indeed, there is a certain kind of positioning that allows for a 'meaningful moment' at a sunset. Poststructuralism has pointed out that such positioning has the trace of history and the postcard on it. Those 'moments' are still possible, but what we are willing to claim, and demand of others, because of them has been brought under scrutiny. Poststructural method has denaturalized the romantic posture, not erased it.

Recently there have been other, more sophisticated, dismissals of poststructural thought in environmental circles. But all of them misunderstand and distort in various ways the potential and the practice of poststructural thought. Neil Evernden, in *The Social Creation of Nature* (1992), provides the most developed example of the rejection of poststructuralism fuelled by an odd but fatal premisse.

First, it is important to note that, like Spretnak, Evernden refuses to relinquish an unironic use of the term *nature*, regardless of the recognition, and even admission, of the complexity, ambiguity and even contradictory usages of the term. He also, like Spretnak, longs for vague concepts, like 'lived experience' (Evernden 1992: 109), to counter sceptical philosophic positions with which he disagrees. Since Evernden ultimately wants to make room for transcendental experiences that escape the human, and therefore are capable of fulfilling the lonely human self and the modern loss of meaning, he must keep nature whole by seeing poststructuralism as just another arrogant humanist attack. Evernden does, indeed, seem to long for a unified experience. He describes the medieval faith in miracles, in the unpredictability of nature, with admiration (ibid. 41). Clearly unhappy with the sense of fluidity (which comes with philosophical scepticism) that excites others, and sounding like a mid-century existentialist, Evernden laments the 'lack of purpose we all experience. That is, the absence of external authority that makes possible this relativistic freedom also removes any given end for the project of human existence' (ibid. 29).

Most disturbing is Evernden's claim that poststructuralism is a humanist, arrogant intrusion into nature. Barthes's attack on the natural, as well as his attack on philosophies like classic humanism that posit a natural and rational foundation, insists that history and ideas are formulated and hide in concepts of the natural, and, therefore, that it is important (as Jameson later says) to historicize nature. Evernden paraphrases Barthes's position: 'If nature is simply a human-made entity, then it must not be permitted to be used as a safe house for social injustices' (ibid. 27). Strangely, instead of seeing this as an opportunity to move deceivers out of the territory of the natural, he sees it as '*another step in the conquest of nature*' (ibid., 28, my emphasis). Barthes's project was meant to liberate us from normalizing values disguised as nature. Evernden mistakenly sees this act of exposure as humanizing and domesticating a wild, transcendent nature. One would think that this occupation of nature, this cultural embedding, would, at the very least, intrigue ecologically minded people. But it irritates ecological and spiritual foundationalists, as well as Marxists.

In the same way that Barthes refuses nature as given, artists in the sixteenth century opposed the seductive techniques of Classicism, and began to draw attention to their technique, away from the clear window of Classical deception. It is this interest in the form as opposed to content, the medium rather than of the message, that begins to dovetail more and more in recent centuries, and define two very different kinds of thinkers. Actually, we see a very condensed form of this in the 30 years that separate impressionism from abstract expressionism.

Before proceeding, it is important to note that, as Gerald Graff (1983) points out, there is nothing intrinsically politically defining about the movement away from foundation to form. A concentration on form can produce Leninists, Bakhtinian carnival revellers, as well as agrarian conservatives (American New Critics). Evernden, however, chooses to see the rhetorical analysis of nature as the overwhelming of substance by form: 'Barthesian thought-police [are] at work weeding nature from our cultural gardens, all but a few fragments have been domesticated' (Evernden 1992: 30). Basically, Evernden complains that his 'nature' is being taken away by speculative, abstract thinking. But even this complaint has the obvious longing for a solidly unmediated reality. Evernden has little to say about the value or object of Barthes's project. He, like others, simply notes that it makes direct contact complicated, if not impossible. He therefore insists, oddly enough, on connecting the poststructural and postmodern moment with a long history of human appropriation.

Embedded within Evernden's discourse is the typical romantic longing for identification with nature, with the wild, a good old-fashioned union with the object. One hears the lament in his voice as he describes the movement from the medieval period to the Renaissance: 'For the medievals . . . to know an object means to negate the distance between it and consciousness; it means in a certain sense, to become one with the object. But as we have seen, this changes with the Renaissance, when there is in effect a withdrawal from the objects of nature and a denial of the propriety of such empathy.' Evernden goes on to lament that truth was then defined as the 'absence of human involvement' (ibid. 85).

Evernden performs his analysis of nature in a very odd, deceptive fashion. In addition to reversing or completely misunderstanding the basis of a Foucauldian, Barthian or poststructural position, claiming as he does that it is a usurping humanism, he uses a constructivist approach when it's convenient, and abandons it when he wants to privilege a 'correct' use of nature. His use of Foucault amounts to three footnotes, but his comments there in reveal why he used a constructivist approach in this odd way. He says that Foucault is 'very useful to the study of the transformation in the concept of nature, but those who have dipped toes into his arcane waters will understand why I am reluctant to pursue this topic beyond the fairly minimal level that seems useful' (ibid. 142, n. 9).

Well, yes, I understand completely. To have used Foucault as a poststructuralist instead of a structuralist would have meant that Evernden would have had to apply constructivist and anti-foundational methods in a more thorough going fashion. Not just as a means to outline past cultures from a privileged vantage point, showing for example where the Renaissance failed, Evernden would have had to go beyond this, and abandon his own need for an untheorized, unidealized wild: something he never does. His main complaint about poststructuralism is, one recalls, that it 'domesticates' by suggesting that our notions of nature are human projections. Asserting that we embed our assumptions in conceptions of the natural is not celebrated by poststructuralism, and it is not done to dominate nature. It is asserted to insist on the notion that we constantly construct the world. It is also asserted as a means of demonstrating that even in moments of apparent tribute to the other, we reveal our desire as we construct a space that frees us. Foucault's insistence that power is everywhere, and that there is no privileged position of calm outside power, is not meant to paralyse either. Foucault puts it this way: 'My point is not that everything is bad, but that everything is dangerous, which is not exactly the same as bad. If everything is dangerous, then we always have something to do. So my position leads not to apathy but to a hyper- and pessimistic activism' (1984d: 343).

Because he does not see this in the poststructural project, Evernden simply responds defensively when he realizes that the realm of unmediated pure experience has been removed. Like a mid-twentieth-century thinker, Evernden never tires of complaining about our desire to control, as though there were a way to perceive without construction and, therefore, without appropriation; mediation and control. This is what Evernden refuses as he privileges Annie Dillard's transcendent experience with a weasel:

> Yet occasionally, an exceptional adult can still encounter an animal in all of its ultrahumanity. . . . She did not observe the behaviors of the beast, did not retain the proper, adult detachment requisite to the study of nature. Instead she momentarily lost her self-consciousness and encountered otherness directly and with astonishment. (Everden 1992: 121–2)

Evernden desperately tries to work his way out of the epistemological trap he sets for himself. He states that the choices are either to make the self into nature – and then we are mechanical and dwell in a realm without subjectivity – or to make nature into the self 'and populate our landscape with the pets and puppets that these pseudo humans inevitable become' (ibid. 108). Actually these positions present many more problems. Nevertheless, Evernden inadvertently points to the solution I want to offer with the help of Foucault.

Evernden knows that 'there is no "nature", and there never has been' (ibid. 99). Yet, as he tries to work from this insight, from the position that states that knowledge is a shaping force and not a window, he clings to a sense of the real that continues to confuse his argument. He ends by countering *common sense*, another word for ideology, or any other theorization of nature, with '*lived experience*' (ibid. 109, my emphasis). So we have inherited knowledge, which is common sense or ideology, and the distortions of science. One wonders what it is that takes the place of these 'false' discourses. It seems to me that this unmediated proposition actually hides other elements that expose themselves throughout the text. For instance, Evernden has a particular penchant for religious experience and the experience of children. In a section entitled 'The Ultrahuman', he theorizes an experience that resembles Dillard's:

> In such instances, we experience . . . the 'wholly other': 'that which is quite beyond the sphere of the usual, the intelligible, and the familiar, which therefore falls quite outside the limits of the "canny", . . . filling the mind with blank wonder and astonishment. . . . All the glorious examples from nature speak very plainly in this sense.' Significantly, this experience is also reported among the important events of childhood. (Ibid. 117)

The romantic bias here hardly needs comment at this point in critical discussions. Nevertheless, it is worth pointing out that post-structuralism is dismissed early in this text, in a distorted manner, and the movement towards reclaiming a significant experience gives the book direction.

It is crucial to note that Evernden has abandoned the references to Barthes and poststructuralism that were his focus in the earlier part of his text. He now takes issue with idealism and materialism, two sides of the Cartesian paradigm. When Evernden theorizes his sense of the epistemological problem, he works with old paradigms, and only vaguely handles the assertions that come from poststructuralism: 'the world is indeed "there" in lived experience, but that experience is not an ephemeral, transparent non-realm between a "subjective" mind and an "objective" world. Nor is it a passive "subjective" report of an autonomously existing "objective" reality' (ibid. 109). Well, of course, there is no argument here. In fact, this is an old argument concerning scientific dualism that hardly has any interest left in it. Evernden goes on with hysterical italics to tell us what *it* is: 'It is *reality*, the only reality that is actually given in experience rather than constructed in experience' (ibid.). This is crucial, because it is the poststructuralist position that abandons dualism, giving us what Evernden asks for from his lived experience. As Mark Poster explains, 'This sensitivity to the ability of language to shape practice is typical of the post-structuralists and exemplifies their rejection of the metaphysical dualism of mind and body, ideas and behavior, consciousness and action' (1987: 116).

Typical of critics who have tried to wrestle with poststructuralist thought, Evernden feels he must reaffirm that the world is *there*, and that it has a particularly vital meaning. Poststructuralism denies none of this. It insists that the world is quite material and *there*, and has meaning for us. The difference is that materiality comes in a context, an interpretation, an interest, and the meaning is irretrievably charged with psychological, cultural and political significance: and there is no relief from this. Evernden is trying to dismiss the poststructural unfairly, by suggesting that it has no concern for the material it is appropriating, and that it is 'nihilistic'.

In addition to intense, unconstructed *reality*, Evernden also proposes nature as the *other*, the strange, the intense. This is where I curiously cross paths and, simultaneously, part company with Evernden. For, although I agree that nature, or experience, can offer unsettling and paradigm-shaking episodes, Evernden, along with Dillard, clearly makes a fetish of this phenomenon. Evernden quotes Merleau-Ponty approvingly: '*to return to things themselves is to return to that world which precedes knowledge*' (1992: 110, my emphasis). Fetishizing otherness, instead of seeing it as a counter to a norm or expectation, Evernden holds out for an experience that is not already written, that is wild and unmediated. He finds himself in the romantic posture of being the ultimate humanist, projecting a world of meaningful intensity available to a momentarily free, transcendent individual. Of course, this is precisely what Foucault and other poststructuralists deny access to. Foucault, in fact, defines nature in a most revealing fashion. Nature is the way in which language works to produce our lives, that which seems normal: 'to know nature is, in fact, to build upon the basis of language a true language, one that will reveal the condition in which all language is possible and the limits within which it can have a domain of validity' (Foucault 1973: 161).

In short, nature, or the world that is ours every day, is linguistic, and, in addition, limited to that language. This situation does not make the world immaterial; it does not make it so plural that one cannot function; it is not nihilism. Further, it does not prevent the experience of change, astonishment and wonder that Evernden's text leans towards and yearns for.

Challenging Deep Ecology and Resistance

Before trying to come to terms with the dynamics of a poststructural nature, one more example is called for. After reading my poststructural attack on the history of the political use of 'nature', George Sessions was kind enough to send along a series of well-written articles he recently published on the topic. In The Wild Duck, Sessions, in an attempt to defend ideas put forth in his Deep Ecology for the 21st Century (1994), continues a similar kind of attack on postmodern treatments of nature as Evernden. In one essay, devoted to a review of Reinventing Nature? Responses to Postmodern Deconstruction, Sessions applauds the essays for assuming that 'the world really does exist apart from humanity's perceptions and beliefs' and for producing a 'thoughtful critique of the views of . . . Foucault' (Sessions 1995b: 14). Once again there is the assumption that the agenda in poststructuralism is to foreground the human and to maintain a 'relativistic moral neutrality' (ibid.). Apparently, when it is stated that there is no nature, no hiding-place for human ideology, no escape to the mountains, no easy reference to an uncomplicated value, there is such a need for defensiveness that poststructuralism is accused of the narcissism it is designed to expose.

In another edition of the same publication, Sessions pushes the same sentiment by claiming that deep ecology 'does not put people first' (1995a: 15), which poststructuralists, by inference, do. As opposed to Stabile, who sees no politics functioning in the post-structural at all, Sessions accuses poststructuralists of adhering to the 'Marxist anthropocentric and relativistic doctrine of the social construction of all knowledge about nature – that Nature is a social category'. Andrew Ross is singled out for subscribing to the Foucauldian notion that ' "what we know about nature is what we know and think about our own cultures" ' (ibid.).

It is clear from recent conferences and publications that the eco-lit constituency is nervous about language having trodden all over the romantic glade of nature. Sessions's title, 'Postmodernism, Environmental Justice, and the Demise of the Ecology Movement?' (1995a) suggests this anxiety. It is easy to identify with thinkers like Sessions, whose sincerity is so evident, and whose indictment of conservative logic and motivations is so agreeable. However, as my opening paragraph stated, this is not enough. The well-documented obscenities of Dan Quayle and Rush Limbaugh aside, this problem persists.

I would now like to turn to addressing some of the problems I have raised. In my 1992 Environmental Ethics article, 'Rethinking Resistance', I outlined the reasons why 'nature' could no longer be used without ironic quotes. My position then, as now, is that such terms are deceptive, in that they try to seduce without argument. Foucault suggested the same thing when he said that power is 'ensured not by rights, but by technique, not by the law, but by normalisation, not by punishment, but by control' (1976: 89). If one agrees that it is natural to be greedy, for example, then all sorts of other behaviour, economic systems included, are much easier to implement. And social policies involving helping people are much more easily dismissed, or, as Foucault points out, those that hold such beliefs are considered insane.

My suggestion was to abandon reference to absolutes, in that they try to bring about change through the use of authority instead of argument. References to the normal, the natural, the obvious, are coercive, and abort fundamental issues regarding the structure of our lives. My point in the article was to demonstrate how resistance theories are as guilty of this process as are dominant power structures. Particularly illustrative of this problem is the classic position of liberal humanist resistance laid out by Theodore Roszak. In accounting for the shared point of resistance occupied by the individual as well as the planet, Roszak defends it this way: 'this right you feel so certain is yours, this right to have your uniqueness respected, perhaps even cultivated, is not an extension of traditional values like civil liberty, equality, social democracy. . . . It *springs* independently, from another, far more mysterious source' (Roszak 1979: 7, my emphasis). In the same way that capitalism establishes a free individual outside the vagaries of history and the social to defend its brutal economic practices, so romantic resistances like those promoted by Roszak play the same game. Roszak feels he must establish his truth as more vital, real, sacred than the one of the dominant structure. The problem is that he uses the same machinery.

I tried to suggest towards the end of the article that there was a form of nature that could still be used effectively while satisfying the sceptical attacks on foundational arguments. If nature could be seen as a force that disrupts, overwhelms, undermines, explodes or otherwise 'makes strange' our ideological consensus, our anthropocentrism, then it is possible to see it as an agent of criticism and deconstruction, as well as of reconstruction. The point was to relieve 'nature' of the burden of carrying mysterious answers to all of our questions, answers that *spring* from the most vague sources of humanist foundational theory. Mostly, however, I have used 'nature' as a force that can empty space, that can clear the ground of ideological occupiers. Somewhat like Evernden's wild nature, I theorized nature as a defamiliarizing, unsettling force; but there is a thread that leads out of this fetish. There is a way to think about how social meaning is generated, how it is contoured, raised, given shape, how it is undermined, and what role 'nature' plays in such a dynamic.

As the phrase 'makes strange' suggests, there is a connection here with the Russian Formalists, especially the development of formalism made possible by the Futurists. One recalls that Tony Bennett (1979), in *Formalism and Marxism*, outlined the way in which the Futurists insisted on a politicized form of defamiliarization that otherwise moves in an art for art's sake direction. In particular, Bennett states that the Futurists 'viewed the devices of defamiliarisation as a means for promoting political awareness by undermining ideologically habituated modes of perception' (1979: 32). This is the dynamic that leads away from essentializing nature, and towards a Bakhtinian, Harawayean (Haraway 1985) and Foucauldean cultural critique and political movement.

If one were to rest with the cultural project of defamiliarization, or making strange, one would find oneself connected to the tradition of the sublime. Perhaps some of this is unavoidable, since, as Poster points out, '[a]n aspect of totalisation necessarily emerges in every effort to counter the prevailing ideology' (1987: 111). The more theoretically appropriate direction, however, is to theorize this *other*, this new information, structure or concept that has infected (to use the language of computer culture referring to the fissuring of a well-running program) the ordinary order of things without grounding it. Bakhtin, I think, accomplishes this with his concepts of carnival and centrifugal as opposed to centripetal power. Like Foucault, Bakhtin builds fluidity and movement into the history of ideas; not teleology or historical determinism, but synchronic junctures, Kuhnian paradigm shifts that, for an instant, stabilize and authorize the natural and the normal for a culture. Bakhtin uses the terms *centripetal* and *centrifugal* to describe how, alongside 'centralisation and unification, the uninterrupted processes of decentralisation and disunification go forward' (1986: 668). This situation is hardly ever quite static, and the forces of multiplicity are always eating away at the walls of the dike. So Bakhtin, like Foucault, insists on the linguistic reality that is, nevertheless, quite material. More interesting, as Bakhtin points out, we have multiple voices within an object: 'Discourse is directed toward an . . . object, naming it, portraying, expressing, and . . . indirectly striking a blow at the other's discourse, clashing . . . within the object itself' (1981: 196). It is from this perspective that Roland Barthes put out the call to 'scour nature . . . to discover History there, and at last to establish Nature itself as historical' (Barthes 1978: 108). But too many critics want to draw an analogy at this point between the wild and the plurality of language, its ambiguity and interrelations, thereby fetishizing nature.

Rethinking Nature with Foucault

What establishes Foucault as the brilliant light on the horizon of recent theorization of resistance is his insistence on re-theorizing power and resistance. Since power is seen as pervasive, not located in specific places, then resistance movements finally find themselves firmly located amidst what they claimed to be outside. Abandoning such self-righteous posturing and the promise of a utopia, Foucault insists that we deal with the material here and now, the synchronic ache. Perhaps Eagleton is partially correct about the genesis of this sentiment, a middle-class capitulation; perhaps it is also maturity, and admission that we are very much part of the problems with which we are concerned. As opposed to leaving the 'cause' behind, as he and many poststructuralists are accused of, Foucault's project is designed to produce a 'reformulation which can unlock the forms of domination inherent in diverse linguistic experiences [and] reveal the significance of new forms of protest' (Poster 1987: 114–15).

Implied by the foregoing discussion, but not quite reached, is Foucault's heterotopia. This is the area of resistance which so many anarchist thinkers have been hovering around, without quite putting it in such useful terms. Bakhtin's notions of heteroglossia, centripetal power, and carnival point to, but ultimately do not include, the urgency and dynamics of resistance suggested by Foucault. Foucault abandons the individual, or the sacred grove that contains mysterious truths. For him, nature, or resistance, must be conceived of as a provisional linguistic space (which structures action, of course, as well as specific physical sites) where some momentary perspective can be assessed and from within which a crisis can occur. It is this borderland that so many critics, such as Haraway (1985), are writing about today. Foucault makes it clear why, so often in the last 200 years, writers have thought of nature as a viable option for society. Heterotopias are places where a site of opposition is created. As William Chaloupka points out, Foucault posits a possible point of opposition, but it is distinctly different from what we are used to in oppositional politics. Like a bubble in molten rubber or rock or steel that is preserved after hardening, these spaces seem to occur as a result of the particular structuring of particular cultural moments: they are not eternal. As Foucault states, 'There are also . . . real places – places that do exist and that are formed in the very founding of society – which are something like counter-sites . . . in which the real sites that can be found within the culture, are simultaneously represented, contested, and inverted' (Foucault 1986: 22). It is also the case, however, that Foucault stated that 'crisis heterotopias', which are 'privileged or sacred or forbidden places, reserved for individuals who are, in relation to society . . . in a state of crisis', are disappearing (ibid. 24–5). Foucault's analysis of the internalization of discipline gives us a better sense of why deviance is less observable. Some would say that Foucault's theories, which have abandoned strong identification to clearly outlined resistance movements, are part of the reason for this. On the contrary, however, one could argue that, because of a new understanding of power, it is easier to see why resistance has been so ineffective. This understanding prepares one to support and comprehend any number of protests emanating from various areas. And indeed, Foucault was interested in supporting the 'new movements' emerging out of the 1960s, such as feminism, gay rights and civil rights. Finally, Foucault explores many unlikely spaces in the social structure where tensions occur and discourses collide, and, therefore, where change is possible. Chaloupka and Cawley point out, in a note, Foucault's interest in Polynesian vacation villages, as ' "a new kind of temporal heterotopia" ' (1993: 23, n. 34). The point here is not to examine this site of nature and nudity, but to point out that resistance and opposition will continue to be produced by the social structure, and that these spaces will occur in places that are different from traditional liberal humanist and Marxist theories.

Heterotopia characterizes the place of the language of resistance quite specifically. Like Bakhtin's object, it is a place full of tension and criss-crossed with cultural dialogue. Wilderness then becomes a cultural space, much to the dismay of critics like Evernden. However, this is a space where, as Chaloupka and Cawley say, 'wilderness may even begin to make sense' (ibid. 14). This is an important point, since the mystical characterizations of nature only serve to mystify and posit positions for new authority. Nature makes sense as a 'response' to culture. Nature may be a place to escape to, but it is not a world elsewhere, another realm, or a place containing sacred ideas or lessons. It is a place to gather strength against the forces of domination, but also a place we have created, and a place to remember that nature has frequently been a weapon of oppression.

Notes

1 This observation concerning the political ineffectiveness of certain kinds of American deconstructive practice is not new. See Scholes 1985: 86–110, which compares de Man to Eagleton. See also Eliss 1989: 74; Eagleton 1983: 142; and Lentricchia 1983: 50–1; also Moi 1985 for a discussion of French versus American applications.

2 Baudrillard's *America* (1988), for instance, is critical of the circularity of simulacra, that which defines current American society. See also, Allison Fraiberg's (1991) discussion of Baudrillard.

3 He does not consider the problems of *rationally* oriented systems such as Nazi Germany or the systematization in the Soviet Union caused. It is typical of this approach to simply point out the distorting and disquieting features of capitalism. Poststructural approaches are quite good at this. They tend to focus on that analysis without the driving force of a better plan or a utopia in the background. This may be exhaustion; it may also be a sobering encounter with the depth of a problem that may be without solution at the moment. No rational programme of nationalism seems likely to be helpful.

4 I have recently made this argument, in 'Jeffers and the Possibilities of Politics', using Robinson Jeffers's use of nature as cultural critique. *Jeffers Studies* is a new journal devoted to the life and writing of Jeffers. It has a printed annual version, but also an electronic version at www.jeffers.org. In a different way from the forthcoming essay I made a similar point in Quigley 1994.

5 Cheney preserves a ground while apparently working within postmodern parameters. The degree to which he is implicated in the romantic grounding is suggested by the fact that he even privileges the child as a superior epistemologist. Will we ever get tired of these old stock manoeuvres?

10

Foucault's Unnatural Ecology

Neil Levy

Contemporary critical theory and the most progressive political practice are today, if not dominated, at least powerfully shaped, by the currents of thought and practice which go under the broad names of the Green movement and of poststructural philosophy. Yet, on the face of it, it would seem that these are movements which stand essentially in opposition to each other. The Green movement's critique of contemporary social formations is often mounted in the name of, or at least informed by, a concept of nature, pure and unsullied, which stands as the ideal and the goal toward which we are urged to move. Poststructural cultural theory, on the other hand, has been profoundly anti-naturalistic. For the poststructuralists, the denomination of any practice, of any state of affairs, as 'natural' has been seen as an ideological move intended to legitimate certain historical and therefore contingent social relations.[1] From the perspective of the Green movement, therefore, poststructuralism must appear dangerously relativistic and abstract, absorbed in arguments about representation, while forests fall. From the poststructural perspective, on the other hand, the language of environmentalism appears hopelessly romantic, and potentially reactionary, in its call for us to return to some putative state of harmony with nature (see chapter 9).

Even at those points where the affinities between poststructural thought and certain currents of environmentalism seem strongest, we should hesitate to conflate their perspectives. One such point concerns the issue of humanism. Poststructuralism develops out of a critique of humanist thought, thus apparently echoing the deep ecological urge to move beyond anthropocentric outlooks. Moreover, for both deep ecology and poststructuralism in general,

many of the negative aspects of Western social and political structures are attributable to the dominance of a type of rationality often
described as 'instrumental', which looks upon the non-human world
as so many tools and resources to be manipulated for human
ends, and sees only those ends which can be measured in terms of
efficiency and economy as being valuable (Soper 1995: 5).

These superficial similarities notwithstanding, however, it would
be a mistake to see Foucault or his poststructuralist colleagues as
lending aid and comfort to the deep ecological project. French
anti-humanism is not ecological eco-centricism; nor does Foucault's
analysis of reason lead to a valorization of non-rational, or natural processes. If Foucault has a contribution to make to the environmental movement, it must be sought elsewhere, in less obvious
places. In what follows, I will first sketch the reasons for my
assertion that Foucault's work is not compatible with deep ecological thought. I will then proceed to show how certain aspects
of his work, especially of the first volume of *The History of
Sexuality* and associated texts, might be extended so as to yield a
relatively 'shallow', or anthropocentric, environmental ethics. This
conclusion may disappoint many deep ecologists, who might have
hoped to find philosophical resources in the work of the reputedly
radical French thinker. Nevertheless, this thought has the advant-
ages of being eminently defensible and practical, as well as con-
sonant with Foucault's work. If it can be shown that it is not deep
enough, I believe, then Foucault, along with much of the Western
rationalist tradition, must be abandoned in the search for an ethic
more appropriate to the dangers we face.

Anti-Humanism and Anthropocentricism

Despite the apparent similarities between at least the rhetorics of
environmental and poststructural thought, their common identification of 'humanism' as their prime enemy does not lead to a
convergence in the solutions they proffer. The French humanist/
anti-humanist and the environmental anthropo/biocentric distinctions are not isomorphic. In fact, in its Foucauldian formulation
at least, the French distinction is a division *internal* to what eco-
philosophy calls 'anthropocentricism'. If Foucault is insistent that
'it is no longer possible to think in our day other than in the void
left by man's disappearance' (Foucault 1989e: 341–2), it is by no

means the biosphere that will replace 'man' as the centre of thought. Instead, what decentres the human is the system of codes which interpret Being to a particular culture at a particular stage in its history: 'The fundamental codes of a culture – those governing its language, its schemas of perception, its exchanges, its techniques, its values, the hierarchy of its practices – establish for every man, from the very first, the empirical orders with which he will be dealing and within which he will be at home' (ibid.).

It is these codes, which divide up and establish the mode of being of reality at a pre-conscious level, which are the primary focus of Foucault's archeological investigations. And while they may not lie within reach of human control, they are thoroughly cultural and historical. As the investigations of the epistemological foundations of natural history and biology in *The Order of Things* make clear, these codes are not themselves natural, but underlie our conception of the natural.[2] If Foucault rejects 'man' as the meaning-bestowing centre of thought, it is not in order to replace 'him' with a non-human substratum or system. Instead, what replaces the individual is the equally human historical sedimentation of meaning and codes which go to make up a culture.

Furthermore, Foucault gives us other grounds for being suspicious of deep ecological positions, at least in so far as the concept of nature remains central to such positions. From Foucault's perspective, any invocation of such a normative notion, which claims to stand apart from the flow of history, is profoundly suspicious. And the concept of nature does seem to be indispensable to the deeper environmental ethics.[3] Why does this river have rights, and not this bulldozer? I presume that the answer will have something to do with the assertion that the river is a natural part of the landscape, whereas the bulldozer is artificial.

Foucault has no deconstructive critique of the concept of nature to offer. Instead, he gives us a description of the way in which the term has functioned in discourse. In the first volume of *The History of Sexuality*, he traces the ways in which the claimed naturalness of sex and sexuality have acted as a powerful mechanism to normalize individuals and populations: 'Situated at the point of intersection of a technique of confession and a scientific discursivity . . . sexuality was defined as being "by nature": a domain susceptible to pathological processes, and hence one calling for therapeutic or normalising interventions' (Foucault 1976: 68).

The naturalization of sexuality has a fourfold function. First, it serves to tie individuals to an identity, an essence which can be expressed or hidden, but cannot be changed. Thus the perverse individual is constituted as an example of a species: homosexuality is defined by 'nineteenth-century psychiatry, jurisprudence, and literature' in all its 'species and subspecies' (ibid. 101). Secondly, by defining this essence as natural, the deployment of sexuality deflects criticism away from itself. What is natural is discovered, not invented. If the naturalization of sexuality is successful, debates over sex can be concerned only with ways in which it should be repressed or expressed, with whether this nature is good or evil, with its importance or triviality. But the more important question: 'Do we *truly* need a *true* sex?' (Foucault 1980d: vii) cannot be asked. That is, the naturalization of sexuality forces us to accept its reality as given, and thus to accept many of the presuppositions it carries along with it.

Thirdly, the naturalization of sexuality provides a powerful justification for intervention in its realm. If sex is natural, if it has a state of health from which it can deviate, a purpose and a function which carry their own normativity within themselves, then it becomes difficult to deny to those who claim knowledge of this state the right to attempt to restore it when it malfunctions. Sexuality may easily become a medical problem under these conditions, a lever with which to institute a regime of policing individuals.

Fourthly, and perhaps most importantly, the establishment of sexuality as our essential nature turns each individual into a self-policing subject. For the deployment of sexuality teaches us, not just that our essence is sexual, but that this essence is – unnaturally – repressed. Thus, for the sake of our mental and physical health, it is incumbent upon us to seek out our sexuality, to track it in its most obscure manifestations and give expression to it. The 'repressive hypothesis', the belief that our sexuality contains our nature, coupled with the conviction that concerning that nature 'we have never said enough' (Foucault 1976: 101), authorizes a more massive, more total and, at the same time, more precise extension of the mechanisms of subjectification than ever before. It is through this mechanism that the apparatus of discipline is extended beyond the criminal and the deviant, to the apparently 'normal'.

All these functions of the naturalization of sex are predicated on the great prestige that the so-called sciences of nature have in our societies. To call something natural is to assert (a) that it holds within itself its own normativity, its state of health, which it is important to preserve, and (b) that the entity so called is essentially outside history. If something is natural, it is eternal and unchangeable, at least in its essential aspects. Foucault's objections to nature, then, like Barthes's objection to myth, lie in nature's transformation of the historical into the eternal.[4]

For these reasons, the term 'nature' has a powerfully negative value in Foucault's writings. But it will immediately be objected that the nature which Foucault critiques and the nature to which environmental ethics has recourse are not the same entity. At the very least, they have a different site. As Jonathan Dollimore has argued, if the evocation of the term 'nature' by the Green movement risks carrying along with it a whole set of reactionary political significations, 'there are obvious and fundamental distinctions which can help prevent that – between human nature and the nature that is destroyed by human culture; between the ecological and the ideological conceptions of nature' (in Soper 1995: 119).

That is, Foucault wishes to deny, not that there is a world outside ourselves, which exists independently of our history, but that we have a nature, an essence, to which we have an obligation to conform. In this sense, he continues the French line of anti-essentialist thought which stretches back to the existentialists. Explicitly, at least, Foucault has nothing to say about nature as it might exist outside of us.[5] However, the distinctions which Dollimore calls upon us to respect are not as easily established as he would seem to believe. Foucault's insistence on the role of cultural codes in constituting our perception of reality by dividing it up and assigning it a mode of being before we can encounter it forecloses the space in which a nature which is independent of us could appear. If there is nature in Foucault's work, we can have no knowledge of it.

The Struggle in Discourse

The further we follow Foucault, it seems, the less he offers us. Culturally, he argues, nature functions negatively, so as to restrict people by coercively assigning them identities. Beneath this culture, however, there is no true nature, 'in itself', to which we can appeal. But perhaps we can follow the model of some feminists, and bracket the question of the existence of nature, just as they have bracketed the question of the definition of 'woman'. Like Spivak, we could rely upon a strategic essentialism, so long as it offers us a useful tool for our cause (Spivak 1984–5). Looked at in this light, Foucault can begin to offer us environmental strategies for resistance which do not rely upon notions as to what nature, in itself, might be, but instead attempt to put the received concept to work without committing us to a belief in an ontological referent for that concept.

The model here, once again, is the discourse of sexuality. We have already seen the way in which the deployment of sexuality worked so as to medicalize homosexuality in the name of a 'normal' sexuality, given 'by nature'. The resistance to such oppressive discourses by homosexuals themselves was itself mounted in the name of precisely the same nature:

> There is no question that the appearance in nineteenth-century psychiatry, jurisprudence, and literature of a whole series of discourses on the species and subspecies of homosexuality ... made possible a strong advance of social controls into this area of 'perversity'; but it also made possible the formation of a 'reverse' discourse: homosexuality began to speak in its own behalf, to demand that its legitimacy or 'naturality' be acknowledged, often in the same vocabulary, using the same categories by which it was medically disqualified. (Foucault 1976: 101)

The discourse of nature is double-edged. It can serve to justify intervention into the sphere of the born deviant, or to proclaim the right to exist of another manifestation of a natural diversity. The concept of the natural can simultaneously signify the primitive, which must be civilized, and the spontaneous, which gives health.

It is this battle over the meaning and functioning of networks of terms which receives, in Foucault's work, the name 'strategy'. It here that the battle in discourse – and through discourse, practice – is joined, not through opposing to the current deployment of sexuality a system of concepts foreign to it, but by reversing certain of its central ideas at strategic points.

It is here, I believe, that Foucault would locate the current state of play in environmental discourse and counter-discourse. Eco-politics is largely a battle over certain key terms, foremost among which is 'nature'. Against the readings of nature as resource to be utilized or danger to be controlled, environmentalists mobilize the largely romantic concept of nature as nurturer and as state of health. This is a genuine, meaningful struggle, through which real gains may be made (and real losses incurred). Despite the deconstructive critiques that can be levelled at this notion, despite its lack of ultimate philosophical justification, environmentalists abandon this – perhaps their most powerful weapon – at the peril of the small gains they have made.

Beyond Nature

Nevertheless, Foucault was never content to remain at this level of the strategic reversal of the concepts employed by the dominant discourse. Such a reversal may constitute a necessary first step toward a discourse of resistance, but it needs to be followed up by the formulation of concepts which to some extent at least break with the presuppositions of the deployment which it opposes. The demand that nature be respected may have a number of positive effects. But it always remains open to recolonization by the very discourse to which it is opposed. The situation is exactly analogous to Foucault's reading of the critique which Reich instituted of the control of sexuality, in the very name of sexuality: 'The importance of this critique and its impact on reality were substantial. But the very possibility of its success was tied to the fact that it always unfolded within the deployment of sexuality, and not outside or against it' (Foucault 1976: 131).

It is necessary, then, to go beyond this strictly reactive stage. In Foucault's view, the inability to formulate a vocabulary which is not simply the reverse of the deployment of sexuality constituted the major failing of the '[h]omosexual liberation movements', which remain 'caught at the level of demands for the right to their sexuality' (Foucault 1980a: 220). Feminism, on the other hand, has been more successful in working through this necessary stage of strategic reversal:

> the feminist movements have accepted the challenge. Are we sex by nature? Well, then, let it be but in its singularity, in its irreducible specificity. Let us draw the consequences from it and reinvent our own type of political, cultural and economic existence. . . . Always the same movement: take off from this sexuality in which movements can be colonised, go beyond them in order to reach other affirmations. (Foucault 1989a: 144)

For Foucault, homosexuals could get beyond strategic reversal by abandoning the question of the homosexual identity, and instead seeking to elaborate new relationships (Foucault 1989c: 203–4). Can environmentalists go beyond the discourse of nature to which they remain mortgaged? I believe that we have already demonstrated sufficiently that a Foucauldian environmental discourse must ultimately abandon such a discourse. But this is a conclusion that others have reached before us; yet so far no new basis for environmentalism has emerged. Perhaps the concept of bio-power, developed by Foucault in his analysis of nineteenth-century medical and governmental discourses, could serve as such a basis.

Bio-Power

Let us return once more to the concept of nature. Besides the deconstructive critique of its foundations, and the historical critique of its functioning, there is yet a third reason to doubt the efficacy of an appeal to nature as an environmental tactic. Consider some definitions of nature advanced by environmentalist philosophers. Nature is that which 'has not been modified by human hand', that which 'is independent of us' (Elliot 1995: 79, 82), that which 'is human neither in itself nor in its origins' (Passmore 1995: 129). Regardless of whether this nature can be conceptually defined, whether an untainted origin or essence could ever be postulated for it, there is good reason to believe that such a nature does not exist today. Given the ubiquity of the human presence on the earth today, as indicated by the effect human activity has on patterns of weather, on the composition of the air, on the amount of ultraviolet radiation, even in places where no human has ever lived and no tree been felled, and given the potential we now have to destroy much of life at a stroke with nuclear weapons, it is not clear that there is any place on the Earth which exists independently of us, which has not been modified by use, or could not be very dramatically further modified.[6] As Bill McKibben has noted, nature in this sense has ended: 'By changing the weather, we make every spot on earth man-made and artificial. We have deprived nature of its independence, and that is fatal to its meaning. Nature's independence *is* its meaning; without it there is nothing but us' (McKibben 1989: 58). We are not in control of the non-human world, because we are unable to predict with any accuracy the effects of our actions upon it. Nevertheless, that world can no longer be said to exist independently of us.

Perhaps, then, we have crossed a threshold similar to that crossed by Western countries in the eighteenth century. At that period in our history, Foucault contends, the basic method of governing underwent a dramatic, and relatively sudden, change. Prior to that time, the fundamental power of the sovereign lay in his or her right 'to *take* life or *let* live' (Foucault 1976: 136). Power in European societies during this period was a 'discontinuous, rambling, global system with little hold on detail' (Foucault 1980b: 151). If it focused upon an individual, it was in order to intervene 'by means of exemplary interventions' (ibid.), most notably, the confiscation of life. For most people, for most of the time, power was a distant rumour; in the rare cases when it manifested itself concretely, it was usually in order to dramatize its might through spectacular punishments ending in death.

But with the growth of new techniques of medico-social intervention at the level, not just of the individual, but of the population, we have the development of a form of power which operates upon life itself, 'that endeavours to administer, optimise, and multiply it, subjecting it to precise controls and comprehensive regulation' (Foucault 1976: 137).

The method of organization of power changed to such an extent that it was now able, not simply to ignore life or to confiscate it, but to make credible attempts to foster it. Power now intervenes continually in the life of every member of the population, for where phenomena of population are concerned, all individuals have the same statistical value. The eye of power is no longer a malevolent gaze, whose attention is to be feared. Instead it is the absence of this fostering power which must be avoided, and political struggles are largely over the claims of competing groups for a greater share of the attention of power.

This new form of power Foucault calls 'bio-power'. And it is perhaps this form of power with which we are dealing in discussing environmental politics. For, after the end of nature as an independent force, it is the non-human world as much as the human which has entered 'into the order of knowledge and power, into the sphere of political techniques' (ibid. 142). Just as the conditions of existence of human life entered for the first time the centre stage of history, as variables subject to intervention by medical authorities, by town planners, by public policy, so the conditions of non-human life have ceased to be 'an inaccessible substrate', and have 'passed into knowledge's field of control and power's sphere of intervention' (ibid.).

It will immediately be objected that, whereas with phenomena of human life we have achieved a degree of control, and can plausibly claim to be able to create environments for ourselves favourable, for example, to the reduction and management of disease, it is radically implausible to see our interventions in the non-human world as examples of our control over it. Were we in charge of the effects of our interventions in the non-human world, we would not be faced with the prospect of global warming, of the hole in the ozone layer, and of the depletion of the biodiversity upon which we ultimately depend. The looming environmental disaster is largely the inadvertent result of attempts to expand our control over the human world, which simply ignored the consequences for the non-human, as well as the longer-term consequences for ourselves. This objection has a certain validity. We cannot overlook the fact that, despite our ability to intervene in any sphere of the non-human world, our ability to calculate the consequences of that intervention remain very limited. Nevertheless, the fact that we have intervened on such a large scale that nature is no longer in principle independent from us by itself entails the extension of bio-power to the non-human world. As Foucault insists, bio-power does not imply control over life; it implies simply that life is no longer inaccessible to our intervention:

> It is not that life has been totally integrated into techniques that govern and administer it; it constantly escapes them . . . the biological risks confronting the species are perhaps greater, and certainly more serious, than before the birth of microbiology. But what might be called a society's 'threshold of modernity' has been reached when the life of the species is wagered on its own political strategies. (Ibid. 143)

Perhaps, then, now that the life of not one species but of all is the stake of our politics, we have crossed a new threshold: the threshold, perhaps, of postmodernity.

The entry of life on to the stage of history changed the stakes and the methods of political struggle. If the dominant powers now operated through the optimization of the conditions for life, then the counter-powers which opposed them utilized the same vocabulary, and fought over the same stakes. Bio-power instituted 'a very real process of struggle; life as a political object was in a sense taken at face value and turned back against the system that was bent on controlling it' (ibid. 145).

Foucault, of course, wished to resist certain features of bio-power, to the extent to which sexuality was the primary means by which power was given access to the smallest recesses of both individuals and of populations, and the form this sexuality took involved the coercive normalization of individuals, as well as an undesirable degree of control over populations. He wished to move beyond a struggle formulated in terms of the life of indi-viduals and populations, their health and their sexualities, to a less coercive way of imagining the autonomy of the subject. To this end, he formulated the aesthetic analogy which he was to develop in the second and third volumes of *The History of Sexu-ality*, which enabled him to think of the individual as needing to be created, rather than brought into harmony with its being. But in the case of a discourse of bio-power which takes as its object of analysis the non-human world, no such problem of essentializing definition arises. Bio-power need not, therefore, have any coercive or normalizing functions when it is turned away from the human and toward the non-human.

The fact that Foucault himself attempted to go beyond bio-power, therefore, need not present a Foucauldian environmental discourse which remains within its framework with any obstacle; for his critique of bio-power was predicated on its coercive effects when applied at the level of individual identity. In fact, Foucault himself, in what appears to be his only pronouncement upon environmentalism, seems to have come to the same conclusion, that it is necessary to remain with the confines of discourses preval-ent today, in order to develop an environmental critique:

> Things being what they are, nothing has, up to the present, proved that we could define a strategy exterior to [the obligation of truth]. It is indeed in this field of obligation to truth that we sometimes can avoid in one way or another the effects of a domination, linked to structures of truth or to institutions charged with truth. To say these things very schematically, we can find many examples: there has been an ecology movement . . . which has often been, in one sense, in hostile relationship with science or at least with a techno-logy guaranteed in terms of truth. But in fact, ecology also spoke a language of truth. It was in the name of knowledge concerning nature, the equilibrium of the processes of living things, and so forth, that one could level the criticism. We escaped then a domina-tion of truth, not by playing a game that was a complete stranger to the game of truth, but in playing it otherwise. (Foucault 1988b: 15)

It may be, then, that it is by applying the very strategies of governmentality which Foucault analysed and critiqued for us that a Foucauldian environmental discourse can find its most potent resource.

Strategies of Governmentality

If our current situation can really be accurately characterized as the extension of bio-power from the realm of population to that of all life, does that entail that the strategies we should be adopting are those of management of the non-human world, as well as that of the human? I believe that it does. But I do not believe that this necessitates, or even makes possible, the genetically engineered, artificial world which McKibben and many others who have advocated non-anthropocentric ethics have feared, the replacement of the natural world with 'a space station' (McKibben 1989: 170). And not just for the reason that, after the end of nature, the artificial/natural distinction is impossible to maintain. The world McKibben fears, in which forests are replaced by trees designed by us for maximum efficiency at absorbing carbon, and new strains of genetically engineered corn flourish in the new conditions brought about by global warming, seems to me unlikely in the extreme. The systems with which we are dealing, the imbrication of a huge variety of forms of life with chemical processes, with meteorological and geographic processes, are so complex, and occur on such scale, that I can see no way in which they could be replaced by artificial systems which would fulfil the same functions. Every intervention we make in that direction has consequences which are so far-reaching, and involve so many variables and as yet undetected connections between relatively independent systems, that they are practically unforeseeable. To replace non-human systems with mechanisms of our own devising would involve thousands of such interventions, each of which would then require follow-up interventions in order to reverse or control their unintended consequences. Even when, and if, our knowledge of the environment were to reach a stage at which we were able to predict the consequences of our interventions, it would be likely to be far easier, and, in the long run, cheaper, simply to turn the already functioning, 'natural' systems to our advantage. No method of reducing the amount of carbon dioxide in our atmosphere is likely to be more effective than preserving the Amazonian rain forest. For this reason, I believe, environmentalists have nothing to fear from such an apparently instrumental approach.

If the 'technological fix' is unlikely to be more successful than strategies of limitation of our use of resources, we are nevertheless unable simply to leave the environment as it is. There is a real and pressing need for more, and more accurate, technical and scientific information about the non-human world. For we are faced with a situation in which the processes we have already set in train will continue to impact upon that world, and therefore us, for centuries. It is therefore necessary, not only to stop cutting down the rain forests, but to develop real, concrete proposals for action, to reverse, or at least limit, the effects of our previous interventions.

Moreover, there is another reason why our behaviour towards the non-human cannot simply be a matter of leaving it as it is, at least in so far as our goals are not only environmental but also involve social justice. For if we simply preserve what remains to us of wilderness, of the countryside and of park land, we also preserve patterns of very unequal access to their resources and their consolations (Soper 1995: 207). In fact, we risk exacerbating these inequalities. It is not us, but the poor of Brazil, who will bear the brunt of the misery which would result from a strictly enforced policy of leaving the Amazonian rain forest untouched, in the absence of alternative means of providing for their livelihood. It is the development of policies to provide such ecologically sustainable alternatives which we require, as well as the development of technical means for replacing our current greenhouse gas-emitting sources of energy. Such policies and proposals for concrete action must be formulated by ecologists, environmentalists, people with expertise concerning the functioning of ecosystems and the impacts which our actions have upon them. Such proposals are, therefore, very much the province of Foucault's specific intellectual, the one who works 'within specific sectors, at the precise points where their own conditions of life or work situate them' (Foucault 1980g: 126). For who could be more fittingly described as 'the strategists of life and death' than these environmentalists? After the end of the Cold War, it is in this sphere, more than any other, that man's 'politics places his existence as a living being in question' (Foucault 1976: 143). For it is in facing the consequences of our intervention in the non-human world that the fate of our species, and of those with whom we share this planet, will be decided.

Notes

1   Thus Kate Soper: 'insofar as theory of sexuality and the body denies a realist conception of nature, it is ... incompatible with ecological thinking' (Soper 1995: 130–1).

2   It is true that some poststructuralists, more closely allied to Heidegger than is Foucault, adopt an even less humanist vocabulary, referring to that which underlies perception, knowledge and even culture, not as a system of codes, but as Being. It remains the case that the primary exemplar of this Being is usually language, which even for Heidegger was 'the house of Being' (Heidegger 1977: 193).

3   There are, of course, alternative foundations for the possibility of an environmental ethics. Unfortunately, none of those which I have encountered survive poststructural critique any better than does 'nature'. For instance, environmentalists sometimes attempt to defend ecosystems on the ground of their beauty (e.g. Sober 1995: 246); enough work has by now been done on the history and ideological functioning of aesthetic criteria (e.g. by Pierre Bourdieu) to make any such appeal problematic in the extreme. Another such putative ground refers to the origin of the natural world (e.g. Elliot 1995: 81; Callicott 1995: 50). Here too we are on shaky ground, given Derrida's critique of the concept of the original and of the authentic. Furthermore, these positions themselves rely upon a notion of nature at some level. It is *natural* beauty that Sober wishes to ground his ethics, and it has by no means been obvious to everyone that such beauty is greater than that of machines (the Italian Futurists are here a case in point). Sober, as much as any environmentalist who relies upon a notion of nature unmediated by aesthetic argument, thus needs criteria to distinguish between the natural world and the artefactual. Similarly, those who would defend the natural on the grounds of its origin stand in need of such criteria.

4   'Semiology has taught us that myth has the task of giving an historical intention a natural justification, and making contingency appear eternal' (Barthes 1978: 142).

5   On the other hand, it is clear that Foucault could not condone any of the many environmental discourses which have recourse to *our* essential nature, such as Callicott's call for us to 'accept and affirm natural biological laws, principles, and limitations in the human personal and biological spheres' (Callicott 1995: 54).

6   There are, of course, alternative definitions of nature which stress, not its independence from us, but our belonging to it. The problem with such definitions is that they do not contain any criteria which would allow us to differentiate between what we may and may not do to the non-human world. As Jan Narveson says, if we are part of nature, this remains true, '[n]o matter what we do to it' (1986: 120).

11

Foucault against Environmental Ethics

Éric Darier

[Nature is] prodigal beyond measure, indifferent beyond measure, without aims or intentions, without mercy or justice, at once fruitful and barren and uncertain.

– Nietzsche

What do we need ethics for?[1] This question could probably summarize Foucault's own interrogation of 'ethics'. Maybe the word *ethics* is so loaded with meaning that it would be better to abandon it altogether and, like Foucault, use other terms like 'aesthetics of existence' or 'practices of freedom'. In fact, Foucault's position was more 'against ethics' (Caputo 1993[2]) or located 'after virtue' (MacIntyre 1981) than the articulation of a yet another 'ethical' theory. If Foucault was critical – or at least suspicious – of 'ethics' in general, he would probably be even more suspicious of most contemporary 'environmental ethics', because of the tendency of advocates to use naturalistic and moralistic justifications. This is what has been called the 'naturalistic fallacy'. The legitimation of most conventional environmental ethical theories seems to rest – in the final instance – on a belief that the alleged 'natural world' should be the source of norms or directions that humans should obey. Like gods and 'objective scientific truth', 'nature' becomes another normative yardstick to impose itself on human behaviour and values. For example, it is in the name of the presumed 'proper' functioning of the 'ecosystem', in the name of 'sustainable development', that humans are now urged to adopt new values and new sets of conduct. Furthermore, as the 'laws of nature' are recognized as applying universally, the norms and solutions which are derived from them also claim to be universal, transcending the cultural and the historical. This is nevertheless what many environmental ethicists would understand by environmental ethics. Maybe surprisingly, many conventional environmental ethicists would condemn the theoretical recourse to a 'naturalistic fallacy' (Sober 1995: 233–8). However, they generally fall back – in the end – into the 'naturalistic fallacy' they themselves condemn. For example, Holmes Rolston seems very clear in his condemnation of the 'naturalistic fallacy'.

> Ethicists had settled on at least one conclusion as ethics became modern in Darwin's century: that the moral has nothing to do with the natural. Science describes natural history and natural law; ethics prescribes human conduct, moral law; and to confuse the two makes a category mistake, commits the naturalistic fallacy. Nature simply is, without objective value; the preferences of human subjects establish value; and these human values, appropriately considered, generate what ought to be. (Rolston 1992: 135)[3]

After denying adopting an ethical justification based on a 'naturalistic fallacy', Rolston tells us that as we prepare to enter the next millennium, 'we must argue from the natural to the moral', and that 'this biological world that *is* also *ought to be*' (ibid.). Rolston becomes much bolder when he declares soon after that, '[f]aced with revolution, ethical conservatives may shrink back and refuse to think biologically, to naturalise ethics in the deep sense' (ibid.). Although Rolston's targets here are anthropocentrists, his argument falls into a naturalistic fallacy of his own ('from the natural to the moral'). What seems to be missing from Rolston's argument is an evaluation of the conditions for the emergence of its own justifications and a heavy dose of much-needed scepticism. Failing to acknowledge that grand universalizing ethical theorizing is itself the product of a specific time and place, Rolston's ethical position becomes just another totalizing theory. His naturalistic ultimate temptation is not, however, unique (Cheney 1989;[4] Hargrove 1989[5]). For example, even Max Oelschlaeger, who is generally more sympathetic to postmodernism than Rolston, feels that 'as opposed to "deconstructive or negative" post-modernism' (Oelschlaeger 1995: 2), 'affirmative post-modernists naturalise the category of "history", so that human beings are described as members of the earth community' (ibid. 7). In this context, the description/prescription by Rolston, Oelschlaeger and others of what environmental ethics *ought* to be leads me to echo David Halperin and ask: what do we need environmental ethics for?

This is where Michel Foucault might help us in recontextualizing 'ethics' and in outlining the conditions for a possible green 'aesthetics of existence', while resisting the temptation to use a naturalistic justification as a foundationalist anchor.[6]

Ethics and Power/Knowledge

One of the current dominant and possible naturalistic justifications for environmental ethics is offered by the natural sciences. Many conventional environmental ethicists would generally agree that the natural sciences' understanding of how the environment functions is more or less accurate, and therefore legitimate as 'truth', and so as a foundation – or at least as a solid starting-point – for environmental ethics. In the late twentieth century, an acceptance of scientific knowledge as a positivist representation of 'reality', of 'truth', is seen as increasingly untenable (Darier 1995). In terms of Foucault's archeology of knowledge (*savoirs*), modern science is more aptly caricatured as a 'will to truth' (Foucault 1973). Like Thomas Kuhn, Foucault argues that 'truth' is context-specific; it emerges from specific world-views ('discourse') or from specific paradigmatic communities (Kuhn 1962). For Foucault, there are only 'games of truth', not absolute 'truth'; knowledge cannot be external and detached from the context of its production. Thus, 'games of truth' are 'an ensemble of procedures which lead to a certain result, which can be considered in function of its principles and its rules of procedures, as valid or not, as winner or loser' (Foucault 1988b: 16). Knowledge is no longer a more or less accurate 'representation' of a presumed fixed, external reality. In some cases, as Latour and Woolgar (1986) have demonstrated, natural scientists are actively engaged in constructing natural 'objects' in the course of their research. In this context, it is futile to expect clear, certain, absolute, universal sets of environmental ethical norms from these contingent, but nevertheless rational in their own terms, 'games of truth'.

The second major challenge to most conventional approaches to environmental ethics is the impossibility of outlining an ethic free from existing relations of power. The omnipresence of un-bracketable relations of power renders this task impossible. In fact, it is the existence of specific relations of power that makes it possible to articulate specific codes of moral conduct. For Foucault, the coexistence of 'games of truth' and 'relations of power' are intimately linked in what he calls 'power/knowledge', a single word underlining the fact that all knowledge is inevitably intertwined with power relations, and vice versa. However, Foucault's approach to 'power' is radically different from what is usually understood by this term, as explained in greater detail in the introduction to this volume. Like Nietzsche, Foucault doesn't define 'power' from the traditional notion of sovereignty as negative and repressive. 'Power' should not be understood as 'domination', although Foucault would not deny the existence of relations of domination in specific cases. Instead, Foucault attempts to go beyond a negative, repressive view of power. He sees power relations as taking place in a non-deterministic 'field of power', and in a non-linear, non-top-down dominating / dominated type of relationship. Thus, 'power is not an evil . . . Power is a strategic game' (Foucault 1988b: 18), as knowledge is a 'game of truth'. Therefore, 'power/knowledge' is the necessary condition for the emergence of any environmental ethic. This means that environmental ethics cannot adequately be conceived in terms of grand universal principles detached from the context of their actual production.

Foucauldian 'Ethics'

Knowing now what ethics is *not* for Foucault, is it possible to examine what it could be, or rather, what the possibilities of non-foundationalist ethics could offer? Just before his death in 1984, Foucault published the second and third volumes of *The History of Sexuality*, in which he explored how 'one can think differently than one thinks, and perceive differently than one sees' (Foucault 1984f: 8). As explained later in more detail, Foucault didn't believe in the existence of a transhistorical, universal human essence. He was strongly opposed to the humanist essentialist project on account of its potential totalizing consequences. This is why Foucault's ethics can be described as being an attempt to outline a 'post-Auschwitz ethic' (Bernauer 1992), which is to say, how it is possible to be 'ethical' after the systematic Nazi effort to erase previously established 'ethics'.

If Foucault rejects the idea of human essence, he keeps the concept of identity. For him, individual identity – or rather, identities, and certainly not essence – is the result of a historical construction emerging from within a specific cultural context. Identity should be understood as what is located within the boundaries which emerge from the socio-cultural milieu, or as what Jacques Lacan would call the 'empty place of the structure' (Sandilands 1995: 80).[7] 'Individuals are therefore the matter on which the work of subjectification is to be carried out. They do not really have any being outside this work' (Jambert 1992: 240). In the case of the Western European experience, Foucault locates the emergence of the identity of the 'modern' subject in the intersection of three axes: '(1) the formation of sciences (*savoirs*) . . . (2) the systems of power that regulate [a] practice, [and] (3) the forms within which individuals are able, are obliged, to recognise themselves as subjects' (Foucault 1984f: 4). The second axis and parts of the third ('individuals . . . are obliged to . . .') are what Foucault calls 'normalization' – that is to say, the process by which individuals are induced to internalize a given set of norms, world-view and expected conduct. Elsewhere, Foucault shows that the internalization of norms by each individual, and by the population in general, was a strategy adopted by the emerging modern European 'states' from the sixteenth century onward. Competing states required greater and more effective control of their populations for military and economic reasons. States became increasingly concerned about all aspects of the life of their populations, especially if they affected the population's biological well-being, as do adequate food supply, reproduction, disease control, health, illness and so on. Ruffié and Sournia (1995) provide an excellent example of a historical study of the culturo-political aspects of 'illness' and 'health' following Foucault. Foucault identified this state preoccupation as 'biopolitics', a concern which 'brought life and its mechanisms into the realm of explicit calculations and made knowledge/power an agent of transformation of human life' (Foucault 1976: 143). The effective control of the population – from the perspective of an instrumental reason of state – required more than the simple use of – or threat of – brutal force. It required instilling self-enforcing, self-imposed mechanisms of social control on the entire social body (*omnes*) and on each individual (*singulatim*) (Foucault 1981c). In the context of this strategy, called 'governmentality', states incorporated 'pastoral' techniques (developed earlier by the Christian Church, like confession and introspection) through the 'social sciences', to achieve greater control of the population through new forms of 'self'-discipline (Darier 1996a).

This necessary digression may enable us to better understand Foucault's deep suspicion of any ethics based on grand universalizing principles whose objectives or consequential 'power effects' might be to increase the normalization of individuals by means of a presumed autonomous expression of their essentialist and humanist subjectivity. In this context, Foucault's *The Use of Pleasure* can be disconcerting for many. Foucault had indeed engaged in another 'theoretical shift', one in which he 'felt obliged to study the games of truth in the relationship of self with self and the forming of oneself as a subject' (1984f: 6). However, Foucault's choice of antiquity as the site for the 'slow formation . . . of a hermeneutics of the self' (ibid.) wasn't a nostalgia for a lost Eden in which social control was less overwhelming than it is in our current societies. Foucault was very clear on this point: 'Nothing is more foreign to me than the idea that philosophy strayed at a certain moment of time, and that it has forgotten something and that somewhere in her history there exists a principle, a basis that must be rediscovered' (1988b: 15). Foucault was not trying to persuade his readers to adopt some idealized Greek ethic *per se*, but to investigate 'if one can think differently than one thinks, and perceive differently than one sees' (Foucault 1984f: 8; Halperin 1990: 62–71).

Beyond Truth, Normalization and Resistance

As mentioned before, there is no universal human essence for Foucault. The essentialist humanist subject is dead, or, more exactly, never existed. Instead, Foucault is interested in examining the conditions for the emergence of specific ways whereby humans constitute their self-identity through the axes of knowledge, power and subjectivity. It is in the context determined by these axes that the process of truth-normalization-resistance takes place. To illustrate the complexity of strategic games of truth, of power/knowledge and resistance, Foucault uses the example of the ecology movement

> . . . which has often been, in one sense, in hostile relationship with science or at least with a technology guaranteed in terms of truth. But in fact, ecology also spoke a language of truth. It was in the name of knowledge concerning nature, the equilibrium of the processes of living things, and so forth, that one could level the criticism. (1988b: 15)

This means that, to Foucault at least, there is no fixed, certain strategic position that a group or individuals can adopt. All the choices present dangers – and opportunities – which have to be reappraised constantly as the configuration of the 'field of power' changes. Every single move by any group, individual or institution alters the dynamics in the 'field of power'. The concept of resistance is hard to define, because what is resisted and who resists constantly change.

Resistance for Foucault is radically different from the way 'liberationists', ranging from early Liberals and Marxists to psychoanalysts, would understand it. 'Liberationist' theory presumed the existence of an irreducible human essence masked and repressed by existing omni-present politico, socio-economic or moralistic values, which need to be lifted as a condition for the realization of human potential. The liberationist position presumed that relations of power are mainly 'negative' – that is, 'repressive' (Foucault 1976). Therefore, for liberationists, the suspension of existing relations of power is a necessary condition for the fulfilment of their objective.

However, Foucault argues that relations of power are largely 'positive' in the sense that they also give identity / identities to individuals, which enables them to act in the world. There cannot be 'liberation' *per se*, because there cannot be 'liberation' in the absence of relations of power. Instead of 'liberation', Foucault preferred the term 'resistance'. The existence of a 'field of power' – and therefore of unbracketable relations of power – is the condition for resistance and, ultimately, the expression of human freedom. Freedom manifests itself through, and because of, relations of power, and certainly not through their absence. In fact, '[t]here cannot be relations of power unless the subjects are free' (Foucault 1976: 12). What Foucault means is that some individuals or groups are able to resist, to challenge and to transgress the boundaries of their given identity / identities. For Foucault, resistance is the obvious manifestation of ultimate human freedom, a freedom grounded in context and in the practices of the transgression of limits, not an ontological and abstract freedom. For Foucault, a person 'does not begin with liberty but with the limit' (Foucault 1972: 578). In this context, one can understand Foucault's critique of foundational identity politics, because for him, 'the target nowadays is not to discover who we are but to refuse who we are' (Foucault 1982: 216).

Consequently, Foucault vehemently refused to offer any explicit grand normative project which could emerge from resistance. While Marx refused to offer a precise description of the future ideal

Communist society on the ground that this task should be left to tomorrow's working class as agents of historical change, Foucault refused for fear of introducing another totalizing project. This fear is understandable in the pessimistic context of the twentieth century, which has witnessed two world wars, systematic genocide in Nazi concentration camps and in Stalinist gulags, nuclear explosions at Hiroshima and Nagasaki, traumatic decolonization wars and the current profound changes in the environment of the planet encouraged by 'integrated world capitalism' (Guattari 1990). Nevertheless, Foucault encourages us 'to promote new forms of subjectivity through the refusal of a kind of individuality which has been imposed on us for several centuries' (Foucault 1982).

This refusal to outline a normative project doesn't mean that Foucault's position is without normative assumptions. On the contrary, Foucault's constant questioning of the self – or, more precisely, the boundaries defining the self – should be seen as one of his core normative assumptions. This is why Lawrence Olivier perceives Foucault as an avowed partisan of nihilism – a nihilism understood as a 'space inside Modernity where thought operates a reflexive turn on itself to interrogate the condition of it own possibility' (Olivier 1995: 17, my translation). This is what Foucault calls 'genealogy', an approach anchored in the constant questioning and transgression of boundaries. This is within the trajectory of the Enlightenment project, but in a radicalized form – 'a self-critical Enlightenment' (Mahon 1992: 179: Foucault 1984h). In light of his genealogical approach, Foucault interprets Kant's critical ontology of ourselves as 'an attitude, an ethos, a philosophical life in which the critique of what we are is at one and the same time the historical analysis of the limits that are imposed on us and an experiment with the possibility of going beyond them' (Foucault 1984h). Foucault uses Kantian reason to question and historicize Kant's own interrogations. Foucault's questions are 'not "What can I know?" but rather, "How have my questions been produced?", "How has the path of my knowing been determined?" Not "What ought I to do?" but rather, "How have I been situated to experience the real?"' (Bernauer 1992: 270–1).

Therefore, Foucault's ethics is 'the practice of an intellectual freedom that is transgressive of modern knowledge-power-subjectivity relations' (Bernauer and Mahon 1994: 152). Foucault believed that through transgression it was possible to go beyond the normalizing effects of knowledge-power-subjectivity and find a relatively autonomous space – a crack in the normalizing *dispositif*

– which would enable each individual 'to give one's self the rules of law, the techniques of management, and also the ethics, the *ethos*, the practice of self, which would allow these games of power to be played with a minimum of domination' (Foucault 1988b: 18).

A Foucauldian Environmental Ethics: An Aesthetic of a Green Existence?

One of the central features of Foucault's ethics, as outlined in *The Use of Pleasure*, is an 'aesthetic of existence', or 'arts of existence', which are 'those intentional and voluntary actions by which men [sic] not only set themselves rules of conduct, but also seek to transform themselves, to change themselves in their singular being, and to make their life into an *oeuvre* that carries certain aesthetic values and meets certain stylistic criteria' (Foucault 1984f: 10–11).

Foucault borrowed this idea of an 'aesthetic of existence' from Nietzsche, for whom aesthetics became not only a strategy of resistance in late modernity, but the only way in which individuals could give meaning to their own life after the death of external referential points, such as 'God' or 'Truth'. For Nietzsche and Foucault, 'we need art not to make us immoral, or to take us beyond the sphere of the ethical, but to enable us to carry on being moral in the fate of our recognition of the terror and absurdity of existence' (Ansell-Pearson 1994: 5).

Before going into further detail about this 'aesthetic of existence', it is important to examine the way in which Foucault mapped the different aspects of ethics as understood since the Greeks (Davidson 1986: 229). The first aspect is 'morality', which is a prescriptive ensemble forming a 'moral code'. In this context, 'morality' is the mechanism by which individuals are normalized. Consequently, 'morality' is 'a set of values and rules of action that are recommended to individuals through the intermediary of various prescriptive agencies such as the family (in one of its roles), educational institutions, churches, and so forth. It is sometimes the case that these rules and values are plainly set forth in a coherent doctrine and an explicit teaching' (Foucault 1984f: 25). Nevertheless, it doesn't necessarily constitute a coherent, 'systematic' ensemble. As in the 'field of power', there are cracks in any moral code which provide possibilities for 'compromises or loopholes' (ibid.). This leads to the second aspect of 'morality', perceived as 'the morality of behaviors', which is the actual 'behavior of individuals in relation to the rules and values that are recommended to them; the word thus designates the manner in which they comply more or less fully with a standard of conduct, the manner in which they obey or resist an interdiction or a prescription; the manner in which they respect or disregard a set of values' (ibid.).

There is a third aspect of ethics, however, which is the reflexive work on, and by, oneself about 'how one ought to "conduct oneself"' (ibid. 26). This third aspect – let's call it an ethics of 'conduct' – is what Foucault is concerned with in the last two volumes of *The History of Sexuality*. This concern for an ethics of conduct doesn't mean that he ignores the other two aspects ('moral code' and 'morality of behaviors'). On the contrary, the first two aspects provide the necessary conditions, in a non-deterministic manner, for an ethics of conduct, an aesthetic of existence. Differences between the three aspects of ethics can be explained by the four levels of the ethical process: (1) the determination of the ethical substance, (2) the mode of subjection, (3) the forms of elaboration of ethical work, and (4) the telos.

The 'determination of the ethical substance' is the 'way in which the individual has to constitute this or that part of himself as the prime material of his moral conduct' (ibid.). The 'mode of subjection' is the 'way in which the individual establishes his relation to the rule and recognises himself as obliged to put it into practice' (ibid. 27). The 'forms of elaboration of ethical work' refer to the way 'that one performs on oneself, not only in order to bring one's conduct into compliance with a given rule, but to attempt to transform oneself into the ethical subject of one's behavior' (ibid. 27–8). Finally, the 'telos' relates to the fact that 'an action is not only moral in itself, in its singularity; it is also moral in its circumstantial integration and by virtue of the place it occupies in a pattern of conduct' (ibid. 28).

What is Foucault telling us here, and how can we understand it in the context of environmental ethics? First of all, for Foucault, for an action to be ethical, 'it must not be reducible to an act or a series of acts conforming to a rule, a law or a value' (ibid.). Simple compliance with an environmental code of conduct is not alone sufficient to make an individual an ethical subject. Secondly, for Foucault, 'self-awareness' is necessary but not sufficient for an individual to engage in 'self-formation as an "ethical subject"' (ibid.). An environmental ethics based only on heightened self-awareness of the natural world is not sufficient. This 'aware-ness' must also lead to the self-formation as an 'ethical subject' which Foucault defined as 'a process in which the individual delimits that part of himself that will form the object of his moral practice, defines his position relative to the precept he will follow, and decides on a certain mode of being that will follow, and decides on a certain mode of being that will serve as his moral goal' (ibid.). This means that individuals must engage in 'practices of the self' which require that they 'monitor, test, improve, and transform' themselves (ibid.). I believe that an environmental ethics *à la* Foucault implies constant 'self-reflection, self-knowledge, self-examination' of the existing limits of what constitutes the 'envir-onment' and the individual's conduct *vis-à-vis* the 'environment' and *vis-à-vis* oneself. Therefore, the objective of a Foucauldian Green aesthetics of existence might not be to 'save the planet' *per se* – although it could well be one of the 'happy' consequences. It is the perpetual process of 'self-reflection, self-knowledge, self-examination', of transforming one's life into an aesthetic of exist-ence, of 'self-overcoming' one's self.[8]

An Example of Foucauldian Politics and Ethical Practices: Gay Resistance and Queer Identity

Foucault's lasting contribution may not be located exclusively in the theoretical and academic debates surrounding the meaning of his voluminous work. On the contrary, one of the most obvious impacts of Foucault has been on the political practices of groups – such as women's or gay and lesbian organizations – engaged directly in struggles. Obviously, the political practices of these groups influence the theoretical work undertaken by feminism and queer theory (Diamond and Quinby 1988; McNay 1992; Ramazanoğlu 1993). Therefore, it is highly pertinent to study more closely the 'Foucault effect' (Burchell et al. 1991) on these groups, and to see if and how Foucault could be relevant to environmentalism. I shall focus here on gay 'ethics', for several reasons – although non-foundationalist feminism would have been another obvious option (Butler 1992; Sandilands 1995). First of all, recent essays have outlined a gay 'ethic' based on Foucauldian ethics (Blasius 1995; Halperin 1995). Secondly, using Foucault, many gay activists have gone beyond naturalist/essentialist argu-ments to justify their activism. It is through acts of resistance that there emerged the conditions for an alternative ethic – let's call it 'queer' – in distinction to the given 'homosexual' identity, and whose motto could be 'identity without an essence'. For Halperin,

> Queer is by definition *whatever* is at odds with the normal, the legitimate, the dominant. *There is nothing in particular to which it necessarily refers.* It is an identity without essence. 'Queer,' then, demarcates not a positivity but a positionality vis-à-vis the normative – a positionality that is not restricted to lesbians and gay men but in fact available to anyone who is or who feels marginalized because or her or his sexual practices: it could include some married couples. (Halperin 1995: 62)

In contrast to this queer 'ethic', most environmental ethicists rarely question their underpinning naturalist / essentialist assumptions, and even more rarely examine their own discourses strategically, rather than substantively. Thirdly, Foucault is less controversial among queer theorists and practitioners than he is among feminists (Ramazanoğlu 1993). Let us remember that the objective here is not to settle theoretical arguments about Foucault, but to give a concrete example of what a Foucauldian understanding of environmental 'ethics' might be.

Would it be possible, following the example of a queer Foucauldian ethics, to imagine an environmental ethics (let's call it a 'Green ethics' to distinguish it from existing environmental ethics) grounded not in naturalist / essentialist assumptions but in practices of transgression of, for example, these naturalist / essentialist boundaries? Would it be possible to imagine a Green ethics based on the transgression of a given subjectivity, such as consumerism (as the 'satisfaction of desire'), to radically change one's own conduct towards a post-consumer identity? Wouldn't the radical questioning and transgression of given subjectivities, such as the consumer subjectivity, be an act of resistance which could lead towards a Green ethics, a Green aesthetics of existence?

Gay Resistance, Not Gay Liberation, as an Aesthetics of Existence

In the first volume of *The History of Sexuality* Foucault challenges what he calls the 'repressive hypothesis' which claims that, since the late nineteenth century, sexuality has been repressed. For Foucault, this scenario of 'repression' doesn't take into account the multiplication of discourses about sexuality, ranging from medical explanations to Freudian and post-Freudian psychoanalysis. Far from being 'repressed', sexuality has been given new forms of expression. Furthermore, it was the creation of the 'homosexual' category by the medical profession which led to the emergence of a new social group called 'homosexuals'. Individuals trapped in the definition of 'homosexual' started to incorporate it as part of their subjectivity. Therefore, it is not surprising that they started to organize themselves politically as 'homosexuals'. However, it was only in the 1970s that organized 'homosexuals' decided to change their name to 'gays and lesbians', to create a tactical rupture between the narrowly defined medical term and the new collective identity they wished to create. The very act of claiming a 'gay or lesbian' identity was an act of resistance – a tactical reversal – to the imposed 'homosexual' label. Yet, at the same time, it was the existence of various discourses about 'homosexuality' which created the conditions for the emergence of the contemporary 'gay and lesbian' movement. The form taken by 'gay and lesbian' politics has been largely a discourse of 'liberation', from oppression and from homophobia. Nevertheless, this 'liberatory' discourse should be seen as a strategy of resistance, of posturing, which is only part of a 'complex strategic situation in a particular society', not some à priori grand project in favour of some universal, transhistoric, transparent and uncensored expression of human sexuality.

This tactic of resistance, not liberation, became more obvious in the political practices of ACT UP (AIDS Coalition to Unleash Power), which have included spectacular actions that 'blocked traffic on San Francisco's Golden Gate Bridge, halted trading on the New York Stock Exchange, and disrupted the broadcast of the CBS Evening News' (Halperin 1995: 23). It is interesting to note that these spectacular actions are a form of 'camp' politics which is the overt, ironic exaggeration of a social role to increase visibility and to undermine dominant, idealized role models. For example, the 'drag queen' manages to attract attention to her/himself (visibility), and to caricature to an extreme the heterosexual model of an ideal feminine body, thus undermining the very possibility of such a heterosexual male fantasy. In the case of ACT UP, the spectacular actions publicly present the 'victims' of AIDS not in a patient role, but, on the contrary, as being very 'impatient'. One of the central objectives of ACT UP is to resist the *dispositif* (apparatus) of normalization which emerges from various problematizations around AIDS. The normalizing *dispositif* surrounding AIDS follows the three axes of knowledge, power and subjectivity identified by Foucault. ACT UP's multiple, diverse political targets represent acts of resistance to the three axes of the *dispositif*. For example, ACT UP challenges simultaneously the monopolistic authority of research and treatment by the medical profession (knowledge) and the legitimacy of public health authorities imposing policies without the active, consenting participation of those directly concerned (power), and promotes a reversal of position, from that of a helpless, passive, shameful AIDS victim (normalized subjectivity) to that of powerful proud activist (subjectivity 'by choice'[9]). The politics, and therefore the practical ethics, of ACT UP is based on constant resistance to the normalization process, because it always transforms and mutates itself. Through this process of constant resistance to forever shifting relations of power, emerge conditions for different subjectivities, different ways of being in the world, a different ethic of existence. This is why Foucault states that resistance is 'not simply a negation but a creative process' (Gallagher and Wilson 1984: 26–30, quoted in Halperin 1995: 60). For Foucault, resistance is a practice of human freedom, a freedom in context, not a grand ontological category, as liberation theorists believe.

Queer Identity as an Identity without Essence, or the Transgression of the Boundaries of Naturalism

One of the reasons why resistance is central to Foucault's political ethics is to avoid having to justify social action by recourse to a foundational essence such as a naturalist category.

History has shown repeatedly that horrors have been committed in the name of universal categories such as 'naturalness', 'progress' and 'liberation'. In the history of political theory, recourse to a foundationally grounded discourse on 'nature' has had many diverse outcomes. For example, Rousseau's interpretation of society and civilization as corrupters of humans' natural good disposition led to the possibility of a majoritarian negotiated social contract to preserve, to a certain extent, the presumed natural good dispositions of humans in the state of nature. On the other hand, for Hobbes, humans were naturally self-interested and selfish, and only an authoritarian Leviathan could keep society from falling into chaos. There are many examples of how abstract naturalistic categories can be used to justify specific socio-political systems. Indeed, it seems that 'nature will justify anything' (Winner 1986: 137). The rejection of foundationalism based on the 'naturalistic fallacy' by some gay and lesbian activists is an attempt to circumvent the pitfalls of such tactics. Whether homosexuality is 'natural' is not an ontological and/or scientifico-rational question, but a choice within a specific context of relations of power. For example, the late nineteenth-century German homosexual rights movement argued that homosexuality was a natural condition, and should therefore be decriminalized. Sadly, the Nazi regime also used a naturalistic argument (homosexuals are indeed members of a natural category – a degenerate 'species') to justify exterminating about 60,000 homosexuals in concentration camps. Other homophobic discourses use the opposing argument that homosexuality is *not* 'natural', because it doesn't result in human reproduction. Therefore the choice of a foundationalist/naturalist category always presents dangers. Halperin suggests that it is a no-win tactical choice for gays and lesbians. There cannot be any external 'rational' adjudicator in the debate about the validity of foundationalist/naturalist categories. In fact, Halperin goes further, and argues that the apparent incoherence of homophobic discourses, through a 'series of double binds', is in fact a subtle *dispositif* to ensure their effective deployment with dire political consequences (Halperin 1995: 33–8; Sedgwick 1990). '[I]f homosexuality *is* an immutable characteristic, we lose our civil rights, and if homosexuality is *not* an immutable characteristic, we lose our civil rights. Anyone for rational argument on these terms?' (Halperin 1995: 34).

Another act of resistance adopted by some gay and lesbian activists consists in a reversal of discourse by questioning the unproblematized norms which enable the identification, definition, medicalization and control of 'abnormalities' such as 'homosexuality'. For example, 'lesbian and gay sexualities may be understood and imagined as forms of resistance to cultural homogenisation, counteracting dominant discourses with other constructions of the subject in culture' (de Lauretis 1991: iii). In this context, the issue is no longer the search for the causes of 'homosexuality', but, on the contrary, the process which makes a norm unproblematized. In practical terms, one of the central questions becomes: how does an individual become 'heterosexual'? This strategy of reversal enables a recontextualization of 'homosexuality' in a broader context. The 'homosexual' category becomes a strategic means to define 'heterosexuality' by creating a negative distance. 'Whatever else you might say about [heterosexuality], at least it's not that.' However, this negative problematization of 'heterosexuality' in opposition to 'abnormal' categories ('it is not that'), creates a void in the 'normal' category of 'heterosexuality'. In turn, this void creates a 'heterosexual anxiety' which could explain homophobia (Morrison 1993–4: 57 in Halperin 1995: 44–5, n. 203). In other contexts of 'normality', it could explain many 'isms', such as sexism, racism and/or xenophobia.[10] However, let us be clear, the statement that the deployment of 'normality' could explain many 'isms' shouldn't be taken as a claim to truth *per se*—despite its seductive and very persuasive logical explanation. On the contrary, it should be taken *tactically* in the overall context of the axes of knowledge, power and subjectivity.

From a Queer Ethics to a Green Ethics

On the basis of the two aspects of queer ethics presented – resistance and non-essentialism – let us examine if and how they could be applicable to Green ethics. The theme of environmental resistance, as ethics, has already been addressed, notably in an article by Peter Quigley in this volume and elsewhere (1990, 1992). For him, 'traditional and contemporary postures of ecological resistance share too many features with the power they wish to oppose', and therefore 'could benefit from a thorough reconsideration in light of poststructural philosophy, which provides the basis for a sweeping resistance movement' (Quigley 1992: 291). Quigley claims that for structuralism there is 'no eternal truth' and no 'transcendent essences', and that what is 'made to seem "natural"' is the result of an 'act of centering and freezing' by 'a power group' (ibid. 293). Quigley sees anthropocentrism as an example of an 'act of centering and freezing' which can be opposed by 'deconstruction', a technique to 'demonstrate the arbitrary nature of this centering', and ultimately forces its dismantling. In practical terms, this means questioning the dominant type of environmental resistance, which advocates a return to a lost, presumably more natural, state as a way of opposing the current degradation of the environment. Quigley correctly identifies this type of resistance in the politics of 'liberation' of the 1960s. It is also precisely this 'liberationist' discourse that Foucault criticized in the first volume of *The History of Sexuality*. Transferring Foucault's argument to the environmental issue, we note that the proliferation of environmental discourse, policies, legislation, political struggles and so on is taking place at the point in history when discourses about human-led environmental changes ('pollution') emerged. Thus, environmentalism might also be, beyond the genuine attempt to prevent 'pollution' and preserve 'nature', a subtle strategy to make the human population adapt to the effective end of 'pristine' nature and the collapse of the previously established distinction between nature and culture. Quigley illustrates this type of 'liberationist' environmental discourse by the example of Theodore Roszak's (1979) argument, which 'posits an eternal essence and suggests that this essence is shared by the unique personality and spirit of nature' (Quigley 1992: 298). However, what is to be resisted, according to Roszak, is defined by clear naturalist boundaries which are themselves not questioned. Quigley's critical analysis follows the same general direction as Foucault's. However, Quigley stops short of giving precise tactical and practical suggestions for an ethics of environmental resistance, despite the fact that there are already existing examples, notably queer ethics.

Green Resistance as an Aesthetic of Existence

It should be obvious by now that a Foucauldian Green resistance is not simply a potential instrument with which to oppose the destruction of 'nature', taken as a pre-given essential category, but is also the ultimate act of human freedom – to constantly question the process whereby essential categories emerge historically, and how human subjectivity and human conduct are constructed in the context of these categories. This constant critique in itself could constitute an aesthetic of existence. A beautiful life worth living is a life of constant self-critique, a work on oneself with regard to the possibilities of thinking differently, of becoming something different from what we have been made, of engaging in the process of construction called 'self-improvement' (Hacking 1986). But how do we know that an act of resistance is 'Green'? As there are no absolute, external referential categories, it is not possible to evaluate in the abstract the degree of 'greenness' of any act of resistance. However, since any action is situated in a

specific context of power relations, it is possible to know if, tactically and at a given time, a Green act of resistance merely legitimizes
the existing system of power relations or if it undermines it.
Because of the extreme fluidity and adaptivity of the relations of
power, a genuine act of Green resistance yesterday could rapidly
become one of the legitimating elements for environmental practices contrary to the intentions of the initial acts of resistance. For
example, the quest for scientific knowledge about the functioning
of the natural environment can be seen as an instrument for
instigating changes in human practices which might otherwise have
arguably dire ecological and human consequences. However, the
same knowledge can also be used to justify the introduction of
changes in social practices *vis-à-vis* the 'environment' which, in
the longer term, could have even worse ecological and/or human
consequences. This is the case with 'conservationism', which wanted
to prevent deforestation, but led to increased exploitation of forests
for commercial and state interests, through greater scientific – and
presumably 'rational' – forest management (Darier 1991). Fire
prevention can be seen as a measure to protect forests (as well as
commercial, fiscal and tourism revenues), but can also lead to
long-term ecological decline if forests are prevented from regenerat-
ing themselves through fire. Therefore, the degree of 'greenness'
of resistance can be measured only in context, not in the abstract.

   In summary, Green ethics based on resistance must be understood as an aesthetic of human existence rooted in a permanent,
radical questioning and re-questioning of the broader conditions
which result in humans seeing the world as they see it, so as to
think differently from the way they now think. It is through this
process of constant hyper-criticism and 'tactical hyper-activism'
(Gandal 1986: 122) that one can question the conditions which
account for one's subjectivity, and start to imagine and build new
kinds of subjectivities. For example, it is through practical opposition to a new landfill site or an incinerator that individuals and
communities may start questioning the conditions which have led
to a 'garbage crisis'. Household recycling can be one technical
alternative which transforms individual subjectivity from 'waste-
ful' consumer to recycling or Green consumer. However, it could
also lead one to re-question the entire process of consumerism,
and why and how individuals are seduced by it. In this case,
opposing a landfill site or incinerator might be a necessary condition for a radical shift from a consumer self to a post-consumer
self, which might be a green self (Conley 1993; Darier 1996b).

Believe in Non-Naturalism, but Tactical Naturalism if Necessary

Even if one adopts a green ethics of resistance, one could still be tempted to ground it in some kind of naturalist certainty. It is at this point that one might see a contradiction between existing environmental struggles and a green Foucauldian ethics. The overwhelming majority of environmental struggles appeal to some kind of 'natural' imperative to justify their actions. It is in the name of some 'natural' law which is violated that the environmental movement is mobilized. It would appear that the discourse of the environmental movement is indeed strongly anchored in naturalistic arguments. On the other hand, a Foucauldian approach challenges foundationalism, including the naturalism of environmentalism.

How can we square this apparent contradiction? Again, we have to go back to Foucault's understanding of discourse and practices, not as the affirmation of absolute truth, but as a strategic game which the existing relations of power forces on the players. As history has shown, naturalist arguments have been powerful strategies to justify virtually any social or economic system. In this context, one can understand that the environmental movement might want to use naturalistic arguments as a political tactic. However, if naturalism can be a powerful tactic, it always includes political dangers. On the one hand, naturalistic arguments have a powerful capacity to seduce and mobilize. On the other hand, the struggle can shift towards the actual content of natural categories which can be discussed *ad nauseam* by scientific experts and counter-experts, without any definitive, absolute certainty. For example, current developments in biotechnologies have exploded the traditional limits between what is 'natural' and what is human-engineered. However, in the context of relations of power, those who resist may not have the choice of political strategies. For example, the procedure of public environmental hearings is an illustration of the structural constraints imposed on environmental groups. Faced with credible-sounding experts and scientific studies presented by advocates of a proposed development, environmental groups are forced to play a tactical game of presenting counter-experts and counter-studies. Because of the degree of inherent uncertainty in any scientific argument, the final decision rests on either the legitimacy of the scientists or the broader state of relations of power.

Nevertheless, the participation of environmental groups in environmental public hearings can also become a site of resistance (Wynne 1982). For example, Richardson, Sherman and Gismondi have documented the detailed struggle of environmental groups and citizens in the context of a public environmental enquiry concerning a $1.3 billion Cdn proposal to build a paper plant in northern Alberta, Canada (Richardson et al. 1993). One argument used by the promoter, Alberta Pacific Forest Industries, to justify the production of bleached paper was demand from the market – more precisely, the demand from 'housewives'. The promoter was trying to argue that the 'market' was imposed on them, and external to their own corporate strategy. It was an obvious attempt at shifting responsibility for environmental damage from the corporation to the consumer. It was also an obvious attempt to 'naturalize' the market, by considering its functions as an imposed imperative – like a law of nature – that one ought to submit to. In response, a local housewife shouted, 'Not this housewife!', to undermine the attempt. Most of the time, the instruments of environmental resistance, like public hearings, are imposed by the overall relations of power. However – and even in generally unfavourable contexts – hearings can be

> moments . . . when less powerful groups undermined the discourses empowered by the dominant groups and in the process constructed counter-discourses of their own. . . . The acts by subordinate groups, of questioning convention, subverting dominant discourses and asserting counter-discourses are highly political. (Richardson et al. 1993)

The recourse to naturalistic arguments by environmentalists is not, however, proof of an inherent naturalism in environmentalism. In large part, it is a tactical game whereby to challenge the legitimacy of what is considered 'natural'. In the process of that challenge or resistance, existing boundaries of what has been constituted as 'nature' are being questioned. The anti-anthropocentrism of deep ecology can indeed appear as the ultimate 'naturalist' discourse, which can present dangers (Luke 1988; Stark 1995). For example, Luke perceives deep ecology as an extreme form of anthropocentrism (an anti-anthropocentric anthropocentrism), which leaves unproblematized the question of who will define and manage the new boundaries of nature, as understood by deep ecology. However, deep ecology can also be a tactical game of counter-discourse to create a radical difference in the existing discursive configuration (Ingalsbee 1996; List 1992). Yet, it could become more than just a counter-discourse: it could also create 'possibilities for . . . new subjectivity to arise' (Richardson et al. 1993).

Conclusion: Do We Need Environmental Ethics?

In order to answer this question, it might be helpful to go back to the mapping of the different types of ethics that Foucault identified: (1) 'morality', (2) 'morality of behaviors', and (3) reflexive work on, and by, oneself about 'how one ought to "conduct oneself"' (Foucault 1984f: 26). Foucault would probably classify most conventional (i.e. foundationalist) environmental ethics in one of the first two types. Indeed, most foundationalist environmental ethics tends to be highly moralistic, unreflexive and uncritical about the full extent of its normalizing effects and how they fit into a disciplinary 'environmentality'. However, the third type of ethics identified by Foucault, which he preferred to call 'an aesthetic of existence' rather than 'ethics', could be the basis for a non-foundationalist environmental ethics or, maybe, as it should be called now, a 'Green aesthetic of existence'. This 'Green aesthetic of existence' doesn't offer solutions to the 'environmental crisis'; it merely suggests the adoption of an 'ethical sensibility' (Connolly 1993a, 1993b), a constant critical, sceptical attitude toward foundationalism and assumed natural categories, a continued transgression of the limits of the conditions that have constructed our current and past subjectivities, a permanent reinventing of ourselves. However, this hyper, constant self-critique doesn't lead to paralysing quietism. On the contrary, it leads to hyper-activism, of reflexive and critical resistance.

Together with so many other resistance movements, such as anti-colonialism, anti-racism, feminism, working-class organizing and queer politics, the environmental movement shares this feature of hyper-activism. However, Foucault's original contribution to a politics of resistance is to add a further reflexive, critical turn. Environmental resistance, inspired by a green aesthetic of existence, includes the questioning of existing dominant discourse and practices around 'nature'. The adoption of naturalistic counter-discourses by environmental groups should be seen as a tactic of resistance rather than a deep ontological and/or metaphysical claim. Affirming counter-essentialist, counter-naturalist alternatives may result in undermining existing dominant discourses about the environment, and thereby creating conditions for the establishment of a permanent critique of all essentialism and naturalism, as a mechanism of deployment of power.

In sharp opposition to many conventional environmental ethical theories, like that of Callicott (1990), a Green aesthetic of existence acknowledges the impossibility of grounding environmental ethics upon an absolute, external, universal and coherent 'truth' about 'nature'. For example, the discourse of 'ecological limits' as a strategy for changing human behaviour might simply reproduce existing relations of power which posit an absolute truth external to humans – God or gods, scientific 'truth' and now an 'ecological imperative'. Foucault would agree with André Gorz, that

> [i]t is important to make sure that the political approach is not presented as the 'absolutely inevitable' product of a 'scientific analysis', to avoid producing a new version of the sort of scientistic and anti-political dogmatism that, in its diamat version, purported to raise political practices and concepts to the level of scientifically proven necessities, thus denying their specifically political character. (Gorz 1993: 55)[11]

The truth-discourse about 'ecological limits' could result in a will to push back these limits even further (a will of 'acting' on these 'external' limits), rather than a will to remain 'within the limits' as an aesthetic of existence. For example, reducing individual energy consumption in the North shouldn't be justified by an imperative / threat like 'global warming' defined by an 'expertocracy' (ibid.), but because one might not want the consumption of large amounts of energy be a defining characteristic of oneself! In the context of rampant consumerism in the North, it is up to us to advance into a Green *askesis* that would make us work on ourselves and invent a manner of being that is still improbable.[12]

Therefore the challenge to environmental activism is not to establish a binding 'ecological rationality' (Dryzek 1990), with even more powerful instruments of control and management, but to acknowledge human freedom, which can manifest itself anywhere, from the outright destruction of the planet to its survival. Maybe it is not environmental ethics we need, but rather, a Green aesthetic of existence. In this case, Foucault is particularly relevant to the task.[13]

Notes

1   This question was formulated by David Halperin while commenting on a previous draft of this chapter.

2   Although Caputo doesn't discuss Foucault specifically, he articulates a 'postmodern ethics' – an ethics of 'dissemination' (1993: 1) which Foucault would probably subscribe to. For Caputo, conventional 'ethics makes safe. It throws a net of safety under the judgements we are forced to make, the daily, the hourly decisions that make up the texture of our lives. Ethics lays the foundation for principles that force people to be good; it clarifies concepts, secures judgements, provides firm guardrails along the slippery slopes of factical life. It provides principles and criteria and adjudicates hard cases. Ethics is altogether wholesome, constructive work, which is why it enjoys a good name. The deconstruction of ethics, on the other hand, cuts this net. Or rather, since deconstruction is not some stealthy, cunning agent of disruption, is not an agent at all, is in a sense nothing at all, it is much more accurate to say that a deconstructive analysis shows that the net is already torn, is "always already" split, all along and from the start. The deconstruction of ethics is ethics' own undoing' (ibid. 4).

3   I am leaving aside some of the problematic issues / assumptions such as: (1) the presumed separation between 'science' and 'ethics', (2) the unresolved question of how we can even pretend to know what 'nature *is*' (presumably for Rolston the unproblematized answer comes from 'science'), and (3) the assumption of a right method ('appropriately considered') to determine 'what *ought* to be'.

4   For a critique of Cheney, see Frodeman 1992, Quigley 1992, and for a general critique, see Quigley's chapter above (ch. 9).

5   The ontological argumentation for the preservation of nature 'is not intended to prove that nature exists, which is *taken as a given*, but to show that humans *have a duty* to act so as to ensure the continuation of nature *in its appropriate, natural forms*' (Hargrove 1989: 191–2, my emphasis). A Foucauldian critique would ask how 'nature' has become an unquestioned 'given', or what led (some?) 'humans' to feel that they 'have a duty to act so as to ensure the continuation of nature', or who is the final authority on what should be considered 'appropriate natural forms'.

6   For Foucauldian – or Foucauldian-inspired – studies around these issues see Davidson 1986; McGee 1994; Michael and Grove-White 1993; Quigley 1992; Szerszynski 1993: 49–88, 235–64; Tully 1998.

7   For a wonderful comparison between Lacan and Foucault, see Rajchman 1991.

8 Nietzsche uses the terms *Selbstaufhebung* and *Selbstüberwindung* interchangeably, and means 'self-dissolution' and 'self-conquest' or 'self-surmounting'. See Ansell-Pearson 1994: 223, n. 1).

9 I used 'by choice' in the same sense as Elspeth Probyn (1995). Probyn makes a distinction between 'for choice' and 'by choice'. The first refers to an individualist, universal, liberal ontological category, while the second refers to the possibility of multiplying choices by problematizing and transgressing the presumed universal, individual, liberal notion of 'choice'.

10 For example, racism cannot be defined positively. In the case of 'white' racism, it is only by opposition to a 'non-white' category that it is definable. Both Said (1978a, 1993), in the context of European colonial empires, and Tully (1993b, 1995), in the context of aboriginal peoples in North America, have performed a tactical reversal by revealing the extent to which 'Western' culture and political systems have incorporated the 'other', while at the same time denying it or failing to recognize it. For example, Tully (1993b) has shown that the political and constitutional concept of 'federalism' so central to contemporary Western political culture, was introduced only in late eighteenth century. The introduction of federalism in to the American Constitution was lifted directly from the existing Iroquois federal system.

11 There seems to be a convergence around the theme of 'self-limitation' even among some post-Marxists. Gorz justifies 'self-limitation as a social project' on the ground that it 'remains the only non-authoritarian, democratic way towards an eco-compatible industrial civilization' (1993: 64).

12 I am adapting Foucault. 'Ascetism as the renunciation of pleasure has had bad connotations. But the *askesis* is something else. . . . We've rid ourselves of asceticism. Yet it is up to us to advance into a homosexual *askesis* that would make us work on ourselves and invent, do not say discover, a manner of being that is still improbable' (Foucault 1989b: 303).

13 I would like to thank the following individuals for helpful comments on previous drafts of this chapter: James Bernauer, Mary Carpenter, Kevin Crombie, David Halperin, Eric Laferrière, Phil Macnaghten and the two anonymous reviewers of the journal *Environmental Ethics*. The usual disclaimers apply.

Bibliography

Abenhaim, Lucien Lewys (1985): 'Travail et santé: dialectique d'un rapport social', in *Traité d'anthropologie médicale, l'institution de la santé et de la maladie*, Sillery: Presses de l'université du Québec.

Adorno, Theodor and Horkheimer, Max (1986): *Dialectic of Enlightenment*, 2nd edn. London: Verso.

Anderson, Chris and Runciman, Lex (eds) (1995): *A Forest of Voices: Reading and Writing the Environment*. Mountain View, Calif. Mayfield Publishing.

Anderson, Lorraine (ed.) (1991): *Sisters of the Earth: Women's Prose and Poetry about Nature*. New York: Vintage.

Ansell-Pearson, Keith (1994): *An Introduction to Nietzsche as Political Thinker*. Cambridge: Cambridge University Press.

Armstrong, Timothy J. (ed. and trans.) (1992): *Michel Foucault Philosopher*. New York: Routledge; Hemel Hempstead: Harvester Wheatsheaf.

Bakhtin, Mikhail (1981): *The Dialogic Imagination*. Austin: University of Texas Press.

Bakhtin, Mikhail (1986): 'Discourse in the Novel', in Adams Hazard and Searle Leroy (eds), *Critical Theory since 1965*, Tallahassee: Florida State University Press.

Barnet, Richard J. (1980): *The Lean Years: Politics in the Age of Scarcity*. New York: Simon and Schuster.

Barret-Kriegal, Blandine (1992): 'Michel Foucault and the Police State', in Armstrong (ed. and trans.), *Michel Foucault Philosopher*, Hemel Hempstead: Harvester Wheatsheaf, 192–7.

Barthes, Roland (1978): *Mythologies*, trans. A. Lavers. London: Paladin.

Bartlett, R. (1990): 'Ecological Reason in Administration: Environmental Impact Assessment and Administrative Theory', in Robert Paehlke and Douglas Torgerson (eds), *Managing Leviathan: Environmental Politics and the Administrative State*, Peterborough, Ontario: Broadview Press, 81–96.

Baudrillard, Jean (1982): 'The Systems of Objects', in *Selected Writings*, Stanford, Calif.: Stanford University Press.

Baudrillard, Jean (1987): *Forget Foucault*. New York: Semiotext(e).

Baudrillard, Jean (1988): *America*. London: Verso.

Beck, Ulrich (1992a): 'From Industrial Society to Risk Society: Questions of Survival, Social Structure and Ecological Enlightenment', *Theory, Culture and Society*, 9, 97–123.

Beck, Ulrich (1992b): *Risk Society: Towards a New Modernity*. London: Sage.

Beck, Ulrich (1994): 'The Reinvention of Politics: Towards a Theory of Reflexive Modernization', in Ulrich Beck, Anthony Giddens and Scott Lash (eds), *Reflexive Modernization: Politics, Tradition and Aesthetics in the Modern Social Order*, Cambridge: Polity, 1–55.

Beck, Ulrich (1995): *Ecological Politics in an Age of Risk*. Cambridge: Polity.

Bednarik, Robert G. (1991–2): 'Rock Art as a Cultural Determinant', *Survey: Bolletino del Centro Studi e Museo d'Arte Preistorica di Pinerolo*, 7–8.

Bennett, Jane and Chaloupka, William (eds) (1993): *In the Nature of Things: Language, Politics and the Environment*. Minneapolis: University of Minnesota Press.

Bennett, Tony (1979): *Formalism and Marxism*. London: Methuen.

Benton, Ted (1994): 'Biology and Social Theory in the Environmental Debate', in Michael R. Redclift and Ted Benton (eds), *Social Theory and the Global Environment*, London: Routledge, 28–50.

Berman, Morris (1981): *The Reenchantment of the World*. Ithaca, NY: Cornell University Press.

Bernauer, James W. (1992): 'Beyond Life and Death: On Foucault's Post-Auschwitz Ethic', in Armstrong (trans.), *Michel Foucault Philosopher*, Hemel Hempstead: Harvester Wheatsheaf, 260–79.

Bernauer, James W. and Mahon, Michael (1994): 'The Ethics of Michel Foucault', in Garry Gutting (ed.), *The Cambridge Companion to Foucault*, Cambridge: Cambridge University Press, 141–58.

Berry, Thomas (1988): *The Dream of the Earth*. San Francisco: Sierra Club Books.

Berry, Wendell (1995): 'Out of Your Car, Off Your Horse', in Anderson and Runciman (eds), *A Forest of Voices*, Mountain View, Calif.: Mayfield Publishing, 698–702.

Bersani, Leo (1995): *Homos*. Cambridge, Mass.: Harvard University Press.

Bird, Elizabeth Ann R. (1987): 'The Social Construction of Nature: Theoretical Approaches to the History of Environmental Problems', *Environmental Review*, 11, 255–64.

Blasius, Mark (1995): *Gay and Lesbian Politics – Sexuality and the Emergence of a New Ethic*. Philadelphia: Temple University Press.

Bocking, S. (1995): 'Ecosystems, Ecologists, and the Atom: Environmental Research at Oak Ridge National Laboratory', *Journal of the History of Biology*, 28(1), 1–47.

Bookchin, Murray (1962): *Our Synthetic Environment*. New York: Knopf.

Bookchin, Murray (1982): *The Ecology of Freedom*. Polo Alto, Calif.: Cheshire Books.

Bookchin, Murray (1990): *Remaking Society*. Boston: South End Press.

Bouchard, Donald E. (ed.) (1977): *Language, Counter-Memory, Practice: Selected Essays and Interviews by Michel Foucault*. Ithaca, NY: Cornell University Press.

Bowerbank, Sylvia (1995): 'Toward the Greening of Literary Studies', *Canadian Review of Comparative Literature/Revue Canadienne de Littérature Comparée*, 22(3–4), 443–54.

Bowler, L. (1993): *The Norton History of the Environmental Sciences*. New York: W. W. Norton and Company.

Bramwell, Anna (1989): *Ecology in the Twentieth Century: A History*. New Haven: Yale University Press.

Brown, Lester. et al. (eds) (1990): *The State of the World*. North Sydney, Australia: Allen and Unwin.

Brown, Lester, Flavin Christopher, and Postel, Sandra (1991): *Saving the Planet: How to Shape an Environmentally Sustainable Society*. New York: Norton.

Brown, Lester R. et al. (1995): *State of the World 1995*. New York: Norton.

Brumley, John H. (1988): 'Medicine Wheels on the Northern Plains: A Summary and Appraisal', *Archaeological Survey of Alberta Manuscript Series*, 12.

Brundtland, Gro Harlem (1985): *Mandate for Change: Key Issues, Strategy and Workplan*. Geneva: World Commission on Environment and Development.

Brundtland, Gro Harlem (1987): *Our Common Future, World Commission on Environment and Development*. New York: Oxford University Press.

Buell, Lawrence (1995): *The Environmental Imagination: Thoreau, Nature Writing, and the Formation of American Culture*. Cambridge, Mass.: Belknap Press.

Burchell, Graham (1991): 'Peculiar Interests: Civil Society and the System of Natural Liberty', in Burchell et al. (eds), *The Foucault Effect*, Hemel Hempstead: Harvester Wheatsheaf, 119–50.

Burchell, Graham, Gordon, Colin and Miller, Peter (eds) (1991): *The Foucault Effect – Studies in Governmentality*. Hemel Hempstead: Harvester Wheatsheaf.

Burks, David Clarke (ed.) (1994): *Place of the Wild: A Wildlands Anthology*. Washington, DC: Island Press.

Butler, Judith (1992): 'Contingent Foundationalism: Feminism and the Question of Postmodernism', in Judith Butler and Joan Scott (eds), *Feminists Theorise the Political*, New York and London: Routledge.

Buttel, Frederick and Taylor, Paul (1992): 'Environmental Sociology and Global Environmental Change: A Critical Assessment', *Society and Natural Resources*, 5, 211–30.

Cairns, John Jr (1995): 'Achieving Sustainable Use of the Planet in the Next Century: What Should Virginians Do?', *Virginia Issues and Answers*, 2(2), 3.

Caldwell, Lynton (1991): 'Globalizing Environmentalism', *Society and Natural Resources*, 4, 259–72.

Callicott, J. Baird (1990): 'The Case against Moral Pluralism', *Environmental Ethics*, 12(2), 99–124.

Callicott, J. Baird (1995): 'Animal Liberation: A Triangular Affair', in Robert Elliot (ed.), *Environmental Ethics*, Oxford and New York: Oxford University Press, 29–59.

Canguilhem, Georges (1988): *Ideology and Rationality in the History of the Life Sciences*. Cambridge, Mass.: MIT Press.

Canguilhem, Georges (1989): *The Normal and the Pathological*. New York: Zone Books.

Capra, Fritjof (1982): *The Turning Point*. New York: Simon and Schuster.

Caputo, John D. (1993): *Against Ethics – Contributions to a Poetics of Obligation with Constant Reference to Deconstruction*. Indianapolis: Indiana University Press.

Carson, Rachel (1962): *Silent Spring*. London: Penguin.

Chaloupka, William (1992): *Knowing Nukes: The Politics and Culture of the Atom*. Minneapolis: University of Minnesota Press.

Chaloupka, William and Cawley, R. McGreggor (1993): 'The Great Wild Hope: Nature, Environmentalism, and the Open Secret', in Bennett and Chaloupka (eds), *In the Nature of Things*, Minneapolis: University of Minnesota Press, 3–23.

Chase, Steve (1991): 'Whither the Radical Ecology Movement?', in Murray Bookchin and Dave Foreman, *Defending the Earth – A Debate between Murray Bookchin and Dave Foreman*, Montreal: Black Rose Books, 7–24.

Cheney, Jim (1989): 'Postmodern Environmental Ethics: Ethics as Bioregional Narrative', *Environmental Ethics*, 11, 117–34. Repr. in Max Oelschlaeger (ed.), *Postmodern Environmental Ethics*, Albany, NY: SUNY Press, 1995, 23–42.

Christoff, Peter (1996): 'Ecological Modernisation, Ecological Modernities', *Environmental Politics*, 5(3), 476–500.

Christopher, Warren (1996a): 'International Environmental and Resource Concerns', *U.S. Department of State Dispatch*, 7(11) (11 Mar.).

Christopher, Warren (1996b): 'Leadership for the Next American Century', *U.S. Department of State Dispatch*, 7(4) (22 Jan.).

Christopher, Warren (1996c): 'Meeting Our Nation's Needs: Providing Security, Growth and Leadership for the Next Century', *U.S. Department of State Dispatch*, 7(14) (1 Apr.).

Clifford, James (1988): 'Histories of the Tribal and the Modern', in Clifford James (ed.), *The Predicament of Culture: Twentieth-Century Ethnography, Literature, and Art*, Cambridge Mass.: Harvard University Press.

Clinton, Bill (1995): 'Address at Freedom House, October 6, 1995 [A White House Press Release]', *Foreign Policy Bulletin* (Nov./Dec.), 43.

Commoner, Barry (1971): *The Closing Circle: Nature, Man and Technology*. New York: Knopf.

Conley, Verena Andermatt (1993): 'Eco-Subjects', in V. A. Conley (ed.), *Rethinking Technologies*, Minneapolis: University of Minnesota Press, 77–91.

Conley, Verana Andermatt (1997): *Ecopolitics – The Environment in Poststructural Thought*. London: Routledge.

Connolly, William E. (1992): 'The Irony of Interpretation', in Daniel W. Conway and John E. Seery (eds), *The Politics of Irony – Essays in Self-Betrayal*, New York: St Martin's Press, 119–50.

Connolly, William E. (1993a): *The Augustinian Imperative: A Reflection on the Politics of Morality*. Newbury Park, Calif.: Sage.

Connolly, William E. (1993b): 'Beyond Good and Evil – The Ethical Sensibility of Michel Foucault', *Political Theory*, 21(3), 365–89.

Connolly, William E. (1995): *The Ethos of Pluralization*. Minneapolis: University of Minnesota Press.

Cook, Deborah (1993): *The Subject Finds a Voice: Foucault's Turn toward Subjectivity*. New York: Peter Lang.

Council on Environmental Quality (1981): *The Global 2000 Report to the President of the United States*. New York: Pergamon Press.

Cramer, J., Eyerman, Ron and Jamison, Andrew (1989): 'The Knowledge Interests of the Environment Movement and its Potential for Influencing the Development of Science', in Stuart Blume (ed.), *The Social Direction of the Public Sciences*, Dordrecht: D. Reidel Publishing Co.

Cronon, William (1993): 'The Uses of Environmental History', *Environmental History Review* (Fall), 1–22.

Cronon, William (1995): 'The Trouble with Wilderness', in William Cronon (ed.), *Uncommon Ground: Toward Reinventing Nature*, New York: Norton.

Crosby, Alfred (1986): *Ecological Imperialism: The Biological Expansion of Europe 900–1900*. Cambridge: Cambridge University Press.

Darier, Éric (1991): 'Une Généalogie du "conservationnisme" et de l'écologie au Canada', *To See Ourselves / To Save Ourselves – Ecology and Culture in Canada, Canadian Issues*, 13, 37–49.

Darier, Éric (1993): 'L'Environnement au Canada: une approche foucaltienne'. (Ph.D. thesis, McGill University, Montreal).

Darier, Éric (1995): 'Environmental Studies in Context: Knowledge, Language, History and the Self', in Michael D. Mehta and Eric Ouellet (eds), *Environmental Sociology: Theory and Practice*, Toronto: Captus Press, 153–69.

Darier, Éric (1996a): 'Environmental Governmentality: The Case of *Canada's Green Plan*', *Environmental Politics*, 5(4), 585–606.

Darier, Éric (1996b): 'The Politics and Power Effects of Garbage Recycling in Halifax, Canada', *Local Environment*, 1(1), 63–86.

Darier, Éric and Shackley, Simon (1998): 'The Seduction of the Sirens: Global Climate Change and Modelling', *Science and Public Policy*, forthcoming.

Davidson, Arnold I. (1986): 'Archeology, Genealogy, Ethics', in David Couzens Hoy (ed.), *Foucault: A Critical Reader*, Oxford: Blackwell, 221–33.

Davies, Stephen (1991): *Definitions of Art*. Ithaca, NY: Cornell University Press.

Davis, Angela (1981): *Women, Race and Class*. New York: Vintage.

Davis, Whitney (1992): 'The Deconstruction of Intentionality in Archaeology', *Antiquity*, 66, 334–47.

Dean, Mitchell (1994a): *Critical and Effective Histories: Foucault's Methods and Historical Sociology*. London: Routledge.

Dean, Mitchell (1994b): ' "A Social Structure of Many Souls": Moral Regulation, Government, and Self-Formation', *Canadian Journal of Sociology*, 19(2), 145–68.

de Certeau, Michel (1984): *The Practice of Everyday Life*. Berkeley: University of California Press.

de Certeau, Michel (1994): 'The Laugh of Michel Foucault', in Smart (ed.), *Michel Foucault – Critical Assessments*, London: Routledge, vol. 1, 195–200.

Defert, Daniel and Ewald, François (eds) (1994): *Dits et écrits*, 4 vols. Paris: Gallimard.

de Lauretis, Teresa (1991): 'Queer Theory: Lesbian and Gay Sexualities: An Introduction', *Differences: A Journal of Feminist Cultural Studies*, 3(2), iii–xvii.

Dempsey, Hugh A. (1956): 'Stone "Medicine Wheels" – Memorials to Blackfoot War Chiefs', *Journal of the Washington Academy of Sciences*, 46(6), 177–82.

Descartes, René (1957): *A Discourse on Method*. London: J. M. Dent and Sons Ltd.

Devall, Bill and Sessions, George (1985): *Deep Ecology: Living as if Nature Mattered*. Salt Lake City: Perigrine Smith.

Diamond, Irene (1994): *Fertile Ground: Women, Earth, and the Limits of Control*. Boston: Beacon Press.

Diamond, Irene and Quinby, Lee (eds) (1988): *Feminism and Foucault – Reflections on Resistance*. Boston: Northeastern University Press.

Dobson, Andrew (1990): *Green Political Thought*. London: Unwin Hyman.

Donnelly, Michael (1992): 'Foucault's Use of the Notion of Biopower', in Armstrong (ed. and trans.), *Michel Foucault Philosopher*, Hemel Hempstead: Harvester Wheatsheaf, 199–203.

Donzelot, Jacques (1979): *Policing the Family*. London: Hutchinson.

Donzelot, Jacques (1993): 'The Promotion of the Social', in Mike Gane and Terry Johnson (eds), *Foucault's New Domains*, London: Routledge, 106–38.

Drengson, Alan (1994): 'The Reflective Ebb and Flow of the Wild', in Burks (ed.), *Place of the Wild*, Washington, DC: Island Press, 75–85.

Dreyfus, Herbert, and Rabinow, Paul (1982): *Michel Foucault: Beyond Structuralism and Hermeneutics*. Hemel Hempstead: Harvester Wheatsheaf.

Dryzek, John S. (1990): 'Designs for Environmental Discourse: The Greening of the Administrative State?', in Robert Paehlke and Douglas Torgerson (eds), *Managing Leviathan – Environmental Politics and the Administrative State*, Peterborough, Ontario: Broadview Press, 97–111.

Dumm, Thomas L. (1996): *Michel Foucault and the Politics of Freedom*. Thousand Oaks, Calif.: Sage.

Eagleton, Terry (1983): *Literary Theory*. Minneapolis: University of Minnesota Press.

Easterbrook, Gregg (1995): *A Moment on the Earth – The Coming Age of Environmental Optimism*. New York: Viking.

Eckersley, Robin (1992): *Environmentalism and Political Theory*. London: UCL Press.

Eder, Klaus (1988): 'Critique of Habermas's Contribution to the Sociology of Law', *Law and Society Review*, 22(5).

Eder, Klaus (1990a): 'The Cultural Code of Modernity and the Problem of Nature: A Critique of the Naturalistic Notion of Progress', in Jeffrey C. Alexander and Piotr Sztompka (eds), *Rethinking Progress: Movements, Forces and Ideas at the End of the 20th Century*, London: Unwin Hyman, 67–87.

Eder, Klaus (1990b): 'The Rise of Counter-Culture Movements against Modernity: Nature as a New Field of Class Struggle', *Theory, Culture and Society*, 7, 28–41.

Eder, Klaus (1993): *New Politics of Class: Social Movements and Cultural Dynamics in Advanced Societies*. London: Sage.

Egerton, J. (1983): 'The History of Ecology: Achievements and Opportunities (Part 1)', *Journal of the History of Biology*, 16(2), 268–71.

Ehrlich, Paul (1968): *The Population Bomb*. New York: Ballantine Books.

Eliss, John (1989): *Against Deconstruction*. Princeton: Princeton University Press.

Ellen, Roy (1996): 'Introduction', in Roy Ellen and Katsuyoshi Fukui (eds), *Redefining Nature – Ecology, Culture and Domestication*, Oxford: Berg, 1–36.

Elliot, Robert (1995): 'Faking Nature', in Robert Elliot (ed.), *Environmental Ethics*, Oxford and New York: Oxford University Press, 76–88.

Engels, Friedrich (1972): *Dialectics of Nature.* Moscow: Progress Publishers.

Éribon, Didier (1991): *Michel Foucault.* Cambridge, Mass.: Harvard University Press.

Éribon, Didier (1994): *Michel Foucault et ses contemporains.* Paris: Fayard.

Evernden, Neal (1992): *The Social Creation of Nature.* Baltimore: Johns Hopkins University Press.

Ewald, François (1991): 'Insurance and Risk', in Burchell et al. (eds), *The Foucault Effect,* Hemel Hempstead: Harvester Wheatsheaf, 197–210.

Faes, Hubert (1992): 'Contrat social et contrat naturel: la nature comme objet de responsabilité', in Pierre Colin, *De la nature: de la physique classique au souci écologique,* Paris: Beauchesne, 121–41.

Fallows, James (1989): *More Like Us: Making America Great Again.* Boston: Houghton Mifflin.

Farr, William (1975): *Vital Statistics: A Memorial Volume of Selections from the Reports and Writing of William Farr.* Metuchen, NJ: Scarecrow Press.

Farr, William (1977): *Mortality in Mid 19th Century Britain.* Farnborough, Hants: Gregg.

Ferry, Luc (1995): *The New Ecological Order,* trans. Carol Volk. Chicago: University of Chicago Press.

Feyerabend, Paul (1981a): *Problems of Empiricism.* Cambridge: Cambridge University Press.

Feyerabend, Paul (1981b): *Realism, Rationalism, and Scientific Method.* Cambridge: Cambridge University Press.

Feyerabend, Paul (1991): *Three Dialogues on Knowledge.* Oxford: Blackwell.

Finch, Robert and Elder, John (eds) (1990): *The Norton Book of Nature Writing.* New York: Norton.

Flathman, Richard (1992): *Willful Liberalism: Voluntarism and Individuality in Political Theory and Practice.* Ithaca, NY: Cornell University Press.

Forbis, Richard O. (1963): 'The Direct Historical Approach in the Prairie Provinces of Canada', *Great Plains Journal,* 3(1), 9–16.

Foucault, Michel (1961) [1965]: *Madness and Civilization.* New York: Pantheon Books; London: Tavistock Publications, 1971.

Foucault, Michel (1963) [1973]: *The Birth of the Clinic: An Archaeology of Medical Perception.* New York: Pantheon Books.

Foucault, Michel (1966) [1971]: *The Order of Things: An Archaeology of the Human Sciences.* New York: Pantheon Books; London: Tavistock Publications, 1970.

Foucault, Michel (1969) [1972]: *The Archaeology of Knowledge.* New York: Harper Colophon; London: Tavistock Publications, 1972.

Foucault, Michel (1970): 'La Situation de Cuvier dans l'histoire de la biologie', *Revue d'histoire des sciences et de leurs applications,* 23(1),

63–92. Repr. in Defert and Ewald (eds), *Dits et écrits 1954–1988*, vol. 2, Paris: Gallimard, 30–66.

Foucault, Michel (1972): 'La Folie, l'absence d'oeuvre', in *Histoire de la folie* (appendix), Paris: Gallimard, 578. Repr. in Bernauer and Mahon, 'The Ethics of Michel Foucault', in Garry Gutting (ed.), *The Cambridge Companion to Foucault*, Cambridge: Cambridge University Press, 1994, 141–58.

Foucault, Michel (1973): *The Order of Things*. New York: Vintage.

Foucault, Michel (1975) [1977]: *Discipline and Punish: The Birth of the Prison*. New York: Pantheon Books; London: Allen Lane.

Foucault, Michel (1976) [1978]: *The History of Sexuality*, Vol. 1: *Introduction*. New York: Pantheon Books.

Foucault, Michel (1977): 'Nietzsche, Genealogy, History', in Bouchard (ed.), *Language, Counter-Memory, Practice*, Ithaca, NY: Cornell University Press; Oxford: Blackwell. Repr. in Paul Rabinow (ed.), *The Foucault Reader*, New York: Pantheon Books, 1984, 76–100.

Foucault, Michel (1980a): 'The Confession of the Flesh', in Colin Gordon (ed.), *Power/Knowledge: Selected Interviews and Other Writings 1972–1977*, New York: Pantheon Books; Brighton: Harvester Wheatsheaf, 1980, 194–228.

Foucault, Michel (1980b): 'The Eye of Power', in Colin Gordon (ed.), *Power/Knowledge: Selected Interviews and Other Writings, 1972–1977*, New York: Pantheon Books; Brighton: Harvester Wheatsheaf, 1980, 146–65.

Foucault, Michel (1980c): 'The History of Sexuality', in Colin Gordon (ed.), *Power/Knowledge: Selected Interviews and Other Writings, 1972–1977*, New York: Pantheon Books; Brighton: Harvester Wheatsheaf, 1980, 183–93.

Foucault, Michel (1980d): 'Introduction', in *Herculine Barbin: Being the Recently Discovered Memoirs of a Nineteenth-Century Hermaphrodite*, trans. R. McDougall, New York: Pantheon, vii–xvii.

Foucault, Michel (1980e): 'The Politics of Health in the Eighteenth Century', in Colin Gordon (ed.), *Power/Knowledge: Selected Interviews and Other Writings, 1972–1977*, New York: Pantheon Books; Brighton: Harvester Wheatsheaf, 1980, 166–82.

Foucault, Michel (1980f): 'Questions on Geography', in Colin Gordon (ed.), *Power/Knowledge: Selected Interviews and Other Writings, 1972–1977*, New York: Pantheon Books; Brighton: Harvester Wheatsheaf, 1980, 63–77.

Foucault, Michel (1980g): 'Truth and Power', in Colin Gordon (ed.), *Power/Knowledge: Selected Interviews and Other Writings 1972–1977*, New York: Pantheon Books; Brighton: Harvester Wheatsheaf, 1980, 109–33.

Foucault, Michel (1980h): 'Two Lectures', in Colin Gordon (ed.), *Power/Knowledge: Selected Interviews and Other Writings, 1972–1977*, New York: Pantheon Books; Brighton: Harvester Wheatsheaf, 1980, 78–108.

Foucault, Michel (1981a): 'Foucault at the Collège de France. I. A Course
Summary: "History of Systems of Thought, 1978"', *Philosophy and
Social Criticism*, 8(2), 236–42.

Foucault, Michel (1981b): 'Foucault at the Collège de France. II. A Course
Summary: "History of Systems of Thought, 1979"', *Philosophy and
Social Criticism*, 8(3), 351–9.

Foucault, Michel (1981c): '*Omnes et Singulatim*: Towards a Criticism of
"Political Reason"', in Sterling McMurrin (ed.), *The Tanner Lectures
on Human Values*, vol. 2, Salt Lake City: University of Utah Press,
225–54.

Foucault, Michel (1982): 'Afterword – The Subject and Power', in Hubert
L. Dreyfus and Paul Rabinow, *Michel Foucault: Beyond Structuralism
and Hermeneutics*, Hemel Hempstead: Harvester Wheatsheaf, 208–26.

Foucault, Michel (1983a): 'How We Behave', interview with Foucault,
Vanity Fair (Nov.).

Foucault, Michel (1983b): 'Structuralism and Poststructuralism: An Interview with Michel Foucault', *Telos*, 55, 195–211.

Foucault, Michel (1984a) [1986]: *The Care of the Self*. New York: Pantheon Books.

Foucault, Michel (1984b): *The Foucault Reader*, ed. Paul Rabinow. New
York: Pantheon Books.

Foucault, Michel (1984c): 'Nietzsche, Genealogy, History', in Paul
Rabinow (ed.), *The Foucault Reader*, New York: Pantheon Books,
76–100.

Foucault, Michel (1984d): 'On the Genealogy of Ethics: An Overview of
Work in Progress', in Paul Rabinow (ed.), *The Foucault Reader*, New
York: Pantheon Books, 340–72.

Foucault, Michel (1984e): 'Space, Knowledge, and Power', in Paul Rabinow
(ed.), *The Foucault Reader*, New York: Pantheon Books, 239–56.

Foucault, Michel (1984f) [1985]: *The Use of Pleasure*. New York: Pantheon Books; London: Viking, 1986.

Foucault, Michel (1984g): 'What is an Author?', in Paul Rabinow (ed.),
The Foucault Reader, New York: Pantheon Books, 101–20.

Foucault, Michel (1984h): 'What is Enlightenment?', in Paul Rabinow
(ed.), *The Foucault Reader*, New York: Pantheon Books, 32–50.

Foucault, Michel (1986): 'Of Other Spaces', *Diacritics – A Review of
Contemporary Criticism*, 16 (Spring), 22–7. Trans. Jay Miskowiec from
1984 'Des espaces autres', *Architecture – Mouvement – Continuité*,
5 (Oct.), 46–9.

Foucault, Michel (1988a): 'An Aesthetics of Existence', in Lawrence
Kritzman (ed.), *Michel Foucault – Politics, Philosophy, Culture –
Interviews and Other Writings 1977–1984*. London and New York:
Routledge, 47–53.

Foucault, Michel (1988b): 'The Ethic of Care for the Self as a Practice
of Freedom – An Interview with Michel Foucault Conducted by
Paul Fronet-Betancourt, Helmut Becker and Alfredo Gomez-Muller on

January 20, 1984', in James Bernauer and David Rasmussen (eds), *The Final Foucault*, Cambridge, Mass.: MIT Press, 11–20.

Foucault, Michel (1988c): 'The Political Technology of Individuals', in Luther H. Martin, Huck Gutman, and Patrick H. Hutton (eds), *Technologies of the Self: A Seminar with Michel Foucault*, Amherst: University of Massachusetts Press, 16–49.

Foucault, Michel (1988d): 'Power and Sex', in Lawrence Kritzman (ed.), *Michel Foucault – Politics, Philosophy, Culture – Interviews and Other Writings 1977–1984*, London and New York: Routledge, 110–24.

Foucault, Michel (1988e): 'Truth, Power, Self: An Interview with Michel Foucault', in Luther H. Martin, Huck Gutman, and Patrick H. Hutton (eds), *Technologies of the Self*, Amherst: University of Massachusetts Press, 9–15.

Foucault, Michel (1988f): 'Practicing Criticism', in Lawrence Kritzman (ed.), *Michel Foucault–Politics, Philosophy, Culture–Interviews and Other Writings 1977–1984*, London and New York: Routledge, 152–6.

Foucault, Michel (1989a): 'The End of the Monarchy of Sex', in Sylvère Lotringer (ed.), *Foucault Live*, New York: Semiotext(e).

Foucault, Michel (1989b): *Foucault Live*, ed. Sylvère Lotringer. New York: Semiotext(e).

Foucault, Michel (1989c): 'Friendship as a Way of Life', in Sylvère Lotringer (ed.), *Foucault Live*, New York: Semiotext(e).

Foucault, Michel (1989d): *Michel Foucault – Résumé des cours 1970–1982*. Paris: Collège de France / Julliard.

Foucault, Michel (1989e): *The Order of Things: An Archaeology of the Human Sciences*. London: Tavistock/Routledge.

Foucault, Michel (1991a): 'Governmentality', in Burchell, et al. (eds), *The Foucault Effect*, Hemel Hempstead: Harvester Wheatsheaf, 87–104.

Foucault, Michel (1991b): 'What Is Enlightenment?', in Paul Rabinow (ed.), *The Foucault Reader*, Harmondsworth: Penguin; New York: Pantheon Books, 1984, 32–50.

Fox, Warwick (1990): *Toward a Transpersonal Ecology: Developing a Transpersonal Ecology*. Boston and London: Shambhala.

Fraiberg, Allison (1991): 'Of Aids, Cyborgs, and Other Indiscretions: Resurfacing the Body in the Postmodern', *Postmodern Culture*, 1(3).

Fraser, Nancy (1989): 'Foucault on Modern Power: Empirical Insights and Normative Confusions', in *Unruly Practices – Power, Discourse and Gender in Contemporary Social Theory*, Minnesota: University of Minnesota Press, 17–34.

Frodeman, Robert (1992): 'Radical Environmentalism and the Political Roots of Postmodernism: Differences that Make a Difference', *Environmental Ethics*, 14, 315–17. Repr. in Max Oelschlaeger (ed.), *Postmodern Environmental Ethics*, Albany, NY: SUNY Press, 1995, 121–36.

Gallagher, Bob and Wilson, Alexander (1984): 'Michel Foucault. An Interview: Sex, Power and the Politics of Identity', *Advocate*, 400 (7 Aug.), 26–30 and 58.

Gandal, Keith (1986): 'Michel Foucault: Intellectual Work and Politics', *Telos*, 67, 121–34.

Gare, Arrane E. (1995): *Postmodernism and the Environmental Crisis*. London: Routledge.

Glacken, Clarence (1967): *Traces on the Rhodian Shore*. Berkeley: University of California Press.

Glotfelty, Cheryll Burgess (1993): 'Teaching Green: Ideas, Sample Syllabi, and Resources', *ISLE: Interdisciplinary Studies in Literature and the Environment*, 1(1) (Spring).

Goldblatt, David (1996): *Social Theory and the Environment*. Cambridge: Polity.

Goldsmith, Edward et al. (1972): *A Blueprint for Survival*. London: Stacey Ltd.

Golley, Frank B. (1993): *History of the Ecosystem Concept in Ecology: More than the Sum of the Parts*. New Haven: Yale University Press.

Gordon, Colin (1980): 'Afterword', in Colin Gordon (ed.), *Power/Knowledge: Selected Interview and Other Writings, 1972–1977*, New York: Pantheon Books; Brighton: Harvester Wheatsheaf, 1980, 229–59.

Gordon, Colin (1986): 'Question, Ethos, Event: Foucault on Kant and Enlightenment', *Economy and Society*, 15(1), 71–87.

Gordon, Colin (1987): 'The Soul of the Citizen: Max Weber and Michel Foucault on Rationality and Government', in Scott Lash and Sam Whimster (eds), *Max Weber: Rationality and Modernity*, London: Allen and Unwin, 293–316.

Gordon, Colin (1991): 'Governmental Rationality: An Introduction', in Burchell et al. (eds), *The Foucault Effect*, Hemel Hempstead: Harvester Wheatsheaf, 1–51.

Gordon, Colin (1996): 'Foucault in Britain', in Andrew Barry, Thomas Osborne and Nikolas Rose (eds), *Foucault and Political Reason – Liberalism, Neo-Liberalism and Rationalities of Government*, Chicago: University of Chicago Press, 253–70.

Gore, Al (1992): *Earth in the Balance: Ecology and the Human Spirit*. Boston: Houghton Mifflin.

Gorz, André (1993): 'Political Ecology: Expertocracy versus Self-Limitation', *New Left Review*, 202, 55–67.

Gould, Stephen Jay (1981): *The Mismeasure of Man*. New York: Nolin.

Graff, Gerald (1983): 'The Pseudo-Politics of Interpretation', in W. J. T. Mitchell (ed.), *The Politics of Interpretation*, Chicago: University of Chicago Press, 145–58.

Greenhouse, Steven (1995): 'The Greening of U.S. Diplomacy: Focus on Ecology', *New York Times*, 9 Oct., 1–12.

Grove, Richard (1990): 'Colonial Conservation, Ecological Harmony and Popular Resistance: Towards a Global Synthesis', in John M. MacKenzie (ed.), *Imperialism and the Natural World*, Manchester: Manchester University Press.

Grove, Richard (1992): 'Origins of Western Environmentalism', *Scientific American*, 266(7), 42–7.

Guattari, Félix (1990): *Les Trois Écologies*. Paris: Galilée.

Gutting, Gary (1989): *Michel Foucault's Archaeology of Scientific Reason*. Cambridge: Cambridge University Press.

Habermas, Jürgen (1981): 'New Social Movements', *Telos*, 490, 33–7.

Habermas, Jürgen (1982): 'A Reply to My Critics', in John B. Thompson and David Held (eds), *Habermas: Critical Debates*, London: Macmillan.

Habermas, Jürgen (1985): *The Philosophical Discourse on Modernity*. Cambridge: Polity.

Habermas, Jürgen (1987): *Theory of Communicative Action*, vol. 2. Boston: Beacon Press.

Hacking, Ian (1986): 'Self-Improvement', in David Couzens Hoy (ed.), *Foucault: A Critical Reader*, Oxford: Blackwell, 235–40.

Halperin, David (1990): *One Hundred Years of Homosexuality and Other Essays of Greek Love*. New York: Routledge.

Halperin, David (1995): 'The Queer Politics of Michel Foucault', in David Halperin, *Saint Foucault – Towards a Gay Hagiography*, New York: Oxford University Press, 15–125.

Hannigan, John A. (1995): *Environmental Sociology: A Social Constructionist Perspective*. London: Routledge.

Haraway, Donna (1985): 'Manifesto for Cyborgs: Science, Technology, and Socialist Feminism in the 1980s', *Socialist Review*, 80, 65–108.

Haraway, Donna (1989): 'Situated Knowledges: The Science Question in Feminism and the Privilege of Partial Perspective', *Feminist Studies*, 14(3), 575–99.

Haraway, Donna (1991): *Symians, Cyborgs, and Women: The Reinvention of Nature*. London: Free Association Books.

Hardin, Garrett (1968): 'The Tragedy of the Commons', *Science*, 162, 1243–8.

Hardin, Garrett (1993): *Living within Limits: Ecology, Economics, and Population Taboos*. Oxford: Oxford University Press.

Hargrove, Eugene C. (1989): *Foundations of Environmental Ethics*. Englewood Cliffs, NJ: Prentice-Hall.

Harris, Richard A. and Milkis, Sidney M. (1989): *The Politics of Regulatory Change: A Tale of Two Agencies*. New York: Oxford University Press.

Hayward, Tim (1994): *Ecological Thought: An Introduction*. Cambridge: Polity.

Heidegger, Martin (1977): 'Letter on Humanism', in David F. Krell (ed.), Frank A. Cappuzi with J. Glenn Gray (trans.), *Basic Writings*, San Francisco: Harper.

Heizer, Michael and Brown, Julia (1984): 'Interview', in Julia Brown (ed.), *Michael Heizer: Sculpture in Reverse*, Los Angeles: Museum of Contemporary Art.

Helvarg, David (1994): *The War against the Greens: The 'Wise Use' Movement, the New Right, and Anti-Environmental Violence*. San Francisco: Sierra Club Books.

Hewitt, M. (1983): 'Biopolitics and Social Policy', *Theory, Culture and Society*, 2(1), 67–84.

Hinchman, Hannah (1991): *A Life in Hand: Creating the Illuminated Journal*. Salt Lake City: Gibbs Smith.

Hindess, Barry (1996): *Discourses of Power: From Hobbes to Foucault*. Oxford: Blackwell.

Hippocrates (1969): *Airs, Waters and Places*. Cambridge: Arabic and English, published for Cambridge Middle East Centre by Heffer.

Hoagland, Edward (1986): 'From the Land where Polar Bears Fly: Review of Barry Lopez, *Arctic Dreams: Imagination and Desire in a Northern Landscape*', *New York Times Book Review*, 16 Feb., 1 and 3.

Honneth, Axel (1986): 'Foucault and Adorno: Two Forms of the Critique of Modernity', *Thesis Eleven*, 15.

Honneth, Axel (1991): *The Critique of Power: Reflective Stages in a Critical Social Theory*. Cambridge, Mass.: MIT Press.

Hubbell, Sue (1986): *A Country Year: Living the Questions*. New York: Random House.

Hulley, Stephen B. (1992): 'Principles of Preventive Medicine', in James B. Wyngaarden, Lloyd H. Smith and Jean-Claude Bennet (eds), *Cecil Textbook of Medicine*, Philadelphia: W. B. Saunders Company, 33–64.

Hutcheon, Linda (1989): *The Politics of Postmodernism*. London: Routledge.

Ingalsbee, Timothy (1996): 'Earth First! Activism: Ecological Postmodern Praxis in Radical Environmentalist Identities', *Sociological Perspectives* (Pacific Sociological Association), 39(2).

IUCN (International Union for the Conservation of Nature) (1980): *World Conservation Strategy*. Gland, Switzerland: International Union for the Conservation of Nature.

IUCN (International Union for the Conservation of Nature), United Nations Environmental Programme, and World Wildlife Fund (1991): *Caring for the Earth: A Strategy for Sustainable Living*. Gland, Switzerland: Earthscan.

Jagtenberg, Tom and McKie, David (1997): *Eco-Impact and the Greening of Postmodernity*. London: Sage.

Jambert, Christian (1992): 'The Constitution of the Subject and Spiritual Practice', in Armstrong (ed. and trans.), *Michel Foucault Philosopher*, Hemel Hempstead: Harvester Wheatsheaf, 233–47.

Jamison, Andrew (1993): 'National Political Cultures and the Exchange of Knowledge: The Case of Systems Ecology', in E. Crawford et al. (eds), *Denationalizing Science*, Amsterdam: Kluwer Academic Publishers.

Jamison, Andrew and Eyerman, Ron (1994): 'The Ecological Intellectuals', in *Seeds of the Sixties*, Berkeley: University of California Press, 64–102.

Jasanoff, Sheila (1990): *The Fifth Branch: Science Advisers as Policymakers*. Cambridge, Mass.: Harvard University Press.

Jasanoff, Sheila (1992): 'Science, Politics and the Renegotiation of Expertise at EPA', *Osiris*, 2nd ser. 7, 95–217.

Kaplan, Robert (1996): *The Ends of the Earth*. New York: Random House.

Kateb, George (1992): *The Inner Ocean: Individualism and Democratic Culture*. Ithaca, NY: Cornell University Press.

Kennedy, Paul (1993): *Preparing for the Twenty-First Century*. New York: Random House.

Killingsworth, J. and Palmer, J. S. (1992): *Ecospeak, Rhetoric and Environmental Politics in America*. Carbondale and Edwardsville: Southern Illinois University Press.

Knorr-Cetina, K. D. (1981): *The Manufacture of Knowledge: An Essay on the Constructivist and Contextual Nature of Science*. Oxford: Pergamon Press.

Knorr-Cetina, K. D. (1983): 'The Ethnographic Study of Scientific Work: Towards a Constructivist Interpretation of Science', in K. D. Knorr-Cetina and M. Mulkay (eds), *Science Observed: Perspectives on the Social Study of Science*, London: Sage, 115–40.

Kritzman, Lawrence (1988): 'Foucault and the Politics of Experience', in Lawrence Kritzman (ed.), *Michel Foucault – Politics, Philosophy, Culture – Interviews and Other Writings 1977–1984*, London: Routledge, ix–xxv.

Kroker, Arthur (1987): 'The Games of Foucault', *Canadian Journal of Political and Social Theory*, 11(3), 1–10.

Kubler, George (1991): *Esthetic Recognition of Ancient Amerindian Art*. New Haven: Yale University Press.

Kubrin, David (1981): 'Newton's Inside Out! Magic, Class Struggle, and the Rise of Mechanism in the West', in Harry Woolf (ed.), *The Analytic Spirit – Essays in the History of Science*, Ithaca, NY: Cornell University Press, 96–121.

Kuhn, Thomas (1962): *The Structure of Scientific Revolutions*. Chicago: University of Chicago Press.

Kwa, Chunglin (1987): 'Representations of Nature Mediating between Ecology and Science Policy: The Case of the International Biological Programme', *Social Studies of Science*, 17, 413–42.

Kwa, Chunglin (1993): 'Radiation Ecology, Systems Ecology and the Management of the Environment', in M. Shortland (ed.), *Science and Nature: Essays in the History of the Environmental Sciences*, London: British Society for the History of Science, 213–49.

Lalonde, Marc (1974): *A New Perspective on the Health of Canadians*. Ottawa: Minister of Supply and Services.

Latour, Bruno (1987): *Science in Action: How to Follow Scientists and Engineers through Society*. Milton Keynes: Open University Press.

Latour, Bruno and Woolgar, Steve (1986): *Laboratory Life: The [Social] Construction of Scientific Facts*. Princeton: Princeton University Press.

Leiss, William (1976): *The Limits to Satisfaction – An Essay on the Problem of Needs and Commodities*. Toronto: University of Toronto Press.

Lemert, Charles and Gillan, Garth (1982): *Michel Foucault: Social Theory as Transgression*. New York: Columbia University Press.

Lentricchia, Frank (1983): *Criticism and Social Change*. Chicago: University of Chicago Press.

List, Peter C. (1992): *Radical Environmentalism – Philosophy and Tactics*. Belmont, Calif.: Wadsworth Publishing Company.

Long, Richard (1986): 'Words after the Fact', in R. H. Fuchs, *Richard Long*, New York: Solomon R. Guggenheim Museum; London: Thames and Hudson.

Lopez, Barry (1986): *Arctic Dreams: Imagination and Desire in a Northern Landscape*. New York: Charles Scribner's Sons.

Luhmann, Niklas (1989): *Ecological Communication*. Cambridge: Polity.

Luhmann, Niklas (1994): 'The Modernity of Science', *New German Critique*, 610, 9–23.

Luke, Timothy W. (1988): 'The Dreams of Deep Ecology', *Telos*, 76, 65–92.

Luke, Timothy W. (1993a): 'Discourses of Disintegration, Texts of Transformation: Re-Reading Realism in the New World Order', *Alternatives*, 130, 229–58.

Luke, Timothy W. (1993b): 'Green Consumerism: Ecology and the Ruse of Recycling', in Bennett and Chaloupka (eds), *In the Nature of Things*, Minneapolis: University of Minnesota Press, 154–72.

Luke, Timothy W. (1994a): 'Placing Powers/Siting Spaces: The Politics of Global and Local in the New World Order', *Environment and Planning D: Society and Space*, 12, 613–28.

Luke, Timothy W. (1994b): 'Worldwatching as the Limits to Growth', *Capitalism Nature Socialism*, 5(2), 43–64.

Luke, Timothy W. (1995): 'On Environmentality: Geo-Power and Eco-Knowledge in Discourses of Contemporary Environmentalism', *Cultural Critique*, Fall.

Luttwak, Edward N. (1993): *The Endangered American Dream: How to Stop the United States from Becoming a Third-World Country and How to Win the Geo-Economic Struggle for Industrial Supremacy*. New York: Simon and Schuster.

Lykke, Nina and Bryld, Mette (1994): 'Between Terraforming and Fortune-Telling – Space Flight and Astrology: Ambivalences of a Post-modern World', in Wendy Harcourt (ed.), *Feminist Perspectives on Sustainable Development*, London: Routledge, 109–27.

Macey, David (1993): *Lives of Michel Foucault*. London: Hutchinson.

MacIntyre, Alasdair (1970): 'Is Understanding Religion Compatible with Believing?' and 'The Idea of a Social Science', in Bryan R. Wilson (ed.), *Rationality*, Oxford: Blackwell, 62–77.

MacIntyre, Alastair (1981): *After Virtue: A Study in Moral Theory*. Notre Dame, Ind.: University of Notre Dame Press.

Macnaghten, Phil and Urry, John (1998): *Contested Natures*. London: Sage.

MacNeill, Jim, Winsemius, Pieter and Yakushiji, Taizo (1991): *Beyond Interdependence: The Meshing of the World's Economy and the Earth's Ecology*. Oxford: Oxford University Press.

Macy, Joanna (1991): 'The Greening of the Self', in *World as Lover, World as Self*, Berkeley: Parallax Press; London: Rider, 1993.

Magne, Martin P. R. and Klassen, Michael (1991): 'A Multivariate Study of Rock Art Anthropomorphs at Writing-On-Stone, Southern Alberta', *American Antiquity*, 56(3), 389–418.

Mahon, Michael (1992): *Foucault's Nietzschean Genealogy – Truth, Power, and the Subject*. Albany, NY: SUNY Press.

Makower, Joel (1993): *The E-Factor: The Bottom-Line Approach to Environmentally Responsible Business*. New York: Times Books.

Marshall, Peter (1992): *Nature's Web – An Exploration of Ecological Thinking*. London: Simon and Schuster.

Marty, François (1992): 'Une Nature que l'homme habite', in Pierre Colin, *De la Nature: de la physique classique au souci écologique*, Paris: Beauchesne, 21–37.

Mathews, Freya (1991): *The Ecological Self*. London: Routledge.

Mazur, Laurie Ann (ed.) (1994): *Beyond the Numbers: A Reader on Population, Consumption and the Environment*. Washington, DC: Island Press.

McCarthy, Thomas (1990): 'The Critique of Impure Reason: Foucault and the Frankfurt School', *Political Theory*, 18(3), 437–69.

McCloskey, Michael (1970): *Ecotactics: The Sierra Club Handbook for Environment Activists*. New York: Pocket Books.

McGee, Glenn (1994): 'The Relevance of Foucault to Whiteheadian Environmental Ethics', *Environmental Ethics*, 16, 419–24.

McIntosh, Robert (1985): *The Background of Ecology*. Cambridge: Cambridge University Press.

McKibben, Bill (1989): *The End of Nature*. New York: Random House.

McLaughlin, Andrew (1993): *Regarding Nature: Industrialism and Deep Ecology*. Albany, NY: SUNY Press.

McMichael, D. J. (1993): *Planetary Overload: Global Environmental Change and the Health of the Human Species*. Cambridge: Cambridge University Press.

McNay, Lois (1992): *Foucault and Feminism: Power, Gender, and the Self*. Cambridge: Polity.

McNeil, Maureen (1993): 'Dancing with Foucault: Feminism and Power-Knowledge', in Ramazanoğlu (ed.), *Up against Foucault*, London: Routledge, 147–75.

McWhorter, Ladelle (1992): 'Guilt as Management Technology: A Call to Heiddeggerian Reflection', in Ladelle McWhorter (ed.), *Heidegger and the Earth: Essays in Environmental Philosophy*, Kirksuille, Mo.: Thomas Jefferson University Press, 1–9.

Meadows, Donella H., Meadows, Dennis L., Randers, Joergen and Behrens, W. (1972): *The Limits to Growth*. New York: Signet.

Merchant, Carolyn (1992): *Radical Ecology: The Search for a Livable World*. London: Routledge.

Merchant, Carolyn (1994): *Key Concepts in Critical Theory – Ecology*. Atlantic Heights, NJ: Humanities Press.

Michael, Mike and Grove-White, Robin (1993): 'Talking about Talking about Nature: Nurturing Ecological Consciousness', *Environmental Ethics*, 15(1), 33–47.

Mies, Maria and Shiva, Vandana (1993): *Ecofeminism*. Halifax: Fernwood Publications.

Miller, James (1993): *The Passion of Michel Foucault*. New York: Simon and Schuster.

Miller, M. (1994): 'Intersystemic Discourse and Coordinated Dissent: A Critique of Luhmann's Concept of Ecological Communication', *Theory, Culture and Society*, 11, 101–21.

Miller, Peter (1987): *Domination and Power*. London: Routledge and Kegan Paul.

Miller, Toby (1993): *The Well-Tempered Subject: Citizenship, Culture, and the Postmodern Subject*. Baltimore: Johns Hopkins University Press.

Mitman, Gregg (1988): 'From Population to Society: The Cooperative Metaphors of W. C. Allee and A. E. Emerson', *Journal of the History of Biology*, 21(2), 173–94.

Moi, Toril (1985): *Sexual/Textual Politics*. London: Methuen.

Moran, Leslie (1996): *The Homosexual(ity) of Law*. London: Routledge.

Morrison, Paul (1993–4): 'End Pleasure', *Gay Liberation Quarterly*, 1, 57.

Moscovici, Serge (1993): 'Filiations intellectuelles et politiques: la polymérisation de l'écologie', in Marc Abélès, *Le Défi écologiste*, Paris: L'Harmattan, 15–26.

Murphy, Raymond (1994): *Rationality and Nature – A Sociological Inquiry into a Changing Relationship*. Boulder, Colo.: Westview Press.

Murray, John A. (1992): 'Introduction', in *Nature's New Voices*, Golden, Colo.: Fulcrum Publishing.

Myers, Norman (1993): *Ultimate Security: The Environmental Basis of Political Stability*. New York: Norton.

Narveson, Jan (1986): 'Against Animal Rights', in Philip P. Hanson (ed.), *Environmental Ethics: Philosophical and Policy Perspectives*, Burnaby B.C.: Institute for the Humanities/Simon Fraser University Publications.

Nietzsche, Friedrich (1909): *The Complete Works of Friedrich Nietzsche*, ed. Oscar Levy, New York: Gordon Press, vol. 9, § 501.

Nietzsche, Friedrich (1956): *The Birth of Tragedy and the Genealogy of Morals*, trans. Francis Golffing. New York: Doubleday.

Nietzsche, Friedrich (1973): *Beyond Good and Evil*. New York: Penguin.

Nikiforuk, Andrew (1992): 'Sacred Circles', *Canadian Geographic*, 112(4), 51–60.

Norris, Christopher (1990): *What's Wrong with Postmodernism*. Baltimore: Johns Hopkins University Press.

Oates, David (1989): *Earth Rising: Ecological Belief in an Age of Science*. Corvalis: Oregon State University Press.

Oelschlaeger, Max (1994): 'The Idea of Wilderness as a Deep Ecological Ethic', in Burks (ed.), *Place of the Wild*, Washington, DC: Island Press, 131–48.

Oelschlaeger, Max (1995): 'Introduction', in Max Oelschlaeger (ed.), *Postmodern Environmental Ethics*, Albany, NY: SUNY Press, 1–20.

Olivier, Lawrence (1995): *Michel Foucault – Penser au temps du nihilisme*. Montréal: Liber.

Oppenheimer, J. Robert (1954): in 'In the Matter of J. Robert Oppenheimer', *USAEC Transcript of Hearing before Personnel Security Board*, Washington, DC.

Pal, Leslie A. (1990): 'Knowledge, Power, and Policy: Reflections on Foucault', in Stephen Brooks and Alain-G. Gagnon (eds), *Social Scientists, Policy, and the State*, New York: Praeger, 139–58.

Palliadino, P. (1991): 'Defining Ecology: Ecological Theories, Mathematical Models, and Applied Biology in the 1960s and 1970s', *Journal of the History of Biology*, 24(2), 223–43.

Parsons, Howard (ed.) (1977): *Marx and Engels on Ecology*. Westport, Conn.: Greenwood Press.

Passmore, John (1995): 'Attitudes to Nature', in Robert Elliot (ed.), *Environmental Ethics*, Oxford and New York: Oxford University Press, 129–41.

Peace, A. (1996): 'Governing the Environment: The Programs and Politics of Environmental Discourse', in Clare O'Farrell (ed.), *Foucault: The Legacy*, Brisbane: Queensland University of Technology.

Pepper, David (1984): *The Roots of Modern Environmentalism*. London: Croom Helm.

Phelan, Shane (1993): 'Intimate Distance: The Dislocation of Nature in Modernity', in Bennett and Chaloupka (eds), *In the Nature of Things*, Minneapolis: University of Minnesota Press, 44–62.

Piasecki, Bruce and Asmus, Peter (1990): *In Search of Environmental Excellence: Moving beyond Blame*. New York: Simon and Schuster.

Popelard, Marie-Dominique (1992): 'De nouveaux rapports entre les sciences et la nature? Considérations épistémologiques', in Pierre Colin, *De la nature: de la physique classique au souci écologique*, Paris: Beauchesne, 41–60.

Porter, Roy (1977): *The Making of Geology – Earth Science in Britain 1660–1815*. Cambridge: Cambridge University Press.

Poster, Mark (1985): *Foucault, Marxism and History*. Cambridge: Polity.

Poster, Mark (1987): 'Foucault and Poststructuralism', in Murray Krieger (ed.), *The Aims of Representation*, New York: Columbia University Press.

Probyn, Elspeth (1995): 'Perverts by Choice – Towards an Ethics of Choosing', in Diane Elam and Robyn Wiegman (eds), *Feminism Beside Itself*, London: Routledge, 261–81.

Quigley, Peter (1990): 'The Ground of Resistance: Nature and Power in Emerson, Melville, Jeffreys, and Snyder' (unpublished Ph.D. dissertation, Indiana University of Pennsylvania).

Quigley, Peter (1992): 'Rethinking Resistance: Environmentalism, Literature, and Poststructural Theory', *Environmental Ethics*, 14, 291–306.

Quigley, Peter (1994): 'Jeffers' Decentering of American Political Rhetoric', in *English Studies and History*, Tampere, Finland: University of Tampere Press.

Quigley, Peter (1995): 'Rethinking Resistance: Environmentalism, Literature and Poststructuralism', in Max Oelschlaeger (ed.), *Postmodern Environmental Ethics*, Albany, NY: SUNY Press, 173–92.

Quigley, Peter (forthcoming): 'Man-Devouring Stars: Jeffers' Decentering of American Political Rhetoric', *Jeffers Studies*. Previously published in *English Studies and History*, University of Tampere Press, Tampere, Finland, 1994.

Rabinow, Paul (1984): 'Introduction', in Paul Rabinow (ed.), *The Foucault Reader*, Harmondsworth: Penguin, 3–29; New York: Pantheon Books.

Rajchman, John (1991): *Truth and Eros – Foucault, Lacan and the Question of Ethics*. London: Routledge.

Rajchman, John (1992): 'Foucault: The Ethic and the Work', in Armstrong (ed. and trans.), *Michel Foucault Philosopher*, New York: Routledge, 215–24.

Ramazanoğlu, Caroline (ed.) (1993): *Up against Foucault – Explorations of Some Tensions between Foucault and Feminism*. London: Routledge.

Ravetz, Jerome R. (1987): 'Usable Knowledge, Usable Ignorance', *Knowledge*, 9, 87–116.

Rawlings, D. L. (1996): 'A Light Green Baroque: Nature Writing at the End of Nature', *Bloomsbury Review*, 16(2).

Redclift, Michael R. (1987): *Sustainable Development: Exploring the Contradictions*. London: Methuen.

Redclift, Michael R. and Woodgate, Graham (1997): 'Sustainability and Social Construction', in Michael Redclift and Graham Woodgate (eds), *The International Handbook of Environmental Sociology*, Cheltenham: Edward Elgar, 55–70.

Reich, Robert (1991): *The Work of Nations: Preparing Ourselves for Twenty-First Century Capitalism*. New York: Knopf.

Richardson, Mary, Sherman, Joan and Gismondi, Michael (1993): *Winning Back the Words – Confronting Experts in an Environmental Public Hearing*. Toronto: Garamond Press.

Rifkin, Jeremy (1984): *Algeny: A New World*. Harmondsworth: Penguin.

Robineau, M. (1922): 'Ostéo-arthrites tuberculeuses et accidents du travail', in *Annales de médecine légale*, 2(3), 153–68.

Rolston, Holmes III (1992): 'Challenges in Environmental Ethics', in David E. Cooper and Joy A. Palmer (eds), *The Environment in Question – Ethics and Global Issues*, London: Routledge, 135–46.

Rorty, Richard (1989): *Contingency, Irony and Solidarity*. Cambridge: Cambridge University Press.

Rose, Nikolas (1990): *Governing the Soul – The Shaping of the Private Self*. London: Routledge.

Rose, Nikolas, and Miller, Peter (1992): 'Political Power beyond the State: Problematics of Government', *British Journal of Sociology*, 43(2), 173–205.

Rosnay, Joël de (1979): *The Macroscope: A New World Scientific System*. New York: Harper and Row.

Ross, Andrew (1988): *Universal Abandon? The Politics of Postmodernism*. Minneapolis: University of Minnesota Press.

Ross, Andrew (1994): *The Chicago Gangster Theory of Life: Ecology, Culture, and Society*. New York: Verso.

Ross, Carolyn (ed.) (1995): *Writing Nature: An Ecological Reader for Writers*. New York: St Martin's Press.

Roszak, Theodore (1979): *Person/Planet: The Creative Disintegration of Industrial Society*. New York: Doubleday.

Rouse, Joseph (1987): *Knowledge and Power: Towards a Political Philosophy of Science*. Ithaca, NY: Cornell University Press.

Rouse, Joseph (1993): 'Foucault and the Natural Sciences', in John Caputo and Mark Yount (eds), *Foucault and the Critique of Institutions*, Pennsylvania State University Press.

Rousseau, G. S. and Porter, Roy (eds) (1980): *The Ferment of Knowledge – Studies in the Historiography of 18th Century Science*. Cambridge: Cambridge University Press.

Ruffié, Jacques and Sournia, Jean-Claude (1995): *Les Épidémies dans l'histoire de l'homme – Essai d'anthropologie médicale*. Paris: Flammarion.

Rutherford, Paul (1993): 'Foucault's Concept of Biopower: Implications for Environmental Politics', in I. Thomas (ed.), *Ecopolitics VI: Interactions and Actions*, Melbourne: Royal Melbourne Institute of Technology.

Rutherford, Paul (1994a): 'The Administration of Life: Ecological Discourse as "Intellectual Machinery of Government"', *Australian Journal of Communication*, 21(3), 40–55.

Rutherford, Paul (1994b): 'Foucault and Ecological Governmentality', paper read at Foucault, Politics and Freedom Conference, April 1994, at the University of Melbourne.

Rutherford, Paul (1994c): 'The Political Economy of Environmental Policy – Review', *Australian Journal of Political Science*, 29(3), 597–8.

Rutherford, Paul (1996): 'Policing Nature: Ecology, Natural Science and Biopolitics', in Clare O'Farrell (ed.), *Foucault: The Legacy*, Brisbane: Queensland University of Technology.

Ryan, Michael (1982): *Marxism and Deconstruction*. Baltimore: Johns Hopkins University Press.

Sachs, Wolfgang (ed.) (1993): *Global Ecology – A New Arena of Political Conflict*. London: Zed Books.

Sadik, Nafis (1994): 'Investing in Women: The Focus of the '90s', in Laurie Ann Mazur (ed.), *Beyond the Numbers*, Washington, DC: Island Press.

Said, Edward W. (1978a): *Orientalism*. New York: Pantheon Books.

Said, Edward W. (1978b): 'The Problem of Textuality: Two Exemplary Positions', *Critical Inquiry*, 4, 673–714. Repr. in Smart (ed.), *Michel Foucault – Critical Assessments*, London: Routledge, 1994, vol. 2, 88–123.

Said, Edward W. (1993): *Culture and Imperialism*. New York: Knopf.

Sale, Kirkpatrick (1993): *The Green Revolution: The American Environmental Movement, 1962–1992*. New York: Hill and Wang.

Sandilands, Catriona (1994): 'Lavender's Green? Some Thoughts on Queer(y)ing Environmental Politics', *Undercurrents* (Toronto), 6 (May).

Sandilands, Catriona (1995): 'From Natural Identity to Radical Democracy', *Environmental Ethics*, 17, 75–91.

Sarup, Madan (1989): *An Introductory Guide to Post-Structuralism and Postmodernism*. Athens, Ga.: University of Georgia Press.

Schneider, William (1990): 'Geographical Reform and Municipal Imperialism in France, 1870–80', in John MacKenzie (ed.), *Imperialism and the Natural World*, Manchester: Manchester University Press.

Scholes, Robert (1985): *Textual Power*. New Haven: Yale University Press.

Sciulli, David (1994): 'An Interview with Niklas Luhmann', *Theory, Culture and Society*, 11, 37–68.

Sedgwick, Eve Kosofsky (1990): *Epistemology of the Closet*. Berkeley: University of California Press.

Seery, John Evan (1990): *Political Returns – Irony in Politics and Theory from Plato to the Antinuclear Movement*. Boulder, Colo.: Westview Press.

Sessions, George (1994): *Deep Ecology for the Twenty-first Century*. Boston: Shambhala.

Sessions, George (1995a): 'Postmodernism, Environmental Justice, and the Demise of the Ecology Movement?', *The Wild Duck: Literature and Letters of Northern California*, June/July.

Sessions, George (1995b): 'Reinventing Nature: The End of Wilderness?', *The Wild Duck: Literature and Letters of Northern California*, Nov.

Sheridan, Alan (1980): *Michel Foucault: The Will to Truth*. London: Tavistock.

Simmons, Ian G. (1993): *Interpreting Nature – Cultural Constructions of the Environment*. London: Routledge.

Simon, Julian L. and Kahn, Herman (1984): *The Resourceful Earth*. Oxford: Blackwell.

Singer, Linda (1993): *Erotic Welfare: Sexual Theory and Politics in the Age of the Epidemic*. New York: Routledge.

Slovic, Scott (1992): *Seeking Awareness in American Nature Writing*. Salt Lake City: University of Utah Press.

Smart, Barry (1983): *Foucault, Marxism and Critique*. London: Routledge and Kegan Paul.

Smart, Barry (1993): *Postmodernity*. London: Routledge.

Smart, Barry (ed.) (1994): *Michel Foucault – Critical Assessments*, 3 vols. London: Routledge.

Smith, N. (1993): 'Social Power and the Domination of Nature', *History of the Human Sciences*, 6(3), 101–10.

Snyder, Gary (1990): *The Practice of the Wild*. New York: North Point Press.

Sober, Elliott (1995): 'Philosophical Problems for Environmentalism', in Robert Elliot (ed.), *Environmental Ethics*, Oxford: Oxford University Press, 226–47.

Soper, Kate (1995): *What is Nature? Culture, Politics and the non-Human*. Oxford: Blackwell.

Soper, Kate (1996): 'Nature/"Nature"', in George Roberston et al. (eds), *Future Natural – Nature / Science / Culture*, London: Routledge, 22–34.

Soulé, Michael E. and Lease, Gary (eds) (1995): *Reinventing Nature? Responses to Postmodern Deconstruction*. Washington, DC: Island Press.

Sparshott, Francis (1982): *The Theory of the Arts*. Princeton: Princeton University Press.

Spivak, Gayatri Chakravorty (1984–5): 'Criticism, Feminism and the Institution', *Thesis Eleven*, 10–11 (Nov./Mar.), 184.

Spretnak, Charlene (1991): *States of Grace: The Recovery of Meaning in the Postmodern Age*. New York: HarperCollins.

Stabile, Carol (1994): *Feminism and the Technological Fix*. Manchester: Manchester University Press.

Stark, Jerry A. (1995): 'Postmodern Environmentalism: A Critique of Deep Ecology', in Bron Raymond Taylor (ed.), *Ecological Resistance Movements – The Global Emergence of Radical and Popular Environmentalism*, Albany, NY: SUNY Press, 259–81.

Stychin, Carl F. (1995): *Law's Desire – Sexuality and the Limits of Justice*. London: Routledge.

Szerszynski, Bronislaw (1993): 'Uncommon Ground – Moral Discourse, Foundationalism and the Environmental Movement' (Ph.D. thesis in sociology, Lancaster University).

Taçon, Paul S. C. (1991): 'The Power of Stone: Symbolic Aspects of Stone Use and Tool Development in Western Arnhem Land, Australia', *Antiquity*, 65, 192–207.

Taylor, Charles (1971): 'Interpretation and the Social Sciences of Man', *Review of Metaphysics*, 24, 3–51.

Taylor, Charles (1980): 'Understanding in the Human Sciences', *Review of Metaphysics*, 33, 25–8.

Taylor, Charles (1985): *Human Agency and Language: Philosophical Papers I*. Cambridge: Cambridge University Press.

Taylor, Charles (1987): 'Overcoming Epistemology', in Kenneth Baynes, James Bohman and Thomas McCarthy (eds), *After Philosophy*, Cambridge, Mass.: MIT Press, 464–88.

Taylor, Charles (1989): *Sources of the Self – The Making of the Modern Identity*. Cambridge, Mass.: Harvard University Press.

Taylor, Paul (1988): 'Technocratic Optimism, H. T. Odum, and the Partial Transformation of Ecological Metaphor after World War II', *Journal of the History of Biology*, 21(2), 213–44.

Terry, Jennifer (1991): 'Theorizing Deviant Historiography', *Differences: A Journal of Feminist Cultural Studies*, 3(2), 55–74.

Thackeray, J. F. (1990): 'On Concepts Expressed in Southern African Rock Art', *Antiquity*, 64, 139–44.

Thomashow, Mitchell (1995): *Ecological Identity: Becoming a Reflexive Environmentalist*. Cambridge, Mass.: MIT Press.

Thurow, Lester (1992): *Head to Head: The Coming Economic Battle among Japan, Europe, and America*. New York: Morrow.

Tilley, Christopher (1991): *Material Culture and the Text: The Art of Ambiguity*. London: Routledge.

Traugott, Joseph (1992): 'Native American Artists and the Postmodern Cultural Divide', *Art Journal*, 51(3), 36–43.

Trombley, S. (1988): *The Right to Reproduce: A History of Coercive Sterilization*. London: Butler and Tanner.

Trombley, S. (1996): *The Human Laboratory*. London: BBC Productions.

Trzyna, Thaddeus C. (1995): *A Sustainable World: Defining and Measuring Sustainable Development*. London: Earthcan.

Tully, James (1993a): 'Governing Conduct: Locke on the Reform of Thought and Behaviour', in James Tully, *An Approach to Political Philosophy: Locke in Contexts*, Cambridge: Cambridge University Press, 179–241.

Tully, James (1993b): 'Rediscovering America: The *Two Treaties* and Aboriginal Rights', in James Tully, *An Approach to Political Philosophy: Questions from Locke in Contexts*, Cambridge: Cambridge University Press, 137–76.

Tully, James (1995): *Strange Multiplicity: Constitutionalism in an Age of Diversity*. Cambridge: Cambridge University Press.

Tully, James (1998): 'An Ethics of Care for the Environment in Conditions of Conflict', in Nicolas Low and Brendan Glesson (eds), *Government for the Environment: Global Problems, Ethics and Democracy* (forthcoming).

Turner, Brian (1984): *The Body and Society*. Oxford: Blackwell.

Turner, Brian (1987): 'The Rationalization of the Body: Reflections on Modernity and Discipline', in Scott Lash and Sam Whimster (eds),

Max Weber: Rationality and Modernity, London: Allen and Unwin, 222–41.

United Nations Population Fund (UNFPA) (1986): *Annual Report 1986*. New York: UNFPA.

Vattimo, Gianni (1992): *The Transparent Society*. Baltimore: Johns Hopkins University Press; Cambridge: Polity. Trans. David Webb from *La società transparente*, Garzanti, 1989.

Vest, Jay Hansford C. (1985): 'Will of the Land', *Environmental Review*, Winter, 321–9.

Visker, Rudi (1995): *Michel Foucault – Genealogy as Critique*. London: Verso.

Vitousek, Peter et al. (1986): 'Human Appropriation of the Products of Photosynthesis', *Bioscience*, 34, 368–73.

Von Maltzahn, Kraft E. (1994): *Nature as Landscape: Dwelling and Understanding*. Montreal: McGill–Queen's University Press.

Waage, Frederick O. (ed.) (1985): *Teaching Environmental Literature: Materials, Methods, Resources*. New York: Modern Language Association.

Waechter, Antoine (1993): 'De l'écologie à la politique', in Marc Abélès, *Le défi écologiste*, Paris: L'Harmattan, 41–5.

Walker, K. (1989): 'The State in Environmental Management: The Ecological Dimension', *Political Studies*, 37, 25–38.

Weale, Albert (1992): *The New Politics of Pollution*. Manchester: Manchester University Press.

Weber, Max (1968): *Economy and Society*. New York: Bedminster Press.

Weeks, Jeffrey (1985): *Sexuality and its Discontents: Meanings, Myths, and Modern Sexualities*. London: Routledge and Kegan Paul.

Westmen, W. E. (1978): 'How Much are Nature's Services Worth?', *Science*, 197, 960–4.

Willers, Bill (ed.) (1991): *Learning to Listen to the Land*. Washington, DC: Island Press.

Williams, Raymond (1976): *Keywords: A Vocabulary of Culture and Society*. London: Flamingo.

Williams, Raymond (1981): *Socialism and Ecology*. London: Socialist Environment and Resources Association.

Williams, Terry Tempest (1992a): 'The Bowl', in John A. Murray, 'Introduction', in *Nature's New Voices*, Golden, Colo.: Fulcrum Publishing, 218–20.

Williams, Terry Tempest (1992b): *Refuge: An Unnatural History of Family and Place*. New York: Vintage.

Wilson, Marie (1989): 'Wings of the Eagle: A Conversation with Marie Wilson', in Judith Plant (ed.), *Healing the Wounds: The Promise of Ecofeminism*, Toronto: Between the Lines, 212–18.

Wilson, Michael (1981): 'Sun Dances, Thirst Dances, and Medicine Wheels: A Search for Alternative Hypotheses', in Michael Wilson, Kathie L. Road and Kenneth J. Hardy (eds), *Megaliths to Medicine Wheels: Boulder Structures in Archaeology, Proceedings of the Eleventh*

Annual Chacmool Conference, Calgary: University of Calgary Archaeological Association, 333–70.

Winch, Peter (1970): 'Understanding a Primitive Society', in Bryan R. Wilson (ed.), *Rationality*, Oxford: Blackwell, 78–111.

Winner, Langdon (1986): *The Whale and the Reactor: A Search for Limits in an Age of High Technology*. Chicago: University of Chicago Press.

Wolf, Stephen, Bruhn, John and Goodell, Helen (1978): *Occupational Health as Human Ecology*. Springfield, Ill.: Charles Thomas Publisher.

Woolgar, Steve (1988): *Science: The Very Idea*. London: Tavistock.

Worster, Donald (1987a): *Nature's Economy*. Cambridge: Cambridge University Press.

Worster, Donald (1987b): 'The Vulnerable Earth: Towards a Planetary History', *Environmental Review*, 11(2), 87–103.

Worthington, Edgar Barton (1983): *The Ecological Century*. Oxford: Oxford University Press.

Wynne, Brian (1982): *Rationality and Ritual: The Windscale Inquiry and Nuclear Decisions in Britain*. Chalfont St Giles: British Society for the History of Science.

Wynne, Brian (1992): 'Carving Out Science (and Politics) in the Regulatory Jungle', *Social Studies of Science*, 22, 745–58.

Wynne, Brian (1994): 'Scientific Knowledge and the Global Environment', in Michael Redclift and Ted Benton (eds), *Social Theory and the Global Environment*, London: Routledge, 169–89.

Yearley, Steven (1992): 'Green Ambivalence about Science: Legal-Rational Authority and the Scientific Legitimation of a Social Movement', *British Journal of Sociology*, 43(4), 511–32.

Young, John (1990): *Sustaining the Earth*. Cambridge, Mass.: Harvard University Press.

Zimmerman, Michael E. (1994): *Contesting Earth's Future – Radical Ecology and Postmodernity*. Berkeley: University of California Press.

Zimmerman, Michael E. (1996): 'The Postmodern Challenge to Environmentalism', *Terra Nova – Nature and Culture*, 1(2), 131–40.

Index

NOTE: Page numbers followed by *n* indicate that information is to be found in a note. All titles indexed are works by Michel Foucault mentioned in the text, except where a different author is given in brackets.